Praise for this book

'*Global Trade* is an interesting new approach to global trade issues – part textbook, part critique of mainstream policies, and part alternative perspective on where we might go from here. All of these angles are desperately needed and they rarely come together in mainstream texts. Here they do, updated for the main debates in not only the corridors of power, but also the halls of academia and the meeting rooms of NGOs. This makes the book extremely valuable.'

Graham Dunkley, author of *The Free Trade Adventure: The WTO, the Uruguay Round and Globalism: A Critique* (2000) and *Free Trade: Myth, Reality and Alternatives* (2004)

About the author

Greg Buckman is former national finance manager of the Wilderness Society of Australia and former treasurer of the Australian Greens. He is also a past co-editor of their magazine, *Green*. He is an economic policy adviser to the Australian Greens and has undertaken extensive economic research, particularly on issues concerning globalisation, poverty, forestry and energy. His long involvement with the environment movement goes back to the successful international fight to save the Franklin River in Tasmania in the early 1980s. He is also the author of *Globalization: Tame it or Scrap it?* published by Zed Books in 2004.

Global Trade
Past Mistakes, Future Choices

Greg Buckman

Fernwood Publishing Ltd
Halifax, Nova Scotia

Books for Change
Bangalore

SIRD
Kuala Lumpur

David Philip
Cape Town

Zed Books
London & New York

Global Trade was first published in 2005 by

In Canada: Fernwood Publishing Ltd,
8422 St Margaret's Bay Road (Hwy 3) Site 2A, Box 5,
Black Point, Nova Scotia, BOJ IBO

In India: Books for Change,
139 Richmond Road, Bangalore 560 025

In Malaysia: Strategic Information Research Development (SIRD),
No. 11/4E, Petaling Jaya, 46200 Selangor

In Southern Africa: David Philip (an imprint of New Africa Books),
99 Garfield Road, Claremont 7700, South Africa

In the rest of the world: Zed Books Ltd, 7 Cynthia Street, London NI 9JF, UK,
and Room 400, 175 Fifth Avenue, New York, NY 100 10, USA
www.zedbooks.co.uk

Designed and typeset in Monotype Bembo by Long House Publishing Services
Cover designed by Andrew Corbett
Printed and bound in the EU by Cox & Wyman, Reading

Distributed in the USA exclusively by Palgrave Macmillan, a division of
St Martin's Press, LLC, 175 Fifth Avenue, New York, NY10010

A catalogue record for this book is available from the British Library
Library of Congress Cataloging-in-Publication Data available

Library and Archives Canada Cataloguing in Publication
Buckman, Greg, 1960–
  Global trade : past mistakes, future choices / Greg Buckman.
Includes index.
ISBN 1-55-266-178-4

ISBN 1-55266-178-4 Pb (Canada)

ISBN 983-2535-72-7 Pb (Malaysia (SIRD))

ISBN 1 84277 578 2 Hb (Zed Books)
ISBN 1 84277 579 0 Pb (Zed Books)

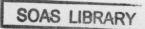

Contents

Figures and Tables

Figures

Tables

To Jill and Ted
whose spirit lives on

Introduction

When I was a youngster in the 1960s and 1970s it was rare to turn a product over and find 'Made in Japan' or 'Made in West Germany' written on it. Thirty years later is rare *not* to turn a product over and find something like 'Made in China' written on it. Today we are all part of a vast global marketplace where the production of something from several thousand kilometres away is now no more out of the ordinary than the production of something from several hundred kilometres away was back in the 1960s and 1970s. To many the emergence of this global marketplace may seem advantageous or at the very least fairly benign. But economics is largely about choices and we have only been able to create this vast global marketplace because we have made particular choices about our environment, the global distribution of income and global economic power relationships. In economics, as in life, choices are rarely fixed however – they often have to be remade according to new and evolving circumstances and limitations. Even though the world has so far chosen to create a vast global marketplace it won't find future choices about whether to expand – or at the very least maintain – the global marketplace as easy to make as they have been in the past. Very real constraints are closing in around the world's global marketplace.

This book is all about the choices that surround global trade. It reflects on the choices made so far and it speculates about the choices of the future. It's a digest of where global trade has come from and where it may go. Trade is not an isolated phenomenon, however, and both its past and its future are inexorably linked to many other influences including technological development, energy use and societal change. The interrelatedness of global trade makes it hard to make the story of trade a simple one but this book has nonetheless attempted to tell the story in clear and concise terms. The first six chapters tell the story of global trade so far while the final four examine its future options and constraints.

Even though the story of global trade has already run for more than five hundred years, the book makes it clear that there is still a lot humankind needs to learn about it and that the story of global trade is therefore a long way from over. There are many more chapters yet to be written.

1

A history of global trade

It is easy to take a given phenomenon and project backwards convincing oneself along the way that it has always been much as it is at present. It is particularly easy to do this with global trade, to kid oneself that today's highly integrated web of global trade must always have been much as it is at present. It is also easy to think that because high-income countries dominate today's world trade they must always have dominated global trade. But both impressions are a long way from the truth. Because these impressions are incorrect it is important to have an understanding of the evolution of global trade so one can have a proper context for the politics of it.

Although *integrated* global trade is a relatively new phenomenon, various forms of trade between different parts of the world have been in existence for a long time; in fact some types of global trade have existed for a very long time. Ivory from Africa has been discovered in Celtic graves in Britain. Volcanic glass mined in prehistoric times in present-day Turkey has been found throughout lands thousands of kilometres from the country.[1] What is new is the highly integrated nature of today's global trade. Today all continents receive goods and services from all other continents but that is something that has only happened over the past few centuries – before that there were only limited trade connections between continents.

Early continental trade networks

European colonisation around the world, which began in the sixteenth century, was the force that first linked together *all* the world's regional trade networks, but before the sixteenth century all continents had their own trade and in some limited instances some continents traded with other specific continents well before Europeans arrived on the scene.

In Asia early trade across the continent was considerably enhanced by the rise of Islam in the seventh century.[2] The spread of Islam meant that safe passage between strategic parts of the continent, such as between the Indian Ocean and the Mediterranean Sea, could be safely made for the first time since the fall of the Roman empire.[3]

In Africa a trade route that crossed the Sahara desert from West Africa to the Mediterranean meant that a connection between Africa and other continents existed a long time before the sixteenth century. The trade route was considerably enhanced by the arrival of camels into Africa in the first century.[4] Key commodities traded via this route were gold, slaves and salt.

In the Americas there was significant trade across its continents before the arrival of Europeans, although the trade was nowhere near as sophisticated as that in Asia, Europe or Africa.[5] The Aztec and Mayan empires conducted trade from about present-day Mexico through to present-day Nicaragua but the trade was limited by the fact that it was conducted separately from local commerce. It tended to focus on luxury goods and was always conducted overland rather than by sea.[6]

In Europe there was a limited amount of trade during the time of the Roman empire, which included the importation of a lot of grain from Egypt, but self-sufficiency was generally then the norm.[7] What trade there was within the continent collapsed after the fall of the Roman empire in the fifth century; later it became divided between the Muslim Ottoman empire in the east and the Christian west, and within the west between the Mediterranean south and the Atlantic north. Trade flourished much more in the Muslim parts of Europe; in the Christian parts rural self-sufficiency still tended to dominate.[8] Until the fifteenth century most European trade pivoted around the Medi-terranean, but after that time it shifted to the Atlantic.[9]

Early trade links between continents

For more than two millennia there was limited trade between Europe, Asia and Africa. Trade is likely to have occurred between the three continents, in fact, as early as prehistoric times: the discovery of luxury items and jewellery made from amber, coral and cowrie shells throughout all three continents suggests there was limited trading between them carried on a very long time ago.[10]

Before the fourteenth century, trade contact between Europe and Asia mainly took place along the so-called Silk Road that was established in the third century and lasted through to the seven-teenth century.[11] Much of the development of the Silk Road was pushed along by the spread of Islam.[12] Trade along the Silk Road mainly involved low-volume/high-profit luxury items such as jade, silk, porcelain and fine textiles. A complete journey along the Silk Road into China could take a long time – often requiring eighteen months to two years to complete.[13] The trade route started to decline between the tenth and thirteenth centuries, and it went into terminal decline in the seventeenth century when the Ming empire in China collapsed.[14] Its collapse stimulated an increase in long-distance maritime trade between the Middle East and India.[15] The swing towards sea-based trade made ports such as Genoa and Venice powerful: Venice had become the commercial centre of Europe by the fifteenth century.[16] Before this swing to Eurasian maritime trade, limited sea-based trade around the landmass had existed but only to a modest degree – as early as the first century the Mediterranean was linked to the Indian Ocean then later to South-East Asia.[17] European ships would take goods to modern-day Egypt, or Israel, then Muslim traders would take them overland to the Red Sea or the Persian Gulf; they would then be shipped on again to ports in India or China.[18]

Trade between Europe and Africa also stretches back a long way. By the eleventh century there were permanent international trading colonies in Syria, North Africa, Byzantium and Western Europe that linked the two continents.[19] By the fourteenth and fifteenth centuries Mediterranean cities such as Barcelona, Venice and Genoa were regularly trading with eastern Mediterranean centres[20] and there had long been trade across the Mediterranean that linked with the trans-Saharan trade route across Africa. The Ottoman empire was also a major conduit for trade between Africa and Europe.

Moves towards European international exploration and trade

During medieval times it seemed that the part of the world most likely eventually to link together all the world's separate continental trade networks was not Europe but China. Beginning in the tenth century the Chinese provinces of Guangdong and Fujian began to engage in a lot of international trade supported by an increasingly large and adventurous Chinese merchant fleet that was mainly based in the ports of Fuzhou, Quanzhou and Guangzhou.[21] Throughout the fourteenth and fifteenth centuries Chinese merchants sailed as far as the east coast of Africa and, some believe, even rounded the Cape of Good Hope.[22] The Chinese suddenly stopped their global exploration in 1433, however, partly because of internal disagreement about the wisdom of expansionism and partly because of the growing Mongol threat to their northern frontiers.[23] In contrast to the Chinese adventurousness, the medieval merchants of Europe were fairly inward-looking and conservative and conducted little trade with the rest of world; it would have seemed unlikely, during those times, that they would ever come to dominate global trade. By the fifteenth century, however, the merchants and mariners of Europe had become much more outward-looking. A key element in their new daring was the development of a type of fully rigged ship that combined the square-rigged tradition of northern Europe with the triangular (lateen) rigged tradition of southern Europe.[24] The new ships could sail closer to the wind, were faster, more manoeuvrable and more seaworthy than previous ships, and they required smaller crews.[25] These ships were known as 'caravels' and were crucial in enabling European exploration of the Atlantic for the first time.[26] When they were combined with better navigation techniques (which also combined northern and southern European traditions), and the establishment of maritime insurance, Europe was ripe to begin exploring the world. Advances in transport technology held the key to European exploration and, eventually, to the Europeans' establishment of a global trade network.

The Portuguese and the Spanish were particularly keen to begin exploiting the new potential that the improved ship design presented. By 1446 the Portuguese had colonised the Atlantic islands of Azores, Madeira, Cape Verde and Canary and were probing the Guinea coast of West Africa, establishing trading posts as they went that were particularly active in the trade of slaves and gold.[27] (Pioneering though the Portuguese undoubtedly were, it is generally forgotten that a full 2,000 years before the Portuguese the Phoenicians had sailed right around Africa.)[28] The Portuguese reached Sierra Leone in 1461, the Congo in 1483 then Bartholomew Diaz rounded the Cape of Good Hope in 1487. Five years later a navigator from Genoa, Christopher Columbus, left Europe, intending to open up a sea route to China and India. Having initially approached the Portuguese, but without success, Columbus was backed by the Spanish who were envious of the maritime success of the Portuguese. He reached Cuba and Haiti but thought he'd reached Japan. Whatever his delusions his 1492 voyage had monumental importance, beginning five centuries of European world domination via trade and colonisation. Six years after Columbus's voyage a Portuguese explorer, Vasco da Gama, reached the east coast of Africa and then India. Once da Gama set foot on the coast of India, Europe had closed its net around the Americas, Africa and Asia. Truly global trade now had the tentacles to reach every corner of the world. There was little doubt that the possibility of greater trade profits was a major motivator for the Portuguese and Spanish – authoritative records from the time make it clear that they would not sail to new lands unless they thought there was a good chance of making money.[29]

A major global economic change that the Portuguese and Spanish discoveries helped to bring on – whose effect is still very much with us today – was the rise of the nation-state. Before the fifteenth century nations as we know them today were relatively insignificant and it was cities that wielded most political power, but after the fifteenth century a new national consciousness began to grow.[30] Economic policies began to be based around the prosperity of nations instead of the prosperity of cities. The rise of nationalism brought with it the start of a trade philosophy known as 'mercantilism' which was a theory that thought it important for nations to secure a surplus of exports over imports.[31]

European global exploration

There was never any humility either in Europe's approach to the new lands it reached or in the way it tried to take over pre-existing local trading networks. From the very start there was local hostility towards the new European trade presence. Arab traders in Mozambique opposed da Gama's attempts to trade along the east coast of Africa, whilst Persians and Arabs resisted his attempts to trade in India.[32] The big advantage the Portuguese had over the Persians and Arabs, however, was their more sophisticated weaponry – an edge that Europe generally held over the rest of the world by the time of da Gama's voyage. Between the twelfth and fourteenth centuries European armaments had gone through quantum leaps in complexity and effectiveness through the development of weaponry such as the crossbow, the longbow and the pike as well as the reinvention of gunpowder (which had earlier been developed by the Chinese).[33] European kings had also developed tax bases that enabled them to finance this more expensive weaponry. Major empires before the modern European empires, such as the Moghul, Ottoman and Ming empires of Asia, had not combined warfare with trade but the Europeans had no compunction about doing so.[34] The result was that when West met East through da Gama's and Columbus's voyages the Europeans could always fall back on the power of the gun to force their way into local trading networks. In the sixteenth century the

Portuguese decided to wage all-out war on the Muslim traders of the Indian Ocean. The same approach was later used by the Dutch and English who would often heavily fortify their trading settlements. No real attempt was made by the Europeans to trade on local terms and it was a given that trade-related violence was acceptable. K. N. Chauduri, author of *Trade and Civilization in the Indian Ocean*, argues: 'the principle of armed trading introduced by the Portuguese conquistadors in the Indian Ocean was taken over by the Dutch and English East India companies without any attempt to find an explicit justification for the practice'.[35] The Spanish were no less violent in the Americas. The Europeans' forced domination of trade in Asia took longer to have the desired effect than their forced domination of trade in the Americas but in the end they won out in both continents. A large part of the reason why Asia took longer to conquer was the fact that Asians shared some of the same Eurasian disease pool as the Europeans and were not devastated by new diseases as the South Americans were; their organisational skills were also a better match for those of the Europeans.[36] Basically, global trade has never been a meeting of equals and that remains as much the case today as it was in the sixteenth century.

World trade in the sixteenth and seventeenth centuries

By the end of the sixteenth century the Spanish dominated trade with the Americas, apart from Brazil, and the Portuguese dominated trade with Africa, Asia and Brazil. Global trade experienced a sharp rise between the mid-fifteenth century and the mid-seventeenth century[37] largely powered by this Iberian domination of global trade links. But by today's standards the trade links were fairly tenuous. A voyage from Lisbon to the west coast of India could take anywhere from six to eighteen months, and no more than about a dozen Portuguese ships did the voyage each year.[38] The voyage from Spain to the Americas only took about half that time, but in the early sixteenth century no more than about one hundred ships completed the voyage each year.[39]

Gold, slaves and pepper dominated trade with Africa while pepper, spices and drugs dominated trade with Asia; sugar and tobacco dominated trade with the Americas. Early in the sixteenth century the Spanish and Portuguese established sugar plantations in the Caribbean and South America; sugar growing is very labour-intensive and its establishment in the Americas was responsible for a sharp rise in the shameful importation of African slaves to the Americas. Roughly 20 million slaves were shipped out of Africa between the mid-fifteenth and mid-seventeenth centuries; about two thirds of those who reached the Americas were used to grow sugar.[40] The Americas were less self-sufficient and more subservient to Europe than Asia was which resulted in European trade surpluses with the Americas but persistent European trade deficits with Asia. To finance the Asian trade deficits, the Spanish and Portuguese took a lot of gold and silver out of the Americas; in fact between 1500 and 1800 some 85 per cent of all the silver mined around the world, and 70 per cent of all the gold mined around the world, came out of the Americas[41] with most of it ending up in Asia. The use of this gold and silver to finance European trade radically changed the face of global trade. Until the sixteenth century most global trade had been done by barter; the South American gold and silver monetarised world trade in a way it had never been before.[42] From the very start Europeans turned their colonies into raw material suppliers and kept most of the value-adding in Europe – another characteristic still very much with us today.

The Spanish and Portuguese domination of Asian and American trade was shortlived. By the early seventeenth century, Spanish expansion throughout the Americas had stalled and Dutch and British traders had taken over much of Portugal's trade with Asia. Part of the reason for the Dutch and British takeover was the superior design of their ships which could move faster and perform better in battle than Spanish or Portuguese ships.[43] The Dutch and British also had a more central geographical position in Europe than the Spanish and Portuguese.

One should not assume, however, simply because Europe dominated trade between continents in the sixteenth century that it was necessarily responsible for producing a lot of the world's traded goods and services. In the sixteenth century India had between 20 and 25 per cent of the world's population and its share of global trade was roughly the same.[44] In fact India was probably the largest exporter in the world between 1500 and 1700.[45]

In Asia throughout the entire seventeenth century as much as three-quarters of Asian exports to Europe were made up of pepper, spices, textiles and silks.[46] Of these, pepper was the main export, particularly during the first half of the seventeenth century. During the early seventeenth century the Dutch had taken over the Portuguese trade in pepper and spices. Most of their trade conquest was carried on through the Dutch East India Company. Formed in 1602, the Dutch East India Company was one of the world's first transnational corporations – until its formation, money had been raised for each individual trade voyage to Asia but its establishment allowed permanent capital to be raised for Asian trade thereby making it more secure. Later in the sixteenth century the English formed their equally formidable English East India Company; the two transnational corporations controlled most of the European trade with Asia until well into the eighteenth century. Eventually there was a plethora of European colonial trade companies which included: the Royal Company of Havana (Spanish), the Royal Company of San Fernando (Spanish), the Royal Company of Barcelona (Spanish), the Hudson Bay Company (British), The Royal African Company (British), the French West India Company and the Franco-African Company. Not only did the Dutch and British displace the Portuguese, they also helped to end the overland Silk Road trade route between Europe and Asia.

The seventeenth century saw not only major changes in the management of global trade, but also major changes in its make-up. Significant changes in European tastes brought enormous changes in the continent's trade with both Asia and America. A major change in the trade with Asia took root in the early part of the century when the English East India Company introduced Indian-made cotton textiles to Britain. Throughout the century the British acquired an ever-growing taste for Indian cotton textiles which gradually ate into the traditional markets for linen and woollen textiles.[47] Another major change in tastes, which took root in the later part of the seventeenth century, was the increasing popularity of tea and coffee in Europe. Coffee took off a bit earlier than tea and was originally sourced from Yemen.[48] Tea initially mainly came from China and during much of the century the Chinese were reluctant to begin a major trade in it but by 1699 the English East India Company had established a tea factory in Canton.[49]

Just as the new European taste for tea, coffee and Indian cotton changed the make-up of Asian trade, a growing European taste for tobacco changed the make-up of trade with the Americas. During the seventeenth century European demand for tobacco grew to seemingly insatiable levels and tobacco cultivation became established in the Americas in much the same way that sugar cultivation had before it.[50] Until the middle of the eighteenth century tobacco and sugar accounted for a full three-quarters of all British imports from the Americas.[51] The surging popularity of both commodities increased the demand for slaves in the Americas, and by the late seventeenth century slaves had replaced gold as the commodity most purchased by Europeans in West Africa.[52] Over 6 million slaves were brought to the United States between 1701 and 1810, or about two-thirds of the total number that ever landed in the Western hemisphere.[53] Throughout the century the Dutch controlled much of the slave trade and had a large share of the overall trade with the Americas, but by the end of the eighteenth century the English were beginning to get the upper hand in the slave trade.

To generalise, between the voyages of da Gama and Columbus and the start of the Industrial Revolution in the eighteenth century, three types of global trade were dominant: slaves (from Africa), gold and silver (from the Americas) and drugs (coffee, tea, sugar, chocolate and tobacco from Asia and the Americas).[54]

As well as the specific changes in the trade between Europe, Asia, Africa and the Americas discussed above, there were some overarching developments throughout the seventeenth century that would eventually have a huge impact on global trade. Bills of exchange had been used since the Middle Ages, but during the second half of the seventeenth century their use became universal throughout Western and Central Europe. These allowed traders to shift money and credits from place to place without running the risks associated with transporting metal currency over vast distances.[55] Another major development was the discovery of the existence of atmospheric pressure, which would be crucial to the development of the steam engine in the eighteenth century. In the mid-seventeenth century Evangelista Torricelli and Otto van Guericke became the first Europeans to prove that atmospheric pressure existed, with von Guericke famously publicly demonstrating that two teams of horses could not separate two hemispheres that had had the air enclosed between them removed. Yet again changes in transport technology would be pivotal in the development of global trade.

Throughout the seventeenth century, relations between the new European trade giants of Holland and Britain were tense. They fought three wars, largely over trade supremacy, in 1652–54, 1664–67 and 1672–78. But by the end of the century a rapprochement had developed between the two countries aided by a marriage between their royal families.[56] By then, however, Britain was vying with France, not Holland, to be the dominant global trade power; Britain eventually prevailed after the final defeat of Napoleon in 1815.

World trade in the eighteenth century

If the sixteenth and seventeenth centuries had introduced new currents to global trade, the eighteenth century brought a tidal wave: in fact by the end of the century global trade had been completely transformed. The biggest change was the dawning of the Industrial Revolution, which coincided with the beginning of a major textile industry in Europe. In the 1760s the turning of cotton into thread was revolutionised by a new spinning machine developed in Britain by Richard Arkwright and the 'Spinning Jenny' invented by James Hargraves.[57] These machines became married to the ground-breaking steam engine invented by James Watt which went into full production in 1774. Watt's machine was a refinement of the atmospheric engines used to pump water from British mines originally invented by Thomas Savery in 1698 then considerably improved by Thomas Newcomen in 1712.[58] The marriage of the new steam and spinning technologies was consummated by the installation of a steam engine in a spinning factory in Nottinghamshire in 1785. This led to a radical reduction in the cost of spun yarn which by 1812 was only one-tenth of its cost three decades before.[59] Before the installation of the steam engine Indian cotton textiles had dominated world textile trade. At its peak India had produced over a quarter of all the world's cloth[60] but the introduction of the new steam engine in Britain devastated the large Indian manufacturers and brutally exposed India to the harsh new realities of global trade politics. This began the sorry tradition of a lot of global manufacturing value-adding being transferred from the poorer to the richer parts of the world.

The Industrial Revolution did much more than wipe out the Indian cotton textile manufacturing industry, it also radically changed the place of Europe in the global trade network. Until the Industrial Revolution the European market didn't necessarily dominate global trade. It was more of a facilitator than a driver of global trade. But once the Industrial Revolution gave Europe a major manufacturing and technological edge over the rest of the world it went from being a trade facilitator to being a generator of global trade and the centre of the global trade network. Global trade after the Industrial Revolution necessarily came to be increasingly channelled through Europe as the continent became the all-powerful beating heart of the world trade system. And the Industrial Revolution also radically changed commerce within Europe itself. Within Europe up until then, businesses were largely self-sufficient and used non-specialised labour; most workplaces took a product from its primary ingredients right through to its final form and most employees were involved with every stage of a product's production. But after the start of the Industrial Revolution European businesses and the labour force became more specialised with employees involved with only particu-

lar parts of the production process, and businesses incre..
only part of overall product development. This is another fe..
global trade that is still very much with us today.

Not only did commerce become more specialised, it also became
more productive. This created surpluses that had to be sold beyond
local markets which drove a need to expand Europe's global trade
network. The higher productivity created a new hunger for raw
materials to feed the newly established factories of the Industrial
Revolution which also drove a major expansion of Europe's trade.

Adam Smith's *Wealth of Nations*

The influence of the Industrial Revolution reached way beyond the
make-up of British and European business. It coincided with the
Enlightenment which put a new emphasis on rationality, science and
the importance of the individual all of which were values crucial to the
success of the Industrial Revolution. The new Enlightenment values
created a new class of philosophers. Until then philosophy had been
dominated by the Church which was often in league with the
monarchy and the landowning nobility who together pushed a creed
of divine rights, family values, loyalty to the crown and duty to one's
country.[61] The Enlightenment philosophers, however, promoted a
belief in rationality, cause–and–effect relationships, organisational efficiency and the entrepreneurial potential of the individual. One of the
new breed of philosophers was Adam Smith, a Scottish national who
originally studied theology. In 1776 Smith published his landmark
opus, *An Inquiry into the Nature and Causes of the Wealth of Nations*
(however during Smith's lifetime his reputation was based more on his
six-volume *The Theory of Moral Sentiments* published between 1759
and 1790).[62] During the eighteenth century economics was considered
a branch of philosophy, and Smith's *Wealth of Nations* book was as
much an exploration of the human psyche as it was a study in what we
would today consider economics. He argued that economic systems
didn't have to rely on altruism and that they should instead capitalise

ation of individuals to get ahead. Smith
affection and support weren't necessary to
He said the collective pursuit of self-interest,
.y, could generate enormous collective wealth
.iould hold societies together. The two best ways
.tive wealth, he argued, were to respect the alloca-
t the free market and to have a high degree of
specia... the workforce. He also argued there should be productive specialisation between countries which necessarily required free
trade. Smith argued that in a free market producers are motivated by a
sort of virtuous self-interest that sees them strive to make the most
desirable goods at the most competitive prices – led by 'an invisible
hand'.[64] He claimed that 'the more efficient distribution of resources
brought about by unimpeded trade would raise productivity all around
and thus increase everybody's purchasing power'.[65] Smith also said
England would be a winner from trade if it imported goods that could
be produced at lower prices in other countries.[66]

Smith's book was an instant success. Its first edition sold out within
six months, and The Wealth of Nations went on to become the definitive text for champions of free trade and free markets – when Ronald
Reagan was elected president of the United States in 1980 many of his
supporters wore ties with the profile of Adam Smith on them.[67] But it
is important to remember that Smith was largely reflecting the mood
of his time, a time that rejoiced in the new-found liberties brought
about by the end of monarchical rule and the potential of new technology, the new Industrial Revolution and new global markets. Smith
was part of a broader eighteenth-century 'Scottish Enlightenment'
school of philosophy that held that society had progressed through
several important historic stages of which the eighteenth century was
a crucial one.[68] Smith never lived to see the downsides of technology,
however – like the greenhouse effect – or the downsides of global
markets – like the Third World debt crisis. Also, Smith's views
assumed perfect markets that knew nothing of monopolistic market
shares held by dominant companies or lop-sided global trade deals
tilted against low-income countries, so his views were very much a

product of their time and don't necessarily connect with today's world.

By the end of the eighteenth century Europe had colonised extensive fertile and mineral-rich areas of the Americas and the Pacific in particular whose colonised area exceeded that of all of Western Europe. These newly colonised areas fed the raw material hunger of Europe's Industrial Revolution. The infamous British coloniser Cecil Rhodes once remarked 'we must find new lands from which we can easily obtain raw materials and at the same time exploit the cheap slave labour that is available from the natives of the colonies'.

In general terms the period up until the end of the eighteenth century saw major changes in the structure of global trade but no quantum change in the volume of global trade. The structural changes that took place during the eighteenth century were mainly to do with the linkage of pre-existing continental trade networks by the Europeans. Right until the end of the eighteenth century the influence of trade was mainly felt at the edges of economic activity because global trade remained largely confined to luxury and high-profit/low-volume goods.

World trade in the nineteenth century

After the end of the eighteenth century world trade entered a new era fundamentally different to everything before. The changes in global trade that had taken place laid the foundations for an explosion in global trade throughout the nineteenth and twentieth centuries. A global trade network had already been established but it only began to carry a significant volume of goods and services after the start of the nineteenth century.

During the nineteenth century the growth of global trade hugely outpaced the growth in worldwide production. By 1913 world output per head of population was 2.2 times what it had been in 1800 whereas the volume of per capita trade was 25 times its 1800 level.[69] In 1800 the total value of global trade was equal to only about three per cent of the value of all the world's combined gross domestic product but by 1913 it had reached 33 per cent[70] – a proportion only slightly less than its level today. Between 1800 and 1913 global trade grew by between 30 and 60 per cent per decade with the highest growth recorded between 1840 and 1870.[71] By contrast, trade volumes in the sixteenth, seventeenth and eighteenth centuries had only increased by about 1 per cent per year.[72] All of this made the nineteenth century a period of some of the fastest growth in global trade ever seen with only the second half of the twentieth century rivalling it.

One of the major drivers of the amazing nineteenth-century growth in global trade was the use of steam power in both sea and rail transport. Just as it had radically reshaped industrialisation in the eighteenth century, steam power radically reshaped trade and transport in the nineteenth century. The first commercial steamship was built in Glasgow in 1812 and operated along the Scottish coast.[73] In 1838 the *Great Western* was launched – the first steam vessel that could cross the Atlantic without refuelling. Steam power hugely increased the carrying capacity of oceangoing ships but they had relatively short ranges and needed frequent stops for coal. By the late nineteenth century Britain had a reliable global network of coal refuelling ports and its domination of steamship technology allowed it to dominate global trade.[74] A major improvement in steam technology came with the development of turbines specifically made for marine propulsion, first used in 1897.[75] Steamships could move at many times the speed of sailing ships and could travel in any weather. They could also carry much larger volumes of freight. They slashed the time it took to travel between Europe and Asia or the Americas with the result that peacetime freight rates fell by 80 per cent between 1815 and 1850 then fell by another 70 per cent between 1870 and 1900.[76]

The development of railways followed a similar trajectory. The first successful railway was developed by George Stephenson in Britain in 1825.[77] After its development there followed a massive laying of railway track and huge speculation in the new railway industry spurred along by rapid advances in metal technology including the discovery of the technique for converting iron into steel in 1856.[78] In the second half of the nineteenth century many high-income countries got caught up in a track-laying frenzy – between 1840 and 1900 the amount of track laid in the US increased 54-fold while in Britain it increased 13-fold.[79]

The upshot of the advances in steam technology was that a much greater range of goods could be profitably traded around the world and many new international business opportunities opened up. Until the nineteenth century international trade had been largely confined to luxury items; steam power made the movement of a broad range of bulk commodities possible for the first time. Instead of only low-volume/high-profit items being traded internationally, many large-volume/lower-profit items could now profitably be moved around the world.

Another major contributor to the nineteenth-century global trade boom was the invention of telegraph communication. The first successful demonstration of electrostatic communication was made in Britain by Francis Ronalds in 1816.[80] By the 1840s electric telegraph communication had become popular, aided by the invention of Morse Code by Samuel Morse in the 1830s. In 1851 Britain and the United States were linked for the first time by an undersea telegraphic cable.[81] In 1876 Alexander Graham Bell developed the first successful telephone.

The combination of the new steam, railway and telegraph technologies had a powerful effect on world trade. Author Philippe Legrain argues that 'steamships, railways and the telegraph made nineteenth century globalisation possible'.[82]

The upshot of the new technology was that global trade experienced a significant deepening. Before the nineteenth century, global trade had been mainly confined to coastal towns and cities and didn't affect inland centres very much; the new steam, railway and telegraph technologies ensured that global trade was able to touch all corners of the world.[83]

Another major development that would have huge implications for global trade was the discovery of oil in the late nineteenth century. The first major oil discovery in the world was made in the US by Edwin L. Drake at Titusville, in Pennsylvania, in 1859.[84] Eleven years later John D. Rockefeller formed the first major oil transnational corporation, the Standard Oil Company. Oil was first discovered in the Baku region of Russia in 1873, and in 1885 the Royal Dutch oil company discovered oil in the Sumatra region of Indonesia.[85] On the back of these discoveries Henry Ford built his first motor car in 1896.

Another major force that slashed the cost of global freight was the building of the Suez Canal between 1859 and 1869. Within three months of its opening the cost of shipping between London and Bombay fell by 30 per cent and the time it took to travel from Marseille to Shanghai fell from 110 days to 37 days.[86] Goods could now move around the world on a scale never dreamed of before.

Ricardo's theory of comparative advantage

The nineteenth century produced a major refinement of Adam Smith's landmark economic philosophies in the form of the economic philosophies of Englishman David Ricardo. Like Smith, Ricardo was a passionate supporter of free trade, but he took Smith's theories further by formulating a theory of *comparative advantage* which he expounded in his 1817 opus *On the Principles of Political Economy and Taxation*. The comparative advantage theory essentially held that even if a country can produce several different goods more efficiently than another country it is advantageous, for both countries, for the more efficient one to specialise in that product that it produces most efficiently (and cheaply) of all. Like Smith, Ricardo is regarded as something of a free trade pin-up boy but also like Smith he largely reflected the influences of his time. When he developed his theory Britain was suffering from high food prices, partly as a result of the Napoleonic Wars, and Ricardo argued that the country could lower this cost by specialising in manufacturing and importing all its food.[87] His comparative advantage theory was underpinned by several assumptions that don't necessarily hold today, however. One was a fundamental assumption that factors of production can not cross national boundaries and that once a country holds a competitive edge in the production of a product it will never lose it. During the nineteenth century this assumption was valid because even though goods had become more mobile global capital had not. Today, of course, capital can move very freely around the world and factors of production can easily move between countries. Comparative advantage has been replaced by *competitive advantage* and as a result Ricardo's theory is no longer particularly valid.

As the Industrial Revolution developed, Europe became more and more entrenched as the centre of global trade. By 1876–1880 Europe accounted for a massive 64 per cent of all the world's exports and 70 per cent of all the world's imports.[88] Within Europe Britain reigned as the dominant trading nation throughout much of the nineteenth century, accounting for nearly half of all the world's imports in the 1850s.[89] The European domination of global trade continued right up until the start of the First World War: Europe still accounted for 59 per cent of all the world's exports and 65 per cent of all the world's imports in 1913.[90] During the nineteenth century Germany, France and the United States all unsuccessfully attempted to challenge Britain's trade dominance. Despite the lack of success of their power plays Britain's domination started to wane with its share of manufactured exports, for instance, falling from 88 per cent of the global total between 1876 and 1880 to 70 per cent by 1913.[91]

One of the most disgraceful chapters in the story of Britain's global trade domination took place between 1839 and 1860 when it waged its Opium Wars with China. Britain had long been frustrated by the restricted access both it and most other European countries had to the Chinese market and also by the trade deficits it routinely ran up with the Chinese. Its answer to both was to introduce Indian-grown opium to China. As Chinese addiction to the drug spread, the Chinese moved to ban it which sparked the wars. The British ended up humiliating the Chinese and as part of its winnings ended up getting access to several Chinese coastal cities as well as taking control of Hong Kong.

During the nineteenth century there were major changes in the make-up of world trade. Raw materials accounted for just under two-thirds of world trade throughout the nineteenth century[92] but towards the end of the century agricultural produce and foodstuffs in general declined in importance while minerals increased their share.[93] The value of the global trade in manufactured goods almost trebled between 1876–80 and 1913.[94] Increasingly throughout the century the emphasis of manufactured trade shifted from textiles towards goods made from metal and other products including chemicals, paper, wood products, clay and glass.[95]

World trade in the twentieth century

Global trade seemed unstoppable during the nineteenth century and the early part of the twentieth century. But after the First World War it hit a wall. After growing by between 30 and 60 per cent per decade during the nineteenth century it grew by only 14 per cent per decade during the period from 1913 to 1937.[96] This rate of growth was much slower than the growth of world output at the time. Global trade was hard hit by the First World War but revived fairly rapidly during the 1920s even though Europe emerged from the war in a vulnerable state with major reconstruction and inflationary pressures upon it. Throughout the 1920s there was a delicate balance of global financial flows between the world's major countries. Europe consistently ran a trade deficit with the United States, whose economy came out of the war relatively unscathed, and the deficits were mainly financed through large flows of US capital that came back to Europe in the form of loans and foreign investment. The delicate financial flows were largely the result of inter-government borrowings used to finance the First World War. Before the war there was little debt between European governments, but during it they borrowed heavily from each other and from the United States in particular. Subsequently they relied on German post-war reparations to finance the debts.[97] This delicate balance came asunder, however, in October 1929 when Wall Street crashed and US investors began calling in their money from overseas. The Wall Street crash kicked off the Great Depression which had a major dampening effect on global trade.

Not only was the pace of global trade expansion significantly affected by the First World War and the interwar years, so too was the ranking of the world's dominant trade powers. The first half of the twentieth century ended European dominance of global trade. In 1913 Europe was responsible for almost two-thirds of global trade but by 1937 it was responsible for just over half.[98] A lot of its trade share went to the US and Japan: North America accounted for just over 13 per cent of global trade in 1913 compared to just under 16 per cent in 1937, while Asia increased its global trade share from about 11 per cent in 1913 to just under 16 per cent in 1937.[99]

One of the most significant areas in which Europe lost its hegemony was the trade in manufactured goods: its global share fell from four-fifths in 1913 to two-thirds in 1937.[100] Britain lost much of its share of manufactured goods trade before the First World War; after the war the rest of Europe also lost out to other producers around the world. The United States emerged from the First World War as a major new player in the trade of manufactured goods, increasing its share of global manufactures trade from 13 per cent in 1913 to 20 per cent in 1937.[101] Within the trade of manufactured products, engineered and metal goods continued to account for a increasingly large share – nearly half by 1937 – while the trade in textiles continued to slide, going from just under 30 per cent in 1913 to just under 20 per cent in 1937.[102]

Raw materials continued to account for about two-thirds of all global-goods trade between 1913 and 1937 but food and agriculture continued to lose importance while minerals continued to gain importance. One of the fastest-growing areas of raw material exports was oil. In 1913 virtually no oil was traded around the world but by 1920 US$1,170 million worth was being traded.[103] Europe was the main importer of oil, and the United States, Dutch Indonesia and Venezuela were the main exporters.

The discovery of oil was a crucial development for global trade. The first drive-in petrol station had been opened in St Louis in the United States in 1907.[104] Oil grew in importance with the development of the 'cracking' process of oil refinement in 1913 as well as the acquisition by Western nations of the first oil concessions in the Middle East in Persia (Iran) in 1901 followed by a major discovery there in 1908 and the granting of an oil concession to Standard Oil of California in 1933.[105] Oil today is vital to world trade, it is the heart that keeps the global trade organ alive.

Other early-twentieth-century developments that would revolutionise global trade were the first flight by the Wright Brothers in 1903, the opening of the Panama Canal in 1914, the development of the diesel engine, the spread of the motor car and the spread of the telephone. The Wright Brothers' flight led to the start of aeroplane passenger travel in Germany before the First World War although it wasn't until the 1960s that declining air travel costs began to make air travel commonplace.[106] The Panama Canal cut about 8,000 nautical miles from the voyage from the east coast to the west coast of the United States. The diesel compression engine (named after one of its major inventors) was more than twice as efficient as the spark engine at converting fuel to effort.[107] It was first developed in 1892 and first fitted to a truck in 1924 – it reduced the fuel costs of trucks to less than half the comparable cost of a spark ignition engine.[108] Diesel engines were also eventually fitted to ships and in the 1920s radically lowered their costs as well.[109] German engineer Gottlieb Daimler had been responsible for developing the petrol-driven engine. In 1886 he attached a four-stroke engine to a bicycle, using an engine concept pioneered by fellow German Nikolaus Otto.[110] Ten years later Henry Ford produced his first car. The famous model T Ford followed in 1908.[111] Ford's early commercialisation of the motor car meant car travel was embraced much earlier in North America than in Europe. In 1912 the invention of the vacuum tube by Lee De Forest allowed the then infant telephone technology to carry calls over long distances (through amplification) which in 1956 led to the laying of the first trans-Atlantic telephone cable – between Scotland and Newfoundland.[112]

The world's economies were hit harder by the Second World War than they had been by the First – and it therefore had a more profound effect on global trade – but the world was generally able to recover from the Second World War more rapidly. Once most of the post-Second World War reconstruction was over, two decades of rapid economic growth began in nearly all the world's economies. High-income economies recorded an average annual growth rate of 4.9 per cent between 1950 and 1970, a rate that towered above the 2.6 per cent averaged between 1870 and 1913 and the 1.9 per cent averaged between 1913 and 1950.[113] This high growth rate resulted in a massive growth of global trade, which between 1948 and 1960 grew on average by just over 6 per cent per year; between 1960 and 1973 it grew by 8 per cent per year.[114] By 1973 trade was five and a half times its 1948 level. But by then the United States and Britain had lost much of their post-war trade dominance (they had accounted for more than half of all high-income country exports in 1950) while Western Europe and Japan had gained greater global trade shares.[115] Japan experienced particularly rapid export growth and nearly quadrupled its share of world exports between 1950 and 1973.[116] In the post-war years manufactured exports gained a much greater share of global exports, rising from 43 per cent in 1950 to 62 per cent in 1973, while food and raw materials declined in trade share falling from 57 per cent in 1950 to 38 per cent in 1973.[117]

The shocks of the seventies and early eighties

In amongst all the economic sunshine of the 1950s and 1960s was a cluster of interrelated dark clouds that remained relatively unnoticed until it was too late. A system of post-war global economic governance – which included the establishment of the International Monetary Fund and the World Bank and a new system of fixed exchange rates – developed at a major world economic conference held at Bretton Woods, in the United States, in 1944 (see Chapter 2) worked well throughout the fifties and sixties but it ultimately sowed the seeds of its own destruction.

One of the destructive seeds was the post-war trade dominance of the United States. As previously discussed, the US finished the Second World War with a giant share of global trade accompanied by large trade surpluses, both of which drove the US's determined post-war support for free trade. But US dominance did not last; the economies of Western Europe and Japan got on their feet again and came to compete more ferociously with the exports of the US. In 1958 the US recorded its first-ever trade deficit since the nineteenth century.[118] By the 1960s its occasional trade deficits were becoming more common and by the 1970s they had become a permanent feature of the US economy. Between 1967 and 1971 the US trade deficit increased from US$2.9 billion to US$19.8 billion.[119] These trade deficits were not helped by the massive debt-financed spending by the US on the Vietnam War which fuelled inflation and ratcheted up US export prices thereby making the country's trade less globally competitive. Nor were US trade deficits helped by the nation's huge oil thirst. Until the 1950s the US had been the world's largest producer of oil and one of its largest oil exporters which helped boost its trade surpluses. But in the 1950s US oil demand began outpacing its production and it started importing oil for the first time (today it imports about half its oil and by 2020 is likely to be importing about two-thirds).

A second seed of destruction lay in the increasing export prices that raw materials (agricultural produce and minerals, mainly) began to command in the 1960s. The unprecedented economic growth of the 1950s and 1960s created a massive demand for raw materials, whose global supply by the end of the 1960s was beginning to fall behind global demand. The net result was a sharp rise in the price of traded raw materials at the start of the 1970s. This did not help the trade balances of high-income countries such as the United States but it did help the trade balances of several low-income countries many of which relied on raw materials for most of their export income. Before the 1970s low-income countries had borrowed very little money from the rest of the world but once their raw material export prices began to climb they started looking like increasingly attractive clients to high-income-country banks which began to court them. The courtship was ultimately consummated with the foreign debts of poor countries more than quadrupling between 1970 and 1980.[120] The consummation was helped by the huge amounts of money that poured into Western banks from Middle Eastern oil producers benefiting from oil price increases throughout the 1970s. High-income-country banks like Citicorp and Bankers Trust came to make up to 80 per cent of their profits from Third World loans.[121] But like the post-war trade luck of the United States, the trade luck of low-income countries was not to last. By the end of the 1970s raw material export prices were beginning to fall and at the same time Paul Volcker, Chairman of the Federal Reserve Bank of the United States, pushed up interest rates – and therefore the debt repayments of poor countries – in an effort to 'blitz' the inflation of the 1970s. These two forces delivered a double whammy to poor countries but their ongoing need to keep financing their foreign debts meant they could not withdraw from the global economy as they had after the Second World War.

Oil experienced sharply increasing prices during the 1970s. During the 1950s and 1960s the world had become increasingly dependent on oil. In Western Europe, for instance, oil only supplied 23 per cent of its energy needs in 1955 but by 1972 it was supplying 60 per cent.[122] The assertiveness of its suppliers was also increasing. In 1960 the world's major oil exporters formed a supply association – the Organisation of Petroleum Exporting Countries (OPEC). In 1970 the Libyan government started pressuring oil companies operating in its country to give it a greater share of both oil revenues and the infrastructure used to extract it (following the rise to power of Muammar al-Qaddafi) a move that was copied by other Middle Eastern countries.[123] The new muscle of oil producers was flexed in a big way in 1973 following the start of the Yom Kippur war between Israel and Egypt/Syria. Oil prices rose in 1973 from US$2.90 per barrel in September to US$11.65 per barrel in December[124] – a move that increased the trade vulnerability of the US and most high-income countries that imported significant volumes of oil. The oil price rises generated a lot of extra revenue for Middle Eastern countries which they invested in a new, lightly regulated, London-based Eurodollar capital market which in turn financed the rapidly increasing lending to low-income countries.

These seeds of destruction coalesced and erupted in the early 1970s and early 1980s and in so doing completely changed the face of the world economy in general and world trade in particular.

As the trade deficits of the United States increased throughout the 1960s, more and more dollars poured out of its economy putting mounting strain on its gold reserves. It became increasingly obvious that its currency was overvalued, so in August 1971 President Richard Nixon unilaterally floated the US dollar and delinked it from the gold standard established at the 1944 Bretton Woods conference. This was a desperate act undertaken with no consultation whatsoever with other major global economies and was a telling indicator of the growing economic insecurity felt by the United States (which continues to this day). It ushered in a new era of floating exchange rates and massive speculation on the world's currency markets (aided by the convertibility of the world's major currencies from the 1950s). It also finally ended the Bretton Woods system which linked all the world's currencies to the US dollar (via fixed exchange rates). It heralded the end of certainty in the world economy and the start of a new era of speculative insecurity. Between 1979 and 1981 there was a second major hike in oil prices – this time coinciding with the fall of the Shah of Iran – which saw prices climb from US$13 to US$34 per barrel.[125] Then in 1982 there was a second major eruption of world economic forces with the start of the Third World debt crisis following default on foreign loans that year by Mexico and Argentina (after its defeat in the Falklands war). Amongst other things the debt crisis radically changed the role of the International Monetary Fund, which went from being a short-term currency crisis lender to a long-term free-market interventionist manager of low-income debtor economies. But more than anything else the de-linking of the dollar and the start of the Third World debt crisis meant, in the long term, that there was much less predictability in the world economy and that low-income countries were necessarily woven into it in a way they had never been before. In the short term these forces were also responsible for a major slowdown in world economic growth throughout the 1970s with a resultant slowdown in the growth of world trade (both fell to half their pre-1970s average).

Throughout the 1980s the growth of global trade remained fairly subdued: it grew by an average of 4 per cent each year between 1980 and 1988 and 4.5 per cent each year between 1973 and 1979; both rates were well down on the eight per cent average annual growth recorded between 1960 and 1973.[126] Another continuing trend during the 1980s was the domination of global trade by high-income countries. In 1980 they controlled 62 per cent of global goods trade and in 1990 they controlled 71 per cent.[127]

A major innovation that ended up radically altering global trade was the development of containerisation on ships. Containerisation was the brainchild of one Malcom McLean who in 1955 hit on the idea of lifting the body of a lorry – after it was unhitched from the driver's cab – on to a ship instead of individually loading its various cargo items.[128] This cut out freight handlers and soon gave way to the use of metal boxes (containers) instead of lorry chassis. In 1965 a standard container design was adopted right around the world.[129] By the 1970s ships solely dedicated to container carriage were dominating world sea freight (which carries about 80 per cent of all the world's trade). The result was that shipping costs fell radically and the amount of sea freight rose steeply. The development of shipping containers ended up having an even greater effect on lowering shipping costs than the development of the diesel engine had.[130] Between 1980 and 1996 the world's container fleet rose from slightly over 500,000 to more than 3 million vessels.[131] During the second half of the twentieth century not only did ships become more numerous, they also became a lot larger (in part as a result of the nationalisation of the Suez Canal by the Egyptian government in 1956 and its closure in 1967 – it reopened in 1975).

A by-product of the fall in shipping costs was the emergence of the global product – which has different parts produced and marketed from a number of countries around the world. One study found that a particular brand of car sold in America, for instance, was produced in nine different countries. Only 37 per cent of the car's production value was accounted for by work performed in the United States; assembly in South Korea accounted for another 30 per cent; 17.5 per cent was components and advanced technology made in Japan; 7.5 per cent was design in Germany; 4 per cent was minor parts made in Taiwan and Singapore; 2.5 per cent was advertising and marketing done in Britain and 1.5 per cent was data processing performed in Ireland and Barbados.[132]

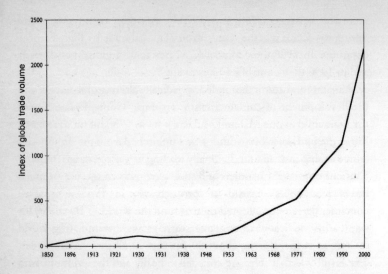

Figure 1.1 Volume of world trade since 1850

Sources: W. W. Rostow, *The World Economy: History and Prospect*, Austin, Texas, 1978, p. 669; C. L. Hottfrerich, *Interactions in the World Economy*, New York, Harvester Wheatsheaf, 1989, p. 2; World Trade Organisation, *Annual Report 2001*, Chart II.i; and Graham Dunkley, *Free Trade: Myth, Reality and Alternatives*, London, Zed Books, 2004, p. 91.

Another trade-impacting innovation that took place during the second half of the twentieth century was the development of jet aeroplanes. Aeroplanes did not progress beyond propeller-based technology until the Second World War when both the United States and Germany developed jet engine technology. During the decade after the war, global airline networks were developed for the first time although not until 1957 could an aeroplane fly non-stop from London to New York.[133] By the time Boeing 707s were crossing the Atlantic in 1958 they were taking only half the time that propeller-driven aeroplanes had taken.[134]

Changing global trade players

Just as the first half of the twentieth century had seen major changes in the makeup of the world's major trading nations the latter part of the century saw yet more major changes. The really big change of the 1980s was the rise of the four East Asian 'tiger' economies of South Korea, Taiwan, Hong Kong and Singapore as major trading nations. Throughout the 1950s and 1960s three of those four economies (excepting Hong Kong) had followed strong import substitution policies but in the 1980s, in particular, they radically changed course and became highly competitive exporting nations. Their competitiveness was often buttressed by large government subsidies. The net result was that they became major global trading nations by the early 1990s: their share of global trade had risen from 2 per cent in 1960 to 9.3 per cent in 1993.[135] In the 1990s Thailand and Malaysia also became increasingly established as major trading nations and by the end of the 1990s China had started to become a very significant global trader. Between 1986 and 2000 the value of China's exports increased eightfold while the total of world exports rose 3.4-fold over the same period.[136]

By the start of the twenty-first century, world trade had reached enormous levels. The value of world exports and imports now equals more than US$13 trillion – equal to 42 per cent of the world's combined gross domestic product.[137] This is an unprecedented level of world trade. By 2000 world trade was twenty times larger than it had been in 1950 while the world's overall production of goods and services was only six times larger.[138] All these growth statistics mask some major imbalances, however. High-income countries still dominate world trade as they did throughout all of the twentieth century. In 2002 developed countries accounted for 63 per cent of the world's exports while developing countries only accounted for 32 per cent.[139] There is also a major imbalance in the make-up of world trade. In recent years manufactured goods have accounted for 61 per cent of world trade but manufactured goods only account for about 20 per cent of the world's total output of goods and services; they therefore

Table 1.1 Timeline of the history of global trade

Prehistoric times	Limited trade between Africa, Europe and Asia
3rd century CE	Silk Road trade route linking Europe with Asia is established (ends in 17th century)
5th century	Limited Roman empire global trade ends with collapse of empire
7th century	Spread of Islam expands continental trade across Asia
10th century	China begins global trading (which finishes in 15th century)
15th century	Euro–Asian trade increasingly goes by sea, making ports like Venice important
1492	Christopher Columbus reaches West Indies
1498	Vasco da Gama reaches east coast of Africa
16th century	Portugal wages war on Muslim traders in Asia; Spain dominates trade with South America, Portugal dominates trade with Africa and Asia; large shipments of slaves leave Africa for American sugar plantations; South American gold monetarises global trade for the first time
17th century	Holland and Britain become the dominant global trade powers; cotton, tea and coffee come to dominate European trade with Asia, while tobacco and sugar come to dominate European trade with America
1602	The Dutch East India company is formed
18th century	Europe colonises vast new lands in the Americas and Pacific
1760s	New cotton spinning technology revolutionises textile production marking the start of the Industrial Revolution
1774	Full production starts of James Watt's new steam engine
1776	Adam Smith publishes *An Inquiry Into the Nature and Causes of the Wealth of Nations*
19th century	Volume of global trade grows at least twentyfold during the century
1812	First commercial steamship is launched
1816	First successful demonstration is made of electrostatic communication which paved the way for telegraph and telephone communication

1817	David Ricardo publishes *On the Principles of Political Economy and Taxation*
1825	First railway begins operation (in Britain)
1839–1860	Opium trade wars between Britain and China
1850s	Britain accounts for half of all global trade
1859	First ever discovery of oil (in Pennsylvania, in the USA)
1869	Suez Canal is opened
1886	Petrol engine is invented
1892	Diesel compression engine is invented
1896	Henry Ford sells the first commercial motor vehicle
1903	First successful aeroplane flight (by the Wright brothers)
1913	Oil 'cracking' process is invented
1914	Panama Canal is opened
1929	Wall Street crash leads begins Great Depression, causing major slowdown of global trade
1950s to 1970s	High world growth rates lead to large increases in global trade
1957	Jet aeroplanes begin flying non-stop between London and New York
1958	The USA records its first trade deficit in the 20th century
1965	Design of shipping containers becomes standardised around the world
1971	US dollar is de-linked from the gold standard
1973 and 1979	First and second world oil price rises result in a slowdown of global trade
1982	Start of Third World debt crisis
2000	Value of global trade reaches US$13 trillion – equal to a record 42 per cent of world gross domestic product

Sources: James D. Tracey (ed.), *The Political Economy of Merchant Empires: State Power and World Trade 1350–1750*, Cambridge University Press, New York, 1991, James D. Tracey (ed.), *The Rise of Merchant Empires: Long-distance trade in the early Modern World 1350–1750*, Cambridge University Press, New York, 1991, Peter J. Hugill, *World Trade since 1431: Geography, Technology and Capitalism*, The Johns Hopkins University Press, Baltimore, 1995 and The Reader's Digest Association, *The Last Two Million Years*, Reader's Digest Services, Sydney, 1986.

account for a disproportionate share of all the world's trade. The reverse is true of services – they account for about 20 per cent of world trade even though their share of the world's total output of goods and services is about 60 per cent.[140] Basically at the start of the twenty-first century the world has an enormous global trade market that has grown to massive proportions but its growth has been unstructured and has major flaws. Today world trade has quantity without necessarily having quality.

Notes

1   James D. Tracey (ed.), *The Political Economy of Merchant Empires: State Power and World Trade 1350–1750*, Cambridge University Press, New York, 1991, p. 422.

2   Kenneth Pomeranz and Steven Topik, *The World that Trade Created: Society, Culture, and the World Economy 1400 to the Present*, M.E. Sharpe, Armonk (New York), 1999, pp. 4,5.

3   Ibid., p. 17.

4   James D. Tracey (ed.), *The Rise of Merchant Empires: Long-distance Trade in the Early Modern World 1350–1750*, Cambridge University Press, New York, 1991, p. 341.

5   Tracey, *The Rise of Merchant Empires*, p. 74.

6   Pomeranz and Topik, *The World that Trade Created*, p. 5.

7   Roger E. Backhouse, *The Penguin History of Economics*, Penguin Books, London, 2002, pp. 25, 27.

8   Ibid., p. 39.

9   Tracey, *The Rise of Merchant Empires*, p. 38.

10   Ibid., p. 422.

11   Tracey, *The Rise of Merchant Empires*, p. 351.

12   Peter J. Hugill, *World Trade since 1431: Geography, Technology and Capitalism*, Johns Hopkins University Press, Baltimore, 1995, p. 106.

13   Tracey, *The Rise of Merchant Empires*, p. 352.

14   Ibid., pp. 351, 365.

15   Ibid., p. 17.

16   Ibid., p. 20.

17   Hugill, *World Trade since 1431*, p. 106.

18   Ibid., p. 110.

19   Tracey, *The Political Economy of Merchant Empires*, p. 436.

20   Tracey, *The Rise of Merchant Empires*, pp. 37,38.
21   Ibid., p. 402.
22   Pomeranz and Topik, *The World that Trade Created*, p. 51.
23   Hugill, *World Trade since 1431*, p. 18.
24   Tracey, *The Political Economy of Merchant Empires*, p. 239.
25   Ibid., p. 240.
26   Hugill, *World Trade since 1431*, p. 107.
27   Reader's Digest Association, *The Last Two Million Years*, Reader's Digest Services, Sydney, 1986, p. 335.
28   Ibid., p. 335.
29   Glyn Davies, *A History of Money: From Ancient Times to the Present Day*, University of Wales Press, Cardiff, 2002, p. 176.
30   Backhouse, *The Penguin History of Economics*, p. 56.
31   Ibid., p. 58.
32   Reader's Digest, *The Last Two Million Years*, p. 335.
33   Tracey, *The Political Economy of Merchant Empires*, p. 25.
34   Ibid., p. 149.
35   Ibid., p. 439.
36   Hugill, *World Trade since 1431*, p. 112.
37   Tracey, *The Rise of Merchant Empires*, p. 37.
38   Ibid., p. 49.
39   Ibid., p. 78.
40   Tracey, *The Political Economy of Merchant Empires*, p. 381.
41   Tracey, *The Rise of Merchant Empires*, p. 224.
42   Pomeranz and Topik, *The World that Trade Created*, p. 180.
43   Hugill, *World Trade since 1431*, p. 51.
44   Tracey, *The Rise of Merchant Empires*, p. 371.
45   Pomeranz and Topik, *The World that Trade Created*, p. 34.
46   Tracey, *The Rise of Merchant Empires*, p. 118.
47   Ibid., pp. 124, 126.
48   Ibid., p. 129.
49   Tracey, *The Political Economy of Merchant Empires*, p. 114.
50   Tracey, *The Rise of Merchant Empires*, p. 57.
51   Ibid., p. 131.
52   Ibid., p. 321.
53   Ibid., p. 288.
54   Pomeranz and Topik, *The World that Trade Created*, p. 84.
55   Tracey, *The Political Economy of Merchant Empires*, p. 283.
56   Hugill, *World Trade since 1431*, p. 120.
57   Reader's Digest, *The Last Two Million Years*, p. 315.
58   Ibid., pp. 313, 314.

59   Ibid., p. 315.

60   Tracey, *The Political Economy of Merchant Empires*, p. 229.

61   Richard Peet (ed.), *Unholy Trinity: the IMF, World Bank and WTO*, Zed Books, London, 2003, p. 5.

62   Backhouse, *The Penguin History of Economics*, p. 121.

63   Ibid., p. 122.

64   Chris Rohmann, *The Dictionary of Important Ideas and Thinkers*, Arrow Books, London, 2002, p. 362.

65   As quoted in Paul Kennedy, *The Rise and Fall of the Great Powers: Economic Change and Military Conflict from 1500 to 2000*, Fontana Press, London, 1988, p. 462.

66   Todd D. Buchholz, *New Ideas from Dead Economists: An Introduction to Modern Economic Thought*, Plume Printing, New York, 1990, p. 29.

67   Ibid., p. 10.

68   Backhouse, *The Penguin History of Economics*, p. 111.

69   A. G. Kenwood and A. L. Lougheed, *The Growth of the International Economy 1820–1990: An Introductory Text* (third edn), Routledge, London, 1992, p. 79.

70   Ibid.

71   Ibid., p 78.

72   Ibid., p. 85.

73   Reader's Digest, *The Last Two Million Years*, p. 315.

74   Peter Hugill, *World Trade since 1431*, p. 151.

75   Reader's Digest, *The Last Two Million Years*, p. 315.

76   Pomeranz and Topik, *The World that Trade Created*, p. 49.

77   Reader's Digest, *The Last Two Million Years*, p. 315.

78   Ibid., p. 315.

79   Hugill, *World Trade since 1431*, p. 174.

80   Reader's Digest, *The Last Two Million Years*, p. 317.

81   Philippe Legrain, *Open World: The Truth about Globalisation*, Abacus, London, 2002, p. 94.

82   Ibid., p. 89.

83   Hugill, *World Trade since 1431*, p. 30.

84   Daniel Yergin, *The Prize: The Epic Quest for Oil, Money and Power*, Free Press, New York, 1991, p. 789.

85   Ibid.

86   Pomeranz and Topik, *The World that Trade Created*, p. 68.

87   Backhouse, *The Penguin History of Economics*, pp. 137, 139.

88   Kenwood and Lougheed, *The Growth of the International Economy 1820–1990*, p. 81.

89   Ibid.

90 Ibid.
91 Ibid., p. 89.
92 Ibid., p. 83.
93 Ibid., p. 88.
94 Ibid., p. 84
95 Ibid., p. 87.
96 Ibid., p. 209.
97 Backhouse, *The Penguin History of Economics*, p. 216.
98 Kenwood and Lougheed, *The Growth of the International Economy 1820–1990*, p. 210.
99 Ibid., p. 211.
100 Ibid., p. 213.
101 Ibid., p. 218.
102 Ibid., p. 219.
103 Ibid., p. 217.
104 Yergin, *The Prize*, pp. 789, 790.
105 Ibid., pp. 789, 790.
106 Hugill, *World Trade since 1431*, p. 249.
107 Ibid., p. 240.
108 Ibid., pp. 240–241.
109 Ibid., p. 32.
110 Reader's Digest, *The Last Two Million Years*, p. 319.
111 Ibid.
112 Hugill, *World Trade since 1431*, pp. 321–322.
113 Ibid., p. 293.
114 Ibid., p. 286.
115 Ibid., p. 289.
116 Ibid.
117 Ibid., p. 290.
118 Joan E. Spero and Jeffrey A. Hart, *The Politics of International Economic Relations* (fifth edition), St Martin's Press, New York, 1997, p. 262.
119 Robbie Robertson, *The Three Waves of Globalisation: A History of a Developing Consciousness*, Zed Books, London, 2003, p. 194.
120 The Worldwatch Institute, *Vital Signs 2003–2004: The Trends that are Shaping our Future*, Earthscan, London, 2003, p. 47.
121 Nicholas Guyatt, *Another American Century?: The United States and the World after 2000*, Zed Books, London, 2000, p. 8.
122 Yergin, *The Prize*, p. 545.
123 Ibid., p. 791.
124 Ibid.
125 Ibid.

126 Kenwood and Lougheed, *The Growth of the International Economy 1820–1990*, p. 286.

127 United Nations Conference on Trade and Development, *Statistics in Brief*, downloaded from www.unctad.org in March 2004.

128 Kate Galbraith (ed.), *Globalisation: Making Sense of an Integrating World*, The Economist/Profile Books, London, 2001, p. 82.

129 Hugill, *World Trade since 1431*, p. 150.

130 Ibid.

131 Galbraith, *Globalisation*, p. 83.

132 Phillipe Legrain, *Open World*, p. 110.

133 Hugill, *World Trade since 1431*, pp. 282–283.

134 Ibid., p. 287.

135 Ibid., p. 232.

136 Based on figures in World Bank, *World Development Report 1988*, Oxford University Press, New York, 1988, pp. 242,243 and World Bank, *World Development Report 2002*, Oxford University Press, New York, 2002, pp. 238, 239.

137 World Bank, *World Development Report 2002*, Oxford University Press, New York, 2002, pp. 237, 239.

138 Emerging-market Indicators, *Economist*, 19 May 2001, p. 108.

139 United Nations Conference on Trade and Development, *Statistics in Brief*.

140 Graham Dunkley, *Free Trade: Myth, Reality and Alternatives*, Zed Books, London, 2004, p. 87.

2

Global trade negotiations

There is little subtlety about the politics of global trade. It is often brutal and frequently reflects broader power dynamics that run through international relations in general. The global trade negotiations held since the Second World War have largely reinforced rather than diluted global power relationships and an understanding of them is essential for an understanding of the future of global trade.

Trade negotiations since the Second World War

Every decade since the end of the Second World War has seen at least one major set of international talks aimed at writing new global trade rules. This level of international trade negotiation is very much a phenomenon of the post-Second World War years. Before the Second World War there were isolated global trade meetings – such as a World Economic Conference held by the League of Nations in 1927 – but they were few and far between.

The Bretton Woods Agreement and the International Trade Organisation

The global trade talks held after the Second World War had their origins in the war itself. As the US/British-led allies became more confident of victory in the war the US and Britain became increasingly concerned about the creation of a stable post-war economic environ-ment that would avoid the excesses of the interwar period (which had, in part, caused the war). Their dialogue on the issue dated from their signing of the Mutual Aid Agreement in 1941 which (although mainly concerned with lend-lease arrangements) committed both countries to post-war economic cooperation.[1] The United States was particularly focused on the potential of trade to create a stable post-war world economy and throughout the war it secured commitments from its allies to a freeing-up of international trade after the war finished.[2]

The foundations of the post-war economic order were laid even before the Second World War had finished, at a conference held in Bretton Woods, New Hampshire (United States), in July 1944 that was attended by 730 delegates from 44 countries (there were only about 55 countries in the world at the time). Although sometimes presented as an exercise in economic democracy, in reality the con-ference was run by the United States which didn't meaningfully negotiate with anyone apart from the British. According to authors Fatoumata Jawara and Aileen Kwa one of the key organisers for the United States, Harry Dexter White, 'was determined to maintain control of the outcome while at the same time creating the illusion that there was genuine participation in the process'.[3] The British and Americans both agreed on the need for general liberalisation after the war – both of trade and of capital mobility – but there was much detail they disagreed on. One of the thornier issues was whether countries that ran up trade surpluses should be treated any differently to countries that ran up trade deficits. The leader of the British delega-tion – the renowned economist John Maynard Keynes – was solidly of the view that they should be treated equally. Keynes argued that countries that ran up trade surpluses should have similar penalties applied to them as countries that ran up deficits (see Chapter 8).[4] Keynes had been partly inspired by a pre-war bilateral barter trade scheme devised by German economics minister, Hjalmar Schacht, which ensured countries stayed in trade balance with each other.[5] The United States, however, would have none of it. They were anticipating major trade surpluses after the war and the idea of trade surplus penalties was abhorrent to them. Dexter White, in particular, had no time for them saying 'we have been perfectly adamant on that point. We have taken the position of no, on that.'[6]

Despite this disagreement on trade surplus penalties the United States was still able to secure agreement to a global foreign exchange system where all the world's currencies would be pegged at a relatively fixed exchange rate to the US dollar which in turn would be convertible into gold. The fixed exchange rate/dollar–gold convertibility system depended on a long-term equilibrium of global balance-of-payments, but the Americans had refused to agree to the mechanism suggested by Keynes that would have delivered such equilibrium so the foundation the Bretton Woods fixed exchange rate house was built on was made of sand. Despite this, however, it remained in place for the next twenty-seven years and did an admirable job of delivering predictability and security before it spectacularly fell apart in the early 1970s.

Despite their lack of agreement on treating surplus and deficit countries equally the British and Americans generally agreed on the desirability of relatively free trade after the war. The US Secretary of State, Cordell Hull, was a particularly strong believer in free trade. Many people, both inside and outside the US, felt that the trade wars of the 1930s had been a major contributor to the Great Depression. There was also agreement on the need for an international body to administer trade after the war, but such a body would necessarily require broader agreement than the Bretton Woods conference could deliver. As part of the preparation for creating such a body a 'preparatory committee' meeting was held in London in 1946; a 'drafting committee' meeting was held at Lake Success in New York in 1947; then a penultimate conference was held in Geneva later in 1947 before a final conference to establish the body was held in Havana between November 1947 and March 1948.[7] The starting point for discussion at these talks was a 1945 US plan for a multilateral convention that would regulate and reduce restrictions on international trade.[8] It proposed rules for many aspects of global trade including tariffs, trade preferences, quantitative restrictions, subsidies and raw material price agreements, and also provided for the establishment of an International Trade Organisation (ITO) that would be the trade 'sister' of the International Monetary Fund and the World Bank (both created at the Bretton Woods conference).[9]

At the Havana conference itself the United States pushed for a system of global free trade based on the Reciprocal Trade Agreements Act deals it had negotiated with selected countries before the Second World War. But the US ran into resistance from low-income countries, particularly South American ones, that wanted trade concessions to aid their development, and from the Europeans, who wanted to continue their pre-war preferential trading agreements.[10] The final conference document, the Havana Charter, was very different to what had originally been envisaged by the United States and was a complex compromise that attempted to satisfy everyone but in the end satisfied no one, least of all the United States. The Americans had particular difficulty with the threat that the International Trade Organisation might pose to their national autonomy fearing it might be able to overrule decisions made by the US Congress. US congressman Robert Loree, chairman of the National Foreign Trade Council, said 'acceptance by the United States of a charter which could be amended without its assent, or over its dissent, would be a most unusual proceeding, involving a sacrifice of sovereignty unprecedented in the history of this country'.[11] After three years of delays, in 1950 US President Truman finally decided to scuttle the Havana Charter and its International Trade Organisation rather than submit the enabling legislation to Congress where it faced certain defeat.[12]

The General Agreement on Tariffs and Trade

Even though the International Trade Organisation did not survive, a supporting agreement developed by the Havana conference – the General Agreement on Tariffs and Trade (GATT) – did. The GATT contained general prohibitions on trade-restricting measures and also had a non-binding mechanism for resolving trade disputes, but its general trade policy coverage was not as comprehensive as the Havana Charter. Unlike the Havana Charter, the GATT did not include provisions covering economic development, raw material price support, restrictive business practices or the trade in services.[13] Like the International Trade Organisation, however, the GATT was framed around a philosophical foundation that said that global trade should be as free as possible and that restricted trade during the 1930s had contributed to the Great Depression.

Although intended as a temporary arrangement, and despite initially including only twenty-three members, over time the GATT became entrenched with its own Geneva-based secretariat. Increasingly the United States saw the GATT as a useful conduit for its post-war agenda of liberalised trade. Immediately after the Second World War a full one-third of all the exports that left the shores of the major high-income countries of the time came from the United States[14] so the US saw its economic future inexorably bound to trade; it also saw trade as a bulwark against communism. It used its large amounts of post-war Marshall Plan aid as a lever for trade liberalisation, particularly in Europe.[15] Through the Marshall Plan and the GATT the US tried to multilateralise the approach it had used in its pre-war bilateral Reciprocal Trade Agreements Act[16] (interestingly, the US is currently swinging back towards bilateral trade deals). As a result the GATT started conducting 'rounds' of international trade negotiations, the first of which was held in Geneva in 1947. Both the Geneva Round and the subsequent eight rounds were strongly promoted by the US.[17] Between the end of the war and the 1970s six trade rounds were held. Although twelve of the original twenty-three signatories of the GATT agreement were low-income countries the GATT was generally viewed with suspicion by low-income countries and was thought to be dominated by high-income countries, particularly the United States and the (then) European Economic Community. The GATT was also often viewed as something of an anti-communist, Cold War institution. As a result the early trade negotiations conducted by

GATT were largely ignored by low-income countries. Most of the early GATT rounds were also relatively short, generally lasting less than two years. The two trade rounds held in the 1960s and 1970s (the sixth and seventh GATT rounds) were longer and much broader, however, and had more than three times the number of participating countries (to some extent because of the increased number of countries in the world, particularly since the 1960s). Aside from the low-income countries' suspicion, in its early years the GATT was relatively uncontroversial, partly because its agreements covered a fairly narrow range of trade issues and partly because adherence to its rulings was effectively voluntary.

The Kennedy Round

The Kennedy Round was the sixth GATT round of trade talks and was much more protracted than earlier rounds – as all subsequent rounds were to be – lasting five years between 1962 and 1967. The Kennedy Round was the most significant of all the rounds held before the 1970s and amongst other things produced agreement to large cuts in tariffs applied to non-agricultural traded products[18] and replaced product-by-product tariff cuts with across-the-board cuts.[19] The Kennedy Round also considered the issue of agricultural tariffs but was unable to reach agreement (an ominous sign of things to come).

While high-income countries were freeing trade through GATT rounds, low-income countries were pursuing a very different strategy. At the 1944 Bretton Woods conference low-income countries asked that development of their economies be given equal status to the reconstruction of Europe. At the Havana conference they also asked for special protection from the forces of free trade through mechanisms such as tariff/quota protection of their 'infant industries' and price support funds for their raw material exports.[20] They were rebuffed at Bretton Woods, and when the US scuttled the International Trade Organisation they ended up being rebuffed at Havana as well. The result was that during the 1950s and 1960s low-income countries abandoned their attempts to influence the global economic agenda and instead turned inwards. South American countries in particular focused on building up local industries behind high tariff barriers and disengaged from the global trade market to a large degree.

The Tokyo Round

In the wake of the first oil price shock, and the delinking of the US dollar, a seventh round of GATT trade negotiations was launched – the Tokyo Round – which began in 1973. Although conducted during more pessimistic times than earlier trade rounds the goals of the Tokyo Round were more ambitious and it included more countries. The round sought further significant decreases in tariffs and quotas as well as tighter regulation of non-tariff barriers to trade.[21] Sixty-two countries had taken part in the Kennedy Round while ninety-nine took part in the Tokyo Round.[22] The Tokyo Round took six and a half years to complete and was largely successful in further reducing tariffs and quotas as well as in increasing the regulation of non-tariff trade barriers. In the crucial area of agricultural trade barrier reduction it was unsuccessful, however. Even though the United States claimed to support liberalisation of agricultural trade, the European Community and Japan did not and liberalisation efforts during the round failed.[23]

Both the Tokyo and Kennedy Rounds included low-income countries in a significant way for the first time although the concessions they were able to negotiate were modest. Starting in the 1950s the low-income country attitude of disengagement from global trade talks relaxed as they became more interested in global trade. As an inducement to participation, the Tokyo Round introduced the concept of longer trade agreement implementation periods for low-income countries. Although a number of low-income countries took part in the Tokyo Round negotiations a large number were not convinced of the worth of the round's final declaration and refused to sign it, thereby keeping themselves out of the GATT system.

The Uruguay Round

Between 1986 and 1993 an eighth round of global trade negotiations was conducted. It was launched at a GATT meeting held in Punta del Este, Uruguay, in September 1986.[24] In the late 1970s and early 1980s the two oil price shocks as well as the apparent success of highly interventionist trade policies – such as those pursued by the Japanese Ministry of Trade and Industry – had created a lot of disillusionment, or at best ambivalence, about free trade,[25] and there was reluctance to start a new round of negotiations. But the new Reagan government in the United States stimulated enthusiasm for the talks.

The Uruguay Round was fundamentally different to the previous seven rounds. Many more countries took place and for the first time low-income countries took a keen interest in the negotiations. In all, 125 countries took part, of which 91 were low-income countries.[26] Only 17 low-income countries had joined the GATT between 1967 and 1987 but between 1987 and 1994 alone another 29 joined the organisation.[27] By the 1980s low-income countries had become quite engaged with global trade as a result of a series of forces that included: a fall in their economic growth rates, the new trade success of several East Asian economies (which started in the 1980s), the need to service their foreign debts, the collapse in raw material prices, and pressure from the IMF and World Bank. The large increase in low-income country participation resulted in negotiations in areas of special concern to them including agriculture and clothing/textile trade.[28] This was seen as a major gain for these countries. High-income countries had special trade issues they wanted considered as well. They successfully lobbied for the introduction of three new major issues into the trade talks: services trade, global intellectual property rights and global trade-related investment. By the 1980s the trade in services had become the most rapidly growing sector of global trade, and high-income countries – who were generally well placed to export an increasing volume of services – wanted it freed up. Major pharmaceutical and finance transnational corporations lobbied the Reagan administration to have intellectual property rights included in the round because they were concerned about their perceived loss of overseas sales in countries that had loose patent laws. Low-income countries were reluctant to have these new issues introduced, however, and only agreed on condition that they were kept separate from the core negotiations on the trade in goods (which they weren't in the end).

Another new area taken on by the round was the tightening of global trade administration and more inflexible enforcement of global trade rulings. In contrast to the voluntary adherence regime of the GATT the Uruguay Round introduced a new compulsory adherence regime to trade disputes rulings to be heard by a new global trade authority, the World Trade Organisation, which replaced the GATT secretariat.

Although originally scheduled to finish by 1990 the Uruguay Round dragged on for another three years and nearly collapsed near its end. The issue of agricultural trade went close to derailing the negotiations. The United States, most low-income countries and the Cairns Group of agricultural free market countries wanted radical reductions in agricultural subsidisation and protectionism but the European Union (EU) and Japan were opposed and frequently held up negotiations over the issue. The EU (France in particular) persistently watered down compromises over farm subsidisation until the final agreement was fairly insignificant. Just as a new US president had been instrumental in starting the round another new US president – Bill Clinton – was instrumental in pushing through final agreement following his perceived success in getting agreement on the establishment of the North American Free Trade Agreement between Canada, the United States and Mexico.[29] The final Uruguay Round agreement was signed on 15 April 1994, in Marrakesh, Morocco. Within its text were several agreements that would have a huge impact on the future of trade. The most significant was agreement to establish the new World Trade Organisation (WTO) from 1995. The agreement also cut tariffs on manufactured products by up to one-third and gradually phased out restrictions on international clothing and textile trade over a ten-year period finishing in 2005. It also included a number of controversial 'side deals'. Some of the most controversial of these were: the Trade

Related Aspects of Intellectual Property Rights (TRIPS) agreement that tightened international patent law, the Trade Related Investment Measures (TRIMS) agreement that prohibited various forms of restriction on foreign investment connected with trade, and the General Agreement on Trade in Services (GATS) aimed at the liberalisation of the trade in services.

The Doha Round

For a short time after the completion of the Uruguay Round it seemed as though free trade harmony had broken out all over the world. This illusion was shattered in 1996 when the first post-Uruguay Round meeting of WTO trade ministers was held in Singapore. Low-income countries had finished the Uruguay Round concerned about the implementation of issues decided during the round, particularly the promised relaxation of high-income country agricultural protectionism and subsidisation. But at Singapore high-income countries made it clear their main priority was not implementation of the Uruguay Round but to push trade negotiations into new areas. At the meeting they identified four new issues they wanted included in the new round that became known as 'the Singapore issues'. They were: investment, competition, government procurement and trade facilitation. Low-income countries were generally loath to take on the new issues and the meeting only agreed to establish working groups on the issues. But at the meeting a fundamental question was posed that would dominate trade talks for the next ten years: should trade talks keep reaching into new areas or should they concentrate on consolidation in existing areas? This issue is a defining point of difference between high- and low-income countries.

The Singapore meeting laid the groundwork for the attempted launch of a new 'Millennium Round' of trade talks at a WTO meeting held in Seattle in November/December 1999. But the new Seattle talks hit a brick wall both internally and externally. Externally 50,000 people took to the streets of Seattle in an unprecedented show of public protest against the talks. Massive crowds met front-line high-tech soldiers and clouds of tear gas. Internally the debilitating factors included: major disagreements about the priorities of the trade talks, poor conference organisation, strong cohesion amongst low-income countries (who had come to the meeting better prepared than they had been for previous meetings), a lack of mediation by the United States host, and serious and unresolved disagreements between high-income countries.[30]

The collapse of the Seattle talks was only viewed as a temporary setback by the WTO which put enormous energy, under its new director Michael Moore, into a fresh attempt at launching a new round (this time called a 'Development Round') at Doha, Qatar, in November 2001. The Seattle failure put a lot of pressure on the Doha meeting, and added pressure came from the terrorist attacks on the World Trade Center and the Pentagon in the United States two months earlier as well as from the fear of an imminent global recession. Most low-income countries did not support launching a new round and most wanted a greater focus on implementation issues from the Uruguay Round. But they were far from united. Some low-income countries, particularly South American ones such as Argentina, Brazil, Paraguay, Uruguay, Bolivia and Chile, could go along with the launch of a new round as long as it included significant agricultural trade reform.[31] After enormous pressure from high-income countries the Doha meeting did, in fact, launch a new round although there was continuing nervousness about it among most low-income countries.

The other main issues discussed at the Doha meeting were: market access and the tariffs on non-agricultural products, agriculture, services trade, the TRIPS agreement, the Singapore issues, implementation issues and special and different treatment for low-income countries.[32] The Singapore issues were particularly divisive. At Doha low-income countries got a commitment that the intellectual property rights agreement as it applied to medicines would be reviewed; they also received a 'waiver' for a pre-existing concessional trade agreement between Europe and a large number of low-income countries in

Africa, the Caribbean and the Pacific but otherwise they only got vague rhetorical acknowledgements of their trade concerns.[33]

The Cancún WTO meeting

In September 2003, almost two years after the start of the Doha Round, a new meeting of WTO trade ministers was held at Cancún, Mexico. Like the Seattle talks the Cancún meeting collapsed. The Singapore issues were again the sticking point. Low-income countries remained opposed to them, and African countries in particular were determined in their opposition, particularly after the United States gave dismissive treatment to a complaint by a number of them about its subsidisation of cotton exports. Cancún marked a major change in the power relationships at world trade talks. Until Cancún low-income countries had generally found it impossible to counter the combined might of the European Union and the United States (although they had some success at Seattle in 1999) but at Cancún they formed an alliance – the G22 – which took the fight to the EU/US axis for the first time. The G22 (which later became the G20) was led by Brazil and India and also included China, Argentina, Bolivia, Chile, Colombia, Costa Rica, Cuba, Ecuador, Egypt, El Salvador, Guatemala, Mexico, Pakistan, Paraguay, Peru, the Philippines, South Africa, Thailand and Venezuela. For the first time, low-income countries were able to use their cohesiveness and their growing trade strength to mount a major challenge to the EU and US. High-income countries could no longer take low-income countries for granted as they had ever since the Kennedy Round in the 1960s.

New issues in the Uruguay Round

The final Uruguay Round agreement signed in 1994 was very long and complex, embracing no fewer than eighteen separate constituent agreements on various trade issues, many of them new. Of the eighteen agreements, the following six were the most controversial:

- Agreement on Trade-Related Aspects of Intellectual Property Rights (TRIPS)

Table 2.1 Timeline of global trade negotiations

1947–48	Talks held in Havana attempt to establish International Trade Organisation (ITO) subject to crucial US approval
1947	First round of global trade talks under General Agreement on Tariffs and Trade is held in Geneva – 23 participating countries
1949	Second GATT round of global trade talks, the Annecy Round, is held – 13 participating countries
1950	US President Truman and the US Congress scuttle the establishment of the ITO
1950	Third GATT round of global trade talks, the Torquay Round, is held – 38 participating countries
1955	The United States is allowed to keep agricultural subsidies despite the apparent conflict with GATT
1956	Fourth GATT round of global trade talks, the Geneva Round, is held – 26 participating countries
1957	The European Economic Community is established despite apparent conflict with GATT
1960–61	Fifth GATT round of global trade talks, the Dillon Round, is held – 26 participating countries
1962–67	Sixth GATT round of global trade talks, the Kennedy Round, is held – 62 participating countries
1973–79	Seventh GATT round of global trade talks, the Tokyo Round, is held – 99 participating countries
1986–93	Eighth GATT round of global trade talks, the Uruguay Round, is held – 125 participating countries
1995	The World Trade Organisation begins operation
1996	High-income countries unveil new trade issues of investment, government procurement, competition and trade facilitation at Singapore WTO meeting
1999	WTO meeting held in Seattle fails to launch proposed new 'Millennium Round' of global trade talks
2001	Ninth GATT round of global trade talks begins at WTO meeting held in Doha – 148 participating countries
2003	WTO trade talks at Cancún collapse over 'Singapore issues'
2004	Framework agreement for Doha Round is agreed to

Source (for GATT Rounds information): Joan E. Spero and Jeffrey A. Hart, *The Politics of International Economic Relations* (fifth edition), St Martin's Press, New York, 1997.

- General Agreement on Trade in Services (GATS)
- Agreement on Textiles and Clothing
- Agreement on Agriculture
- Agreement on Trade-related Investment Measures (TRIMS)
- Agreement on the Application of Sanitary and Phytosanitary Measures

The TRIPS Agreement

The TRIPS agreement was, and still is, one of the most contentious agreements struck during the Uruguay Round. Its aim was to bring all WTO members into a global patent regime under which global patent holders could be satisfied that their intellectual property rights were being honoured throughout the world by all WTO members. The TRIPS agreement largely got into the Uruguay Round as a result of intense lobbying of the Reagan administration by a number of large US software, pharmaceutical and chemical companies which wanted the administration to quantify the amount of revenue they claimed they were losing from patent piracy.[34] Originally the TRIPS agreement was simply going to be an attempt to coordinate internationally patent laws to stop counterfeiting and copying etcetera, but it ended up becoming a comprehensive agreement covering the trade in protected intellectual-property-related goods and services.[35] Although at first glance the idea of global coordination of trade in copyrighted goods and services seems reasonable, there was considerable concern about what effect the TRIPS agreement would have on the availability of affordable essential medicines as well as on access to plants and genetic material traditionally used in low-income countries. Before the TRIPS agreement, mainly Third World-based makers of generic medicines had been able to market them at a fraction of the price they sold for in high-income countries. Indian generic drug companies, for instance, were able to sell anti-retro viral triple therapies against AIDS for less than US$1,500 in low-income countries whereas patented equivalents sold for between US$10,000 and US$15,000.[36] This alarmed large transnational corporation drug companies who, fearful of losing a lot of their international market share, created the TRIPS agreement as insurance against this. Following the signing of the TRIPS agreement there was a backlash against it, particularly after a coalition of 39 drug companies took the South African government to court in 2001 after it allowed generic HIV/Aids drugs to be made available in the country. The backlash produced general agreement that there needed to be a relaxation of the TRIPS deal particularly in the way it applied to essential medicines, although the US wanted a narrow relaxation applicable only to a few specific diseases such as tuberculosis, malaria and Aids. One of the few victories for low-income countries at the Doha meeting was agreement on a fairly broad relaxation of the TRIPS agreement. However low-income countries without any generic drug manufacturing capacity were left with a cumbersome system for obtaining these drugs that involved a compli-cated licensing system coupled with guarantees that the generic drugs would not be re-exported.

The TRIPS agreement could also restrict access to plants and genetic material traditionally used in low-income countries. Patents have already been issued in Europe, and in the US, for products and formulas long known to farmers in low-income countries and long considered public property there. US companies have already patented the Mexican Yellow Enola Bean, Basmati rice and selected maize genes, while a European company has patented a process for extracting medical substances from the Indian neem tree, a process known to Indian farmers for centuries.[37]

The General Agreement on Trade in Services

Services are the fastest-growing area of global trade. In 1985 total global trade in services was worth US$373 billion but by 2001 it was worth US$1,446 billion; today it accounts for about a fifth of all world trade.[38] High-income countries – particularly the United States and the European Union – dominate the global trade in services and, unsurprisingly, had tried since at least the early 1980s to get services trade included in global trade negotiations; they succeeded in the Uruguay Round. In 2001 the United States and the high-income countries of Western Europe together accounted for 64 per cent of all the world's service exports.[39] A major force behind the inclusion of the GATS agreement was lobbying by large finance companies including American Express, Credit First Suisse Boston and the American International Group. Low-income countries put up strong resistance to the GATS agreement during the Uruguay Round, however. They didn't want it linked to other agreements and they wanted an assessment of the agreement's impact before it was signed. In the end they got neither, and they only reluctantly agreed to it as a trade-off for greater access to high-income-country agricultural markets under the Agreement on Agriculture. High-income countries originally wanted a 'negative list' approach to the GATS agreement under which it would be assumed that a specific service industry in a specific country was open to international competition unless quarantined by that country. Low-income countries got this changed to a 'positive list' regime under which a service industry would not be opened unless specifically nominated by its country. A cumbersome bidding regime was also set up to implement the GATS agreement: WTO member countries would nominate specific service sectors they wanted other specified countries to open up, then the specified country would come back with an offer based on concessions it felt it could win from the first country in other service sectors. It was agreed at the Doha meeting that the requests phase would be finished by the end of June 2002 and the offers phase would finish at the end of March 2003 but at the time of writing the response had been underwhelming and many major WTO members had yet to make GATS offers. Many members are waiting to see what agricultural trade concessions high-income countries are willing to make before they make GATS offers. Low-income countries are reluctant to open up service sectors that are of interest to high-income countries, such as financial, professional, courier and transport services, while high-income countries are reluctant to open up sectors that are of interest to low-income countries by, for example, allowing low-income-country professional people to work in high-income countries.[40] The Doha Round framework agreement, finalised in mid-2004, came up with a new GATS negotiations deadline of May 2005. The 2004 framework agreement used wording that contradicted the supposedly voluntary nature of the GATS agreement by saying 'members who have not yet submitted their initial offers must do so as soon as possible'.

Low-income countries are concerned that the GATS agreement could eventually lead to the privatisation of essential government services such as water and electricity supply, health and education. About half of all the foreign direct investment that goes into low-income countries is associated with service industries,[41] so many low-income country governments see the GATS agreement as a backdoor way of foreign investors getting control of government services. There is some ambiguity about the applicability of the GATS agreement to government services but it definitely applies where a government sells a service – so water and electricity supply could easily be targets. An oft-quoted example of the devastating impact that service privatisation can have in low-income countries is the water supply privatisation undertaken by the Bolivian government in the city of Cochabamba in 1999 under pressure from the World Bank. A consortium led by a subsidiary of the Bechtel transnational corporation won the contract and promptly raised water prices by as much as 400 per cent.[42] This caused huge protests in 2000 and 2001 until finally a hitherto reluctant Bolivian government cancelled the privatisation contract, to which Bechtel responded with a US$25 million lawsuit for loss of profits.[43] In recent years more global trade issues involving services have been challenged through the WTO. In 2004, for instance, the United States successfully challenged the right of Mexico to regulate Mexico's domestic telecommunications industry and Antigua and Bermuda successfully challenged the right of the US to regulate the US gambling industry.

The Agreement on Textiles and Clothing

Textiles and clothing is one of the few trade areas in which low-income countries have long enjoyed a competitive advantage. Textiles manufacturing is generally labour-intensive and often uses raw materials, such as cotton, that are grown in relative abundance in low-income countries. Clothing and textile export industries have traditionally been viewed as a reliable early rung on the ladder of low-income country industrialisation and were used by countries such as Japan and Hong Kong when industrialising after the Second World War. Unhappily for low-income countries, clothing and textiles is also a major sector in high-income countries and manufacturers in those countries have long felt threatened by exports from low-income countries. This fear has been expressed through a series of discriminatory 'export restraint' agreements between high- and low-income countries that date back to the first such agreement struck between Japan and the US in 1957. The agreements struck since have embraced a number of major textile exporting and importing nations and include the Short-Term Agreement of 1961, the Long-Term Agreement of 1962 and the Multifibre Agreement of 1973 (which like the Long-Term Agreement of 1962 was renewed several times).[44] These agreements generally restrained textile exports by allocating export quotas to specific countries. Since these agreements were unambiguously aimed at restraining exports from low-income countries their termination was a major inducement used to get low-income countries involved in the Uruguay Round. The Agreement on Textiles and Clothing negotiated during the round stated that the liberalisation of the sector was to be phased in in four stages that would take effect in 1995, 1998, 2002 and 2005. The 1995 stage would liberalise 16 per cent of 1990 exports (by volume), the 1998 stage a further 17 per cent, the 2002 stage another 18 per cent and the final 2005 stage the final 49 per cent.[45] Unfortunately the Agreement on Textiles and Clothing was not specific about which clothing and textile products high-income countries had to open up in each stage; they were largely allowed to determine for themselves what items were first exposed to this liberalisation. The result was that rich countries were highly selective in the import restrictions they elected to lift: liberalisation often occurred in categories that poor countries don't compete in – such as parachutes and felt hats – or in areas that have little added value. By January 2002 only 12 per cent of the liberalisation in the US and 18 per cent of the liberalisation in the European Union had been applied to higher-value textile products.[46] This has created a lot of mistrust between low- and high-income countries. Many low-income countries feared that after the sector was fully liberalised in January 2005 many high-income countries will go back on what they agreed to. As if to confirm this fear, in mid-2005 the United States government introduced 'safety quotas' that may last until 2008 and limit annual import volume increases to 7.5 per cent on seven types of Chinese imports, among them textiles including trousers, shirts and underwear.[47] After large increases in Chinese textile imports into Europe in early 2005 the (new) European Union trade representative, Peter Mandelson, started building a similar case for protectionist measures saying 'Europe cannot stand by and watch its [textile] industry disappear.' Many low-income countries also fear the full liberalisation of the trade in textiles will result in China and India grabbing a lot of global market share from other low-income countries (see Chapter 4).

The Agreement on Agriculture

Agriculture was, and remains, easily the most contentious issue in both the Uruguay and Doha Rounds. The Doha Round could collapse over agriculture and the Uruguay Round went very close to collapsing over it. The Uruguay Round was only got back on track by negotiations between the United States and the European Union at Blair House in Washington in December 1993 which originally agreed to reduce agricultural subsidies by 21 per cent over six years then watered this down after resistance from the European Union (particularly from France).[48] Even though agriculture was of vital importance to low-income countries they were not involved in these crucial negotiations.

High-income countries are sensitive about agriculture because they dominate the global trade in it and their dominance shows little sign of waning. In 2000 a full 64 per cent of all the global imports of agricultural raw materials came from developed countries, slightly up on the 61 per cent that came from them in 1980. By way of contrast, in both 2000 and 1980 developing countries were the source of only 30 per cent of the world's traded agricultural produce.[49]

The final Uruguay Round Agreement on Agriculture had three fundamental pillars. One was market access: high-income countries agreed to reduce agriculture import tariffs by 36 per cent over six years and low-income countries agreed to lower their import tariffs by 24 per cent over ten years.[50] The second pillar was export subsidisation: high-income countries agreed to reduce the value of their export subsidies by 36 per cent, and their volume by 24 per cent, over six years; low-income countries agreed to make 24 per cent and 10 per cent cuts to value and volume respectively over a ten-year period.[51] The third pillar concerned cuts to domestic support. High-income countries agreed to cut total domestic farm support by 20 per cent over six years while low-income countries agreed to cut it by 13 per cent over ten years.[52]

For the purposes of applying the agreement, agricultural subsidies were separated into three categories: an 'amber box' that covers all trade-distorting domestic support, a 'blue box' that covers payments linked to indicators such as the area of a farm or the number of its animals but which (supposedly) limit production and therefore (supposedly) have a limited trade effect, and a 'green box' covering those subsidies that do not distort trade.[53] The agreement also said WTO members could not challenge each other's agricultural subsidies through the WTO dispute process until the end of 2003.

At first glance the agricultural subsidy reductions seemed reasonably ambitious but, as with the clothing and textile agreement, the devil was in the detail and high-income countries have exploited that detail to the hilt. The perilous detail in the agriculture agreement comes in the treatment of the boxes. None of the subsidies in the blue box have to be cut at all. The blue box was a last-minute addition to placate the European Union which argued that the other cuts in the agreement would have a detrimental effect on its farmers. But the green box too is unaffected by the agreement, which means that only the amber box is affected. In the years since the agreement on agriculture came into effect high-income countries have made an art form of juggling the box classification of their agricultural subsidies. The European Union has progressively moved subsidies out of the amber box and into the green and blue boxes, and from the very start the US made sure that most of its subsidies fell into the green box. The net result of all the shifting has been that nothing stopped high-income countries from raising the value of their farm support paid between 1999 and 2001 by 9 per cent compared to its 1986–1988 value.[54] In 2002 the US Congress even passed a new Farm Bill that provided US$175 billion in assistance to farmers over ten years,[55] and in late 2002 the (then) member states of the European Union agreed that agricultural assistance under its Common Agricultural Policy would rise from the current €43 billion level to about €49 billion by 2013.[56] Most of these subsidies go to large, industrial-scale farms and not to smaller, more sustainable farms. In 2002 industrial-scale farms in the US received US$7.8 billion in subsidies or 65 per cent of total US government farm payments; almost 30 per cent of the subsidies went to the largest 2 per cent of farms with over 80 per cent going to the largest 30 per cent.[57]

In addition to its blatant increases in farm subsidisation the US has a system of 'export credits' that extends government-backed bank loans with low interest rates to farmers; these loans are effectively a form of subsidy but the US has so far refused to classify them as such. Further violation of the spirit, if not the letter, of the Agreement on Agriculture takes place in the form of a high level of dumping of subsidised agricultural exports by high-income countries, particularly the EU and US, and in the form of manipulation of the agreed tariffication process by high-income countries where at the start of the agreement they set very high tariffs so that the agreed tariff cuts will have little final effect.[58] The tariffication process has been further weakened by aggregation of different tariffs that disguise tariffs applied to the most sensitive products[59] (in an echo of the violation technique used on the clothing and textile agreement).

Agricultural subsidisation remains a very, very vexed issue. The whole future of WTO trade agreements largely rests on the future of agricultural subsidies and their place in global trade agreements. Low-income countries see them as a major barrier to greater trade wealth, and high-income countries see them as a way of preserving an important part of both their culture and their industry base. In many ways the very tolerance of agricultural subsidies is contrary to the bedrock philosophy of the WTO, but in 1955 the United States threatened to leave the GATT unless a permanent exemption was granted to its agricultural subsidies and they have been tolerated within the GATT/WTO system ever since.[60]

It is often claimed that government support for agriculture in high-income countries exceeds US$300 billion per year. This statistic needs to be treated with caution. It is a statistic generated each year by the Organisation for Economic Cooperation and Development (OECD). For 2002 they claim the support amounted to US$311 billion, or nearly US$1 billion per day. This figure is not the amount actually spent by high-income countries on farm support, however. It is mainly generated by comparing the price of agricultural produce in OECD countries with the prices that would be paid if their farm trade was completely open and cheaper agricultural produce could be bought in those countries. So it is mainly an expression of how much more OECD consumers pay for their farm produce rather than an indicator of actual farm subsidy payments. The difference is keenly illustrated by the European Union's agricultural subsidies. In 2003 actual spending by the European Union on agricultural subsidies came to US$54 billion but the OECD claims its total (effective) subsidisation was US$121 billion, more than twice the amount actually paid.[61]

In July 2004 WTO members met in Geneva to hammer out a framework for the negotiations over the Doha Round following the collapse of negotiations at the Cancún meeting the previous September. As always, negotiations over agricultural trade were central to the framework negotiations. The key negotiations were held between the EU, the US, Australia, India and Brazil. Although the talks produced an agreement that kept the Doha Round alive, the agricultural part of it was deeply flawed and looked as though it would still allow significant evasion by high-income countries. Among its flaws were:

- a new category of 'sensitive' agricultural industries, such as rice in Japan and dairy in Switzerland, that high-income countries could continue to apply significant protection to (this was included to win over countries such as Japan);

- no reduction in green box subsidies and an expansion of blue box subsidies to include some new US subsidies. The EU and US refused to consider any overall capping and reduction of blue box subsidies. With respect to blue box subsidies the agreement even said 'in cases where a member has placed an exceptionally large percentage of its trade-distorting support in the blue box, some flexibility will be provided on a basis to be agreed to ensure that such a member is not called upon to make a wholly disproportionate cut';

- domestic support for agriculture, including blue box support, in the first year and throughout the implementation period of the agreement, to be reduced by 20 per cent (but still to be able to end up equalling 80 per cent of its current level);

- the 20 per cent reduction in domestic support to be based on allowable subsidies – not on actual subsidies (which are generally lower than the allowable subsidies) – which means that the US and EU will be able to lower the overall cap on their permissible agriculture subsidies without lowering the amount of subsidisation they actually pay out. In the US the Bush administration, for instance, was confident it could meet the 20 per cent farm subsidy reduction without touching the amount it pays out because it spends well below WTO limits;[62]

- a commitment by the EU to eliminate its export subsidies but the lack of an agreed timetable for the elimination – it was made clear that it was dependent on other countries doing the same. The French agriculture minister, Herve Gaymard, thought the end date for export subsidies would not be before 2015 or 2017;[63]

- no formula for reduction of agricultural import tariffs; instead the agreement simply developed guiding principles;

- no special treatment extended to cotton subsidisation which had played a major part in the collapse of the Cancún talks (although high-income countries said they would consider giving its blue box subsidisation specific attention and the US made vague commitments about speeding up reduction of its cotton subsidies). Cotton subsidies were the subject of a WTO ruling against the US in April 2004;

• no specific preservation of low-income country preferential trade agreements such as the one between the European Union and African, Caribbean and Pacific countries (the Cotonou agreement).

Basically the Geneva framework agreement did nothing to stop further exploitation of the blue and green box subsidisation system by high-income countries, and it looks set to continue the problems of the Uruguay Round. The then trade representative for the US, Robert Zoellick, told congressman Tom Daschle that the framework agreement 'will not weaken our ability to support our farmers'.[64] Even the conditional pledge by the European Union to eliminate its export subsidies is much less generous than it appears. In 2004 European Union export subsidies accounted for just €3 billion of its annual €45 billion farm subsidy programme.[65] The EU and the US together spend US$70–80 billion each year on agricultural subsidisation and the Geneva agreement did very little to curb that spending. By 2005 agricultural trade was once again shaping up as the lynch pin to the successful conclusion of a trade round, in this case the Doha Round. Many low-income countries were reluctant to make commitments about freeing up trade in services and non-agricultural goods before high-income countries made genuine commitments about freeing up agricultural trade.

The Agreement on Trade-related Investment Measures (TRIMS)

The TRIMS agreement seeks to eliminate the trade-distorting effects of foreign investment restrictions in either low- or high-income countries. Within 90 days from the start of the WTO on 1 January 1995 member countries were supposed to identify and eliminate measures that were inconsistent with the agreement; high-income countries had two years to eliminate them while most low-income countries had five years (with the least developed low-income countries having seven).[66] Most high-income countries – the US and Japan in particular – were keen to have the TRIMS agreement included in the Uruguay Round. Foreign investment, particularly in low-income countries, often has little, if any, spin-off benefit attached to it for local businesses. In an effort to change this, some low-income countries in the past have attached local content rules to foreign investment in their economy that obliged foreign investors to buy a certain proportion of their content from local suppliers. Such local content rules have been fairly common in the car making industry, and countries such as South Korea, China and Malaysia have used them to ensure that they get a significant benefit from foreign investment.[67] But high-income countries hate local content rules and have consistently fought them and challenged them through the WTO. Since the TRIMS agreement began, the car making industry has attracted the most challenges lodged by high-income countries against low-income countries about breaches of the agreement. Between 1995 and February 2002, 11 complaints were lodged by countries including Japan, the US and the EU against the local content rules of the car making industries of four low-income countries that have large future potential car markets: Brazil, Indonesia, India and the Philippines.[68] In 1997 a WTO dispute panel upheld a Japanese complaint about the Indonesian car making industry which it held to be in violation of the TRIMS agreement.[69] A major problem with the TRIMS agreement is that more and more foreign direct investment in low-income countries is associated with mergers and acquisitions of locally owned businesses. Mergers and acquisitions rose from an average 22 per cent of foreign direct investment in low-income countries between 1988 and 1991 to 72 per cent between 1992 and 1997.[70] So the TRIMS agreement effectively conspires with the increasing amount of overseas takeover activity to ensure that low-income countries get no local benefit from foreign investment. Unsurprisingly, although originally viewed somewhat benignly by low-income countries, the TRIMS agreement is these days viewed by them with a lot of suspicion.

The Agreement on the Application of Sanitary and Phytosanitary Measures

The sanitary and phytosanitary agreement (SPS agreement) seeks to facilitate trade by eliminating differences in food, animal and plant regulation. It sets criteria that WTO member countries must follow with regard to domestic policies that affect human health.[71] The agreement also applies to the use of exhaustible natural resources. A country can adopt a health standard that is different to those agreed under the SPS agreement but if it does so it has to justify it, and justification generally means that it does not set up 'unnecessary obstacles to international trade'.[72] The SPS agreement has been criticised both by groups within the global justice movement (sometimes known as the antiglobalisation movement) and by low-income countries. Groups in the global justice movement argue the agreement represents a 'race to the bottom' and makes trade a barrier to adopting stringent health standards. Low-income countries argue the agreement is often used by high-income countries as a form of protectionism. They argue that high-income countries often use the agreement as an excuse to bar imports from low-income countries knowing that low-income countries often do not have the resources to meet the standards set by high-income countries.

New issues in the Doha Round

The Singapore issues

As previously mentioned (see pages 58 and 59), the Singapore issues (sometimes just known as the 'new issues') – investment, competition, government procurement and trade facilitation – were introduced into global trade negotiations during a WTO meeting of trade ministers held in Singapore in 1996. The European Union was the original backer of these issues at the 1996 meeting[73] although they came to be enthusiastically embraced by nearly all high-income countries, especially the US, the EU, Japan, Switzerland and Australia.[74] The US, however, was less enthusiastic about the investment and competition parts of the Singapore issues than the EU was.[75] Low-income countries were generally opposed to the Singapore issues, seeing them as an unnecessary expansion of global trade rules, although during the 2001 Doha meeting of the WTO Columbia, Uruguay and Peru supported starting negotiations over the Singapore issues while India, Zimbabwe, Nigeria, Kenya, Senegal, Malaysia, Indonesia, Thailand, Egypt, Jamaica, Cuba, St Lucia, St Vincent and Belize all remained trenchantly opposed to them.[76] The 1996 WTO meeting in Singapore only agreed to set up working groups into the four issues. At the 2001 WTO meeting in Doha the issues were hotly disputed. Those who backed the new issues thought the Doha meeting made a clear decision to start negotiating on the issues at the 2003 WTO meeting in Cancún while those opposed thought the Doha meeting only agreed to make a decision at Cancún about whether negotiations should start or not. In the end the Singapore issues ended up being a very sensitive issue at Cancún that, along with agricultural subsidies, were responsible for the collapse of the Cancún talks. At Cancún the European Union offered to withdraw the investment and competition issues in the face of unrelenting opposition from the new G22 alliance of low-income countries. By 2004 it appeared as though only the trade facilitation issue had any serious chance of remaining in the Doha Round negotiations, though many high-income countries (the EU in particular) have kept talking about having 'plurilateral'/two-speed trade agreements where WTO members can retain the option to sign up to the Singapore issues if they wish. Many high-income countries, particularly the US, have included the Singapore issues in their bilateral trade agreements regardless of their reception in the Doha Round. Although three of the four Singapore issues now seem to have dropped out of the Doha Round the framework agreement for the round agreed to in July 2004 did not specifically delete the issues, leaving the (small) possibility they could be revisited in the future. Because the Singapore issues retain some potency it is worth briefly examining them.

Investment

The investment Singapore issue is an attempt by high-income countries to protect the (perceived) rights of foreign investors. Global foreign investor agreements go back as far as the eighteenth century. Since the Second World War various parts of the United Nations have attempted to codify the rights of foreign investors on at least three occasions.[77] The year before the 1996 WTO Singapore meeting the Organisation for Economic Cooperation and Development launched its own foreign investor agreement – the Multilateral Agreement on Investment – which was backed by the US Council for International Business but which met with considerable public resistance and was finally dropped in 1998. The United States had originally wanted the investment Singapore issue to cover all types of foreign investment including purchases of shares, bonds and other financial instruments[78] but in the end it applied just to foreign direct investment (that is, to direct foreign ownership of businesses etcetera rather than indirect holdings). Investment as a trade issue is generally opposed by most low-income countries, and at the 2001 Doha meeting India, China, Cuba, Pakistan and Zimbabwe tried to relate the issue to the obligations, rather than the rights, of foreign investors (much to the chagrin of high-income countries).[79]

Competition

The competition Singapore issue is closely linked to the investment issue. Like the investment issue the aim of the competition issue is to give foreign companies the same rights as local companies. Historically the issue has been much kicked around by both low- and high-income countries. In 1980, high-income countries refused to sign up to a UN protocol on the codification of competition practices that low-income countries wanted to make legally binding[80] but by 1996 they were keen on the idea as a way of increasing market access in low-income countries. Most low-income countries do not have competition policies of their own; instead their governments generally intervene directly if they think there has been competitive malpractice. By 1990 only 16 low-income countries had competition policies. Most high-income countries have only adopted competition policies relatively recently – in the case of Japan and the EU during the last fifty years.[81] Most low-income countries think WTO competition policies could be used to wipe out their locally owned industries and are therefore suspicious of them. Their suspicion is heightened by the proposal to include in the investment Singapore issue a clause that would allow foreign investors to sue a government for lost profits if it felt its profit-making opportunities were being unreasonably curtailed (as happened in the infamous 2000 case in which the US Metalclad corporation successfully sued a Mexican council for lost profits (under the North American Free Trade Agreement) after it was denied permission to establish a toxic waste dump).[82]

Government procurement

The government procurement Singapore issue is only meant to relate to transparency in government procurement (purchasing). Low-income countries, however, fear that the possible introduction of the issue into the Doha Round could, in future, open their government purchasing to fully-blown international competition. Globally, government procurement accounts for a huge share of the overall purchase of goods and services. Non-defence procurement by all the world's governments is estimated to be worth about US$1,500 billion each year.[83] In high-income countries government procurement is equal to about 10 and 20 per cent of gross domestic product while in low-income countries it is equal to about 9 and 13 per cent.[84] A voluntary government procurement agreement was inserted into the Uruguay Round agreement but was only signed by a few high-income countries.

Trade facilitation

Trade facilitation is the least contentious of the Singapore issues and seems likely to survive the Doha Round. The issue is concerned with the harmonisation and standardisation of trading procedures around the world. Traditionally trade facilitation has not been part of global trade negotiations and has instead been managed by the World Customs Organisation, the United Nations Conference on Trade and Development, and the United Nations Economic Commission for Europe.[85] In 1996 transnational corporations began arguing that much more work needed to be done on trade facilitation, claiming that costs associated with border delays, excessive documentation and lack of automation in many countries etcetera were making trade unnecessarily expensive.[86] The danger for low-income countries is that the measures transnational corporations want them to implement could be quite expensive and could reduce the transparency of global trade. Amongst other things, reduced trade transparency could reduce the ability of low-income countries to control transnational corporation transfer pricing – which has a huge influence on where transnational corporations report their profits (and therefore where they pay their taxes).[87] High-income countries are demanding that the transfer price valuations supplied by transnational corporations be simply accepted without question by host governments even though this policy was rejected in both the Tokyo and Uruguay Rounds.[88]

Other new issues: labour and environment clauses and electronic commerce

There are three other new issues that, from time to time, high-income countries show interest in including in WTO trade negotiations: labour and environment clauses and electronic commerce.

Labour clauses are clauses that would allow a country to restrict imports from another country that allowed dubious labour practices such as child labour. The possibility of introducing such clauses into new trade rounds was raised at the 1996 WTO meeting in Singapore, and the US also raised it at the failed WTO meeting in Seattle in 1999. On both occasions the idea did not get support – the Singapore meeting decided labour clauses should remain the province of the International Labor Organisation. Low-income countries view labour clauses quite cynically and generally feel they amount to yet another form of high-income country protectionism.

Environment clauses are somewhat like labour clauses in as much as they would generally allow a country to restrict imports from another country that had dubious environmental standards. The European Union has been the main champion of their inclusion in trade negotiations. Environment clauses cover a plethora of sub-issues, including the relationship between environmental trade measures and multilateral environment agreements, the environmental impact of process and production methods, the use of eco-labelling, the application of the environmental precautionary principle and the access to, and liberalisation of, trade in environmental technology.[89] Generally high-income countries want to be able to more easily apply environmental standards to trade and want to export their environmental technology more freely. Low-income countries again see the potential for more high-income country protectionism in such measures and want to be able to develop their own environmental technology instead of importing it from high-income countries.

Despite low-income country resistance to labour and environment clauses being attached to trade agreements, in October 2004 the European Union announced it would include such clauses in future preferential trade arrangements made with low-income countries. Pascal Lamy, the then EU trade commissioner, said low-income countries that implement the Kyoto protocol and other international treaties on human rights, labour standards and the environment would be rewarded with lighter tariff burdens.[90]

Electronic commerce was first raised as a potential new WTO trade issue in 1998. It mainly covers services delivered via computers and the Internet. High-income countries see a lot of export potential for themselves in electronic commerce and have already negotiated a provisional WTO agreement that such computer-based services should be able to enter a country free of any charge or tariff.[91] The United States has traditionally been a keen champion of duty-free electronic commerce and has pushed the measure very assertively at the WTO. This measure threatens to reduce the ability of low-income countries to develop their own electronic commerce industries and also eliminates their ability to raise revenue from the taxation of electronic commerce-based trade.

Negotiating tactics within the WTO

Because international trade now accounts for a large proportion of the world's economic activity there is a huge amount at stake in global trade negotiations. It is not surprising that countries with a large amount of trade and economic clout are generally more than willing to use it during global trade negotiations to get their way.

Debt relief, aid or trade preferences pressure

High-income countries in particular are not adverse to using fairly blunt negotiating tactics during trade talks such as using debt relief or aid or preferential trade deals – and the threat of their withdrawal – to win low-income countries across to their point of view. The Doha Round has been plagued with debt relief/aid/preferential trade bribery. Tactics used during the round so far include:

- before the 2001 WTO meeting in Doha the US tried to bribe India, which it had often found obstructionist in past trade negotiations, with US$450 million in bilateral tariff cuts;[92]

- the US signed trade and investment deals with eight West African countries before the Doha meeting;[93]

- the European Union used its preferential trade deal with African, Caribbean and Pacific countries to get their support for the Singapore issues during the Doha meeting;[94]

- Pakistan was given debt relief and preferential textile trade rights by the US in return for its support at the Doha meeting;[95]

- before the Doha meeting the EU trade minister, Pascal Lamy, made many trips to low-income countries reminding them of the importance of various preferential trade agreements they had with the EU as a way of getting their support for the Singapore issues;[96]

- before the 2003 WTO meeting at Cancún, Tanzania and Kenya were threatened with the loss of preferential trade arrangements unless they dropped their opposition to high-income-country trade positions;[97]

- Japan used several threats of withdrawal of foreign aid to get low-income-country compliance with its positions at Cancún;[98]

- the US threatened Uganda with withdrawal of concessionary trade arrangements when it considered joining general African opposition to high-income-country trade positions at Cancún;[99]

- just before the Doha Round's framework agreement was agreed in July 2004 the US gave Brazil, a key player in the framework's formulation, its second-highest agricultural import quota;[100]

- also just before the finalisation of the July 2004 Doha framework agreement the EU withdrew US$60 million in aid to Kenya which had led a walkout of low-income countries at Cancún.[101]

Pressure on trade ministers

Another blunt negotiating tactic sometimes used by high-income countries during WTO negotiations is to go over the head of the low-income-country trade minister taking part in the negotiations if her or his position is not agreeable to them. Phone calls are made to senior government officials back home who in turn pressure their trade ministers to change their positions. The US is a well-known practitioner of this tactic and is known to keep a blacklist of WTO trade ambassadors it would like to see removed.[102] At least five WTO ambassadors who have been unpopular with the US were removed after the 2001 Doha meeting.[103] One trade ambassador who lost his job in this way was the WTO trade ambassador for the Dominican Republic, Dr Frederico Cuello.[104]

Green room and mini ministerial decision making

Another common tactic used to pressure low-income countries during WTO negotiations is to exclude them from pivotal 'green room' talks that take place during negotiations and to also exclude them from 'mini ministerials' that take place before major WTO meetings. Green room meetings are small group meetings occurring during WTO negotiations that tend to make the key decisions of the meeting – there is a lot of pressure to agree to green room meeting decisions once they have been made. Mini ministerials are informal meetings of WTO trade ministers arranged by specific countries before WTO meetings which, although not formally endorsed by the WTO, nonetheless can be crucial in determining positions and alliances before major WTO meetings. The most influential WTO members – the EU, the US, Japan and Canada (known as 'the Quad') – nearly always attend every green room meeting and mini minister-ial, but low-income countries tend to be invited only if they represent a strategic alliance of other low-income countries; otherwise they don't get a look-in. During the final, all-important green room meeting of the Doha meeting half the high-income countries present at the meeting were included in the green room negotiations but less than one eighth of all the low-income countries were included.[105] At the mini ministerials held before the Doha meeting in Mexico and Singapore all the Quad members were invited and about a quarter of other high-income WTO members got invitations but only 3 per cent of least-developed-country WTO members were invited to attend.[106]

WTO rulings

One of the 18 specific agreements that made up the Uruguay Round was the Dispute Settlement Understanding. This agreement funda-mentally changed the way global trade disputes are settled. During the reign of the GATT trade disputes were settled diplomatically. This allowed a resolution that produced clear winners and losers but meant that more neutral outcomes were generally explored first. The diplo-matic cushioning of GATT dispute outcomes was further enhanced by a need for all rulings to be adopted by consensus by the GATT – in theory this meant that a country with a ruling against it could block such a ruling, though in practice this seldom happened. The Dispute

Settlement Understanding made trade disputes much more adversarial. Under the new rules all WTO disputes are taken to a three-person WTO-appointed panel that makes a ruling. The rulings normally have compliance deadlines and if these are not met financial compensation or retaliatory trade sanctions can be imposed against the country against whom the ruling has been made. The rulings can be appealed to another WTO-appointed body although, in practice, very few WTO rulings are overturned by the appeal body – in the nine-year history of the WTO to 2004 only two rulings have been overturned.[107] Once a ruling has been appealed no further appeals can be made outside the WTO system.

Much of the WTO dispute resolution system is cloaked in secrecy. All documents are confidential unless a government chooses to release its dispute documents.[108] Representations by third parties, such as non-government organisations or businesses (*amicus* briefs), are not allowed unless they form part of a government's case.[109] There is also a lack of transparency associated with the people who hear the disputes. The panellists are selected from a roster of people who have past experience in trade law and international commerce, but this narrow set of qualifications frequently fails to cover the broad spectrum of issues that WTO disputes often touch on.[110] The panellists produce a single ruling that all of them put their names to so one never knows what the specific opinion of each individual panellist is.[111]

Bringing a dispute before the WTO takes a lot of time and money so, unsurprisingly, the main plaintiffs are high-income countries. Between January 1995 and January 2003 some 63 per cent of the 279 WTO challenges heard were brought by high-income countries with the United States, the European Union and Canada being the top three plaintiffs.[112] As of January 2003 no least-developed country had brought a challenge to the WTO. In most cases the challenger wins. In 85 per cent of the completed cases heard between January 1995 and January 2003 the WTO ruled in favour of the challenger; in cases where a high-income country is pitted against a low-income country the rate is even higher – 94 per cent.[113] A minor consolation for low-income countries, however, is that most cases are brought by high-income countries against other high-income countries and only about a quarter of all cases are brought by high-income countries against low-income countries.[114]

Low-income countries fear the WTO disputes process is allowing high-income countries gradually to chip away at what remaining rights the low-income countries have under international trade law. In 1996 the US government challenged a European Union trade measure that gave preferential access to bananas grown in Africa, the Caribbean and the Pacific. The US was acting on behalf of the Chiquita transnational corporation which was excluded from the EU arrangement. The WTO ruled in favour of the US and the EU was eventually forced to give some of its preferential access to US and Latin American producers.[115] In 1997 the US mounted a challenge against the Indian government after its parliament temporarily refused to pass legislation giving effect to the TRIPS agreement. The WTO ruled against India and it was forced to agree to TRIPS-related patent applications made before its parliament eventually passed the TRIPS legislation. It was also forced to change its TRIPS legislation so that genetically modified seeds could be introduced into the country.[116]

The retreat from trade multilateralism

Although the increased number of countries that participated in the Uruguay and Doha rounds and the ever-expanding reach of trade agreements leave the impression that the world has never embraced multilateral trade negotiations with the same passion as it has over the past two decades, in fact a steady retreat away from trade multilateralism is underway. Increasingly major trading countries are embracing regional or bilateral trade deals (see below) and are only using multilateral WTO trade negotiations as a fallback position. The catalyst for this retreat from multilateralism was the rise of Japan as a major trading nation in the 1970s and the end of the Cold War in the late 1980s. Before Japan became a major trading nation Western Europe and the United States maintained a cosy and fairly cooperative attitude to global trade politics which was considerably enhanced by their common hostility to the Soviet Union. But Japan's rise upset the balance and introduced a much more competitive atmosphere into global trading relations. The United States became increasingly threatened by the impact of Japanese exports into the US economy and by the early 1980s was accusing Japan of pursuing a deliberate strategy of 'deindustrialising' it. This led to the imposition of US 'voluntary export restraints' and large punitive trade duties on Japan (under the infamous section 301 of the 1974 US Trade Act) despite their conflict with the rules of the GATT. During the 1980s the US also entered into a ferocious agricultural subsidy war with the European Economic Community and signed a free trade agreement with Canada in 1988. This led to a fair degree of reluctance by the Western Europeans (and many low-income countries) to participate in the Uruguay Round, but they ended up participating in it because they feared the United States would otherwise retreat into protectionism, thereby closing off the world's largest marketplace to them. But despite the launch of the Uruguay Round both Western Europe and the United States began working on trade agreements that were outside the reach of the Round. In 1987 the Single European Act came into force which sought to create free movement of capital, goods, services and people between the members of the European Union by 1992, and in the same year the United States began negotiating with Canada and Mexico over the North American Free Trade Agreement which came into force in 1994. Separate to these developments a host of new regional and bilateral trade agreements came to be negotiated around the world with the result that after covering about 10 per cent of global trade in 1990, regional and bilateral trade deals had come to cover about 30 per cent of global trade by 2003.[117] Underlying these developments was the United States view that whilst they had been prepared to make many trade concessions and wholeheartedly embrace multilateralism during the Cold War, partly in the interests of anti-Soviet solidarity, they were not prepared to be so flexible after the fall of the Berlin Wall; the US saw the post-Cold War environment as a case of 'every person for themselves'. None of these developments mean that the world's major trading countries are on the verge of leaving the WTO – far from it – but they do mean that these countries do not assign the same importance to WTO/GATT negotiations that they used to; increasingly they put their trade eggs in several other trade-deal baskets.

Regional trade deals

A key tenet of WTO membership is that no country is allowed to extend any trade benefit to any other WTO member, or group of members, that it does not extend to all members. This should, by rights, mean that regional and free trade deals should not be able to exist between WTO members, but they do and they are spreading like wildfire. As of June 2004 no less than 284 regional trade agreements and free trade agreements had been notified to the WTO – most of them bilateral deals. The mushrooming of these deals is the clearest expression there is of the global retreat from multilateral trade negotiations.

The tolerance of such arrangements goes back to the formation of the European Union in 1957 (then known as the European Economic Community, EEC) which created a customs union amongst its members. The EEC members threatened to leave the General Agreement on Tariffs and Trade unless a blind eye was turned to its customs union, and ever since both the GATT and the WTO have had to tolerate them. [118] In addition to the European Union, other major global regional free trade agreements around the world include: the North American Free Trade Agreement (between Canada, the US and Mexico, created in 1994), the ASEAN free trade agreement (signed between South-east Asian countries in 1992 and reinforced by the Bali Concord Two signed in 2003), the South American Mercosur free trade agreement (between Argentina, Brazil, Paraguay and Uruguay, signed in 1995), the Cotonou Agreement signed between the EU and seventy-seven African, Caribbean and Pacific countries (signed in 2000), the Central American Free Trade Agreement (between Guatemala, Honduras, El Salvador, Nicaragua and the US, signed in 2004), the South Asian Free Trade Agreement (between

India, Pakistan, Bhutan, Nepal, the Maldives, Sri Lanka and Bangladesh, signed in 2004) and the Pan Arab Free Trade Area agreement (signed in 2003). There is also the free trade agreement between the members of the Asia-Pacific Economic Cooperation group in which high-income countries have undertaken to cut all their tariffs by 2010 and low-income countries have undertaken to cut them all by 2020. In addition a plethora of bilateral free trade deals now exist such as the ones between the US and Singapore, Chile, Australia, Saudi Arabia, Israel, Jordan and Morocco; between Japan and Mexico; between China and Indonesia; between Singapore and Japan and Australia; and between Australia and New Zealand.

Discussions are currently taking place about the following future agreements:

- the proposed (controversial) Free Trade of the Americas Agreement which is meant to embrace all the countries of North and South America (except Cuba), due to be signed in 2005 (although negotiations are currently stalled);

- a proposed free trade agreement linking ASEAN with China, Japan, India, South Korea, Australia and New Zealand;

- various free trade deals between the European Union and Africa and the United States and Africa including a free trade agreement between the US and the Southern African Customs Union (which includes South Africa, Botswana, Namibia, Lesotho and Swaziland);

- proposed US free trade agreements with Thailand, Colombia, Peru, Ecuador, Bolivia, and Panama;

- a proposed free trade agreement between the US and various Middle Eastern countries;

- a linking of the South American Mercosur and Andean economic communities.

There seems to be no end to the regional and bilateral free trade deals that can be negotiated. In trade terms the world is increasingly tied

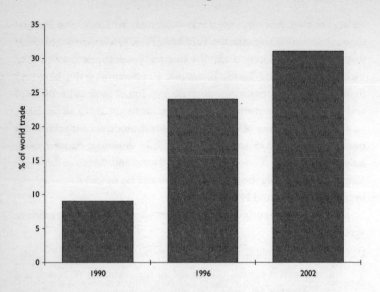

Figure 2.1 Percentage of world trade covered by regional trade agreements

Source: The World Bank and the *Economist*, 20 November 2004, p. 76.

together by WTO agreements augmented by a complicated mat of regional and bilateral trade deals.

Often the regional and free trade deals pit very unequal countries against each other. They are frequently used by high-income countries to gain influence they cannot gained through regular WTO agreements. The Free Trade of the Americas Agreement is widely viewed as a form of trade colonisation by the US of South America; the European Union Cotonou Agreement is sometimes seen as a form of European trade colonisation of Africa, the Caribbean and the Pacific; the trade arrangements that exist between the US and many African countries through the US African Growth and Opportunity Act is an attempt to wield US influence throughout Africa. One of the most conspicuous attempts to use bilateral trade deals to influence the trade politics of low-income countries was the threat by the US to review its trading relationship with Guatemala, Peru, Ecuador, Colombia and Costa Rica unless they left the G22 alliance of low-income countries that successfully stood up to high-income countries at the 2003 WTO meeting at Cancún. The move was successful although Thailand and the Philippines resisted similar pressure and stayed in the G22. Bilateral trade deals are also used to further issues that high-income countries cannot progress through regular WTO negotiations – the US, for instance, has included some of the Singapore issues in its bilateral free trade deals.

High- and low-income country global trade shares

At the end of the day the amount of clout different countries, or groups of countries, can exert in global trade negotiations often depends on the amount of trade they do and their shares of the global trade market. There is no doubt that high-income countries enjoy the lion's share of global trade and therefore most of the influence associated with it. In 2001 some 64 per cent of the world's exports came from developed countries and only 31 per cent came from developing countries (the balance of about 5 per cent came out of Eastern Europe).[119] Developed countries also dominate the flow of the world's imports – in 2001 they purchased 67 per cent of the world's imports while developing countries purchased 29 per cent.[120]

There are a number of major concerns about the low-income countries' share of the global trade market. One is that it is not increasing over time. In 1980 developing countries accounted for 28 per cent of world exports and in 1990 they accounted for 24 per cent; over the past two decades they have never had a global export share that has exceeded 32 per cent.[121] This may shortly change, however, with the rapidly increasing trade being done by countries like China, India, Brazil and Mexico. A second major concern is that several major low-income-country regions are experiencing smaller and smaller shares of the world export market. Africa is being hit the hardest – between 1980 and 2000 its share of global exports fell from 4.62 per cent to 1.84

per cent.[122] It is not alone: West Asia's share of global exports fell from 9.97 per cent to 3.97 per cent over the same period while Oceania's share fell from 0.11 per cent to 0.06 per cent.[123] As these regions have experienced shrinking shares of the global export market, other low-income countries have enjoyed increased shares. The share of global exports coming out of Southern and Eastern Asia shot up from 7.97 per cent in 1980 to 19.97 per cent in 2000[124] – this is great for the countries in that part of Asia but other low-income countries are missing out on increased exports, and export income is becoming increasingly concentrated amongst a select few low-income countries.

There is some hope for low-income countries on the global trade front, however. During the 1990s exports from developing countries grew more quickly than those from developed countries (9.1 per cent versus 5.5 per cent), although during the 1980s they had grown less quickly (3.2 per cent versus 7.5 per cent).[125] This means that when the 1980s performance is combined with the 1990s performance developing countries recorded roughly the same growth as developed countries over both decades. Another ray of hope for low-income countries comes from the fact that they are increasingly exporting a larger share of the world's manufactured exports. In 1980 only 10.5 per cent of the world's manufactured exports came from developing countries but by 2000 29.5 per cent did.[126] This increase does not mean, however, that a lot more manufactured export income is flowing to low-income countries. As discussed in Chapter 4, much evidence suggests that most manufactured value adding still takes place in high-income countries with only the low-value-added, labour-intensive parts being performed in low-income countries.

Different trade patterns of high- and low-income countries

The global trade of high- and low-income countries differs in more than just scale and share, however – it also differs in several qualitative ways. Another defining difference between them is the extent to which high- and low-income countries trade with neighbouring, similar high- or low-income countries. High-income countries do this a lot whilst low-income countries tend not to trade to a significant extent with other nearby low-income countries. In 2001 the total exports of the European Union that went to other EU countries equalled 61 per cent of all its exports that year; similarly 55 per cent of all the exports leaving the three countries that belong to the North American Free Trade Agreement (Canada, the US and Mexico) went to one of the other two members.[127] In contrast 21 per cent of all the exports from the countries that make up the Mercosur free trade area (Argentina, Brazil, Paraguay and Uruguay) went to one of the other three members, 15 per cent of the exports of the Central American Common Market stayed within the group, 22 per cent of the exports of the countries that make up the Association of South-East Asian nations stayed within its grouping, and just 14 per cent of all the exports from the countries that make up the West African Economic and Monetary Union stayed within that group.[128]

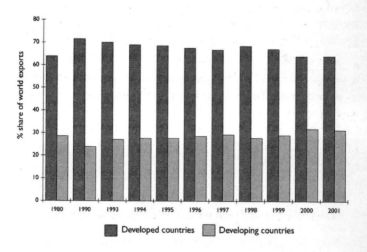

Figure 2.2 Developed and developing countries' shares of world exports

Source: *UNCTAD Handbook of Statistics 2002*, United Nations, New York and Geneva, 2002, p. 14.

Basically there is nothing particularly gracious or dignified about global trade politics. Everyone is out to get as much as they can by whatever means they can. Global trade negotiations are far from civil and involve a lot of brinkmanship and use of brute force. Global trade is not conducted on a level playing field, although in recent years low-income countries have had some success in correcting the tilt against them (but structurally the global trade market remains well and truly balanced against them). There is a long way to go before the global trade market can be called fair, and at the moment there appears to be no great momentum in that direction.

Notes

1   A. G. Kenwood and A. L. Lougheed, *The Growth of the International Economy 1820–1990: An Introductory Text* (third edn), Routledge, London, 1992, p. 235.
2   Joan E. Spero and Jeffrey A. Hart, *The Politics of International Economic Relations* (fifth edn), St Martin's Press, New York, 1997, p. 50.
3   Fatoumata Jawara and Aileen Kwa, *Behind the Scenes at the WTO: The Real World of International Trade Negotiations*, Zed Books, London, 2003, p. 81.
4   Ibid., p. 162.
5   Robert Skidelsky, *John Maynard Keynes 1883–1946: Economist, Philosopher, Statesman*, Pan Books, London, 2004, p. 672.
6   Ibid., p. 165.
7   Richard Peet (ed.), *Unholy Trinity: The IMF, World Bank and WTO*, Zed Books, London, 2003, p. 149.
8   Spero and Hart, *The Politics of International Economic Relations*, p. 51.
9   Ibid.
10 Ibid.
11 Peet, *Unholy Trinity*, p. 149.
12 Spero and Hart, *The Politics of International Economic Relations*, p. 53.
13 Ibid.
14 Kenwood and Lougheed, *The Growth of the International Economy 1820–1990*, p. 289.
15 Spero and Hart, *The Politics of International Economic Relations*, p. 54.
16 Ibid., p. 55.

17   Ibid.

18   Ibid., p. 57.

19   Robert Gilpin, *The Challenge of Global Capitalism: The World Economy in the 21st Century*, Princeton University Press, Princeton, 2000, p. 64.

20   Spero and Hart, *The Politics of International Economic Relations*, p. 161.

21   Ibid., p. 80.

22   Ibid., p. 56.

23   Ibid., p. 81.

24   Ibid., p. 82.

25   Peet, *Unholy Trinity*, p. 152.

26   Spero and Hart, *The Politics of International Economic Relations*, pp. 125, 240.

27   Ibid., p. 239.

28   Ibid., p. 83.

29   Ibid., p. 85.

30   Bhagirath Lal Das, *The WTO and the Multilateral Trading System: Past, Present and Future*, Zed Books, London, 2003, p. 15.

31   Jawara and Kwa, *Behind the Scenes at the WTO*, p. 54.

32   Ibid., p. 25.

33   Ibid., p. 120.

34   Vandana Shiva, *Protect or Plunder? Understanding Intellectual Property Rights*, Zed Books, London, 2001, p. 19.

35   Linda Weiss et al., *How to Kill a Country: Australia's Devastating Trade Deal with the United States*, Allen and Unwin, Sydney, 2004, p. 123.

36   Kevin Watkins et al., *Rigged Rules and Double Standards: Trade, Globalisation and the Fight against Global Poverty*, Oxfam International, Washington DC, 2002, p. 213.

37   Ibid.

38   United Nations Conference on Trade and Development, *UNCTAD Handbook of Statistics 2002*, United Nations, New York and Geneva, 2002, pp. 2 and 208.

39   Ibid., p. 208.

40   The Washington Trade Daily, 'Problems with Services', published by Deb Foskey via WTO Watch email list (debf@webone.com.au), 17 December 2004 (No. 281), p. 1. (For archive copy see www.nwjc.org.au/avcwl/lists/archives.html).

41   Kamal Malhotra (ed.), *Making Global Trade Work for People*, Earthscan, London, 2003, p. 267.

42   Lori Wallach and Patrick Woodall/Public Citizen, *Whose Trade Organisation?: A Comprehensive Guide to the WTO*, The New Press, New York, 2004, pp. 125–126.

43   Ibid.

44   Malhotra, *Making Global Trade Work for People*, p. 168.

45   Ibid., p. 172.

46   Watkins, *Rigged Rules and Double Standards*, p. 108.

47   'A knotty problem', *Economist*, 4 June 2005, p. 72.

48   Spero and Hart, *The Politics of International Economic Relations*, p. 86.

49   United Nations Conference on Trade and Development, *UNCTAD Handbook of Statistics 2002*, p. 108.

50   Action Aid/Azione Aiuto, *The WTO Agreement on Agriculture*, 2003, p. 3, downloaded from www.actionaid.org in 2004.

51   Ibid.

52   Ibid.

53   Ibid., p. 5.

54   Ibid., p. 6.

55   Ibid., p. 7.

56   Ibid., p.8.

57   The Agribusiness Examiner, 'Bush administration accused of creating two rural Americas', published by Deb Foskey via WTO Watch email list (debf@webone.com.au), 19th September 2004 (No. 272), p. 1. (For archive copy see www.nwjc.org.au/avcwl/lists/archives.html).

58   Action Aid/Azione Aiuto, *The WTO Agreement on Agriculture*, p. 9.

59   Ibid., p. 10.

60   Lal Das, *The WTO and the Multilateral Trading System*, p. 21.

61   'Agricultural subsidies', *Economist*, 3 July 2004, p. 92.

62   Doug Palmer, 'Kerry buys into Bush WTO Agriculture 'Framework' trade deal', published by Deb Foskey via WTO Watch email list (debf@webone.com.au), 5th September 2004 (No. 271), p. 1. (For archive copy see www.nwjc.org.au/avcwl/lists/archives.html).

63   Devinder Sharma, 'WTO: The Dope Trick', published by Deb Foskey via WTO Watch email list (debf@webone.com.au), 26 August 2004 (No. 270), p. 2. (For archive copy see www.nwjc.org.au/ avcwl/lists/archives.html).

64   Ibid., p. 1.

65   'From Cancún to can-do', *Economist*, 15 May 2004, p. 69.

66   Malhotra, *Making Global Trade Work for People*, p. 236.

67   Ibid., p. 246.

68   Ibid., p. 240.

69   Ibid., p. 241.

70   Ibid., p. 243.

71   Wallach and Woodall, *Whose Trade Organisation?*, pp. 55–56.

72   Lal Das, *The WTO and the Multilateral Trading System*, p. 42.

73   Jawara and Kwa, *Behind the Scenes at the WTO*, p. 39.
74   Ibid., p. 94.
75   Ibid., p. 40.
76   Ibid., p. 93.
77   Malhotra, *Making Global Trade Work for People*, p. 237.
78   Jawara and Kwa, *Behind the Scenes at the WTO*, p. 239.
79   Ibid., p. 240.
80   Malhotra, *Making Global Trade Work for People*, p. 288.
81   Ibid., p. 291.
82   Wallach and Woodall, *Whose Trade Organisation?*, p. 270.
83   Malhotra, *Making Global Trade Work for People*, p. 297.
84   Ibid.
85   Ibid., p. 304.
86   Ibid.
87   Jawara and Kwa, *Behind the Scenes at the WTO*, p. 243.
88   Chakravarthi Raghavan, 'From euphoria over Doha talks, to 'ownership' and advocacy?', published by Deb Foskey via WTO Watch email list (debf@webone.com.au), 16 August 2004 (No. 269), p. 1. (For archive copy see www.nwjc.org.au/avcwl/lists/ archives.html).
89   Lal Das, *The WTO and the Multilateral Trading System*, pp. 111–118.
90   Tobias Buck, 'EU to offer rewards to good, poor countries', published by Deb Foskey via WTO Watch email list (debf@webone.com.au), 29 October 2004 (No. 277), p. 1. (For archive copy see www.nwjc.org.au/avcwl/lists/archives.html).
91   Lal Das, *The WTO and the Multilateral Trading System*, p. 137.
92   Jawara and Kwa, *Behind the Scenes at the WTO*, p. 93.
93   Ibid., p. 174.
94   Ibid., p. 156.
95   Ibid., p. 174.
96   Ibid., p. 162.
97   Kanaga Raja, 'North attempts to split developing country alliances', published by Deb Foskey via WTO Watch email list (debf@webone.com.au), 30 July 2004 (No. 266), p. 2. (For archive copy see www.nwjc.org.au/avcwl/lists/archives.html).
98   Ibid.
99   Ibid., p. 4.
100   Devinder Sharma, 'WTO Framework: A Promise Belied', self-published, August 2004, p. 4, (available by emailing to:dsharma@ndf.vsnl.net.in).
101   Ibid.
102   Jawara and Kwa, *Behind the Scenes at the WTO*, p. 151.
103   Ibid.

104 Kanaga Raja, 'North attempts to split developing country alliances', p. 2.
105 Jawara and Kwa, *Behind the Scenes at the WTO*, p. 133.
106 Ibid., p. 61.
107 Wallach and Woodall, *Whose Trade Organisation?*, p. 246.
108 Ibid., p. 245.
109 Ibid., p. 248.
110 Ibid., p. 246.
111 Ibid., p. 248.
112 Ibid., pp. 244, 245.
113 Ibid., p. 244.
114 Ibid.
115 Ibid., pp. 178–180.
116 Ibid., pp. 202–203.
117 'Exclusive', *Economist*, 20 November 2004, p. 76.
118 Lal Das, *The WTO and the Multilateral Trading System*, p. 21.
119 United Nations Conference on Trade and Development, *UNCTAD Handbook of Statistics 2002*, p. 14.
120 Ibid., p. 15.
121 Ibid., p. 14.
122 Ibid.
123 Ibid.
124 Ibid.
125 Ibid., p. 16.
126 Ibid., p. 108.
127 Ibid., p. 35.
128 Ibid.

3
High-income countries and trade

High-income countries dominate the politics of global trade. A profile of the attitude of high-income countries towards trade negotiations and trade in general tells a lot about the realpolitik of global trade.

Trade fights between high-income countries

Although high-income countries generally sort out their differences before key WTO negotiations, and are generally keen to present a united face at such talks, the reality is that most of the world's trade is conducted between high-income countries and therefore a lot of differences exist between them about trade policy. In 2001 some 64 per cent of all the world's exports came out of high-income countries while 67 per cent of all the world's imports went into high-income countries.[1] This means there is a lot at stake in the trade between high-income countries. And there has been no lack of vexed trade politics between them.

Much of the aggravation has been expressed through challenges mounted by one high-income country against another through the WTO trade disputes settlement process. One commonly challenged issue is US trade law. For a long time a US statute known as the Foreign Sales Corporation Act has exempted the overseas sales of US transnational corporations from US company tax. In the late 1990s the European Union challenged the act, and in 2000 the WTO ruled the scheme was discriminatory and said it had to be abolished. The US, however, stalled implementation of the WTO decision, and by early 2004 the EU was threatening to apply retaliatory trade sanctions unless it complied. A similar case brought to the WTO in 2001 involved a US law known as the Byrd Amendment. This law gives the proceeds from extra import duties imposed on goods imported into the US at (what are deemed) unreasonably low prices to those US companies that first identified the dumping. The WTO found the law to be illegal and gave the US until late 2003 to get rid of it. The US failed to do so, and in 2004 the WTO authorised the European Union, and other complainants, to impose retaliatory tariffs on the US.[2]

Another commonly challenged issue has been discriminatory purchasing laws. In 1996 the US state of Massachusetts introduced a selective purchasing law that discriminated against goods from the military-governed country Myanmar (Burma). In 1997 both the EU and Japan challenged the law through the WTO arguing it was anti-trade. In the end the law was defeated through internal US constitutional challenges but the WTO challenge hastened its demise.[3] A similar situation occurred in the US state of Maryland: its senate rejected legislation that would have banned state government contracts with firms that did business with the (then) repressive regime in Nigeria after the US State Department testified that the legislation would violate international trade rules.[4]

Other issues that have attracted WTO challenges between high-income countries have included attempts to prop up domestic industries. With the US economy in recession and a glut of steel flooding on to the world steel market, in 2002 US President George W. Bush imposed a 30 per cent tariff on steel imported into the US. The tariff was immediately challenged by the EU, and in 2003 the WTO ruled that the tariff was illegal and had to be scrapped (which it was shortly thereafter). Yet another source of US/EU trade tension is the amount of subsidy each claims the other gives to its airline industry. The US claims that the European Airbus corporation is subsidised through government provision of capital needed for the development of new aircraft, while the EU claims that the US Boeing corporation unfairly benefits from the high level of spending by the US space department NASA and the US Defense Department.[5] In 2005 this issue was taken to the WTO.

The US has been particularly hostile to the EU's agricultural policies. In 1988 the EU banned the sale of beef from cattle treated with artificial hormones that have been linked to cancer and have been shown to have genotoxic effects. The US had long opposed this policy and in 1996 challenged the ban through the WTO at the behest of the US National Cattlemens Association.[6] In 1997 the WTO ruled that the ban was forbidden and that the EU must open its markets to hormone-treated beef – a decision upheld in a 1998 appeal. Instead of complying with the decision the EU undertook further risk assessments of the hormones, but the US refused to consider the new assessment findings and was given permission by the WTO to impose retaliatory trade sanctions.[7] By late 2003 the EU had still not lifted the ban but had changed its laws in a way it claimed complied with the ruling. The US said the EU had still not properly complied and refused to lift its retaliatory tariffs.[8]

A really big issue of future trade conflicts between the US and the EU will be genetically modified organisms (GMOs). The US has always had a relaxed attitude towards genetically modified food and has included it in food aid given to African countries but the EU has a more cautious approach. In 1990 the EU introduced stringent regulations about the introduction of GMOs under which about twelve GMOs were subsequently released but in 1999 it halted the approval of new GMO releases pending the adoption of policies on GMO segregation and labelling.[9] In 2001 new EU GMO regulations were released but they contained flaws that prompted six EU member states to declare that they would continue to prohibit new GMO releases until the flaws were fixed (which they subsequently were in EU legislation released for comment in 2003). By late 2002, however, the US had become sufficiently annoyed with the EU attitude towards GMOs to start preparing a WTO challenge to the EU GMO laws. The US delayed the challenge to allow it time to woo EU support for its invasion of

Iraq in early 2003, but in May 2003 it announced it would go ahead with the challenge. This got under way in June 2004, and if it succeeds it will signal to the world that deep concerns over the impact of new food technology cannot be allowed to stand in the way of the almighty force of global trade.

Until the Uruguay Round there had been tacit agreement between the US and the EU that world trade negotiations would not include agriculture (even though agriculture had been covered, at least in principle, by the 1947 General Agreement on Tariffs and Trade (GATT)). In 1955 the US had even threatened to leave the GATT unless US agricultural subsidies were exempted from the GATT regime.[10] The agreement unravelled, however, during the 1980s when the US and EU became locked in an intense farm subsidy battle that produced large farm surpluses that both sides were desperate to export.[11] The upshot was that the US joined with low-income countries in pushing for agriculture to be included in the Uruguay Round and these days it generally supports more radical cuts in farm subsidies than the EU does although, in the end, both sides still often come to an arrangement that allows them to retain most of their subsidies.

High-income country disputes over agricultural trade are not confined to the EU and the US. For a long time Australia has not allowed the import of uncooked salmon. In 1996, after the US and Canada requested Australian access for their uncooked salmon, Australia decided it would not allow the salmon in. It based its decision on a risk assessment that identified some 20 bacteria not present in Australian salmon but present in Canadian salmon.[12] In response in 1997 Canada challenged the decision at the WTO and was joined by the US. In June 1998 the WTO ruled against Australia, a decision that was upheld on appeal in November 1998.[13] Despite several attempts by Australia to interpret the WTO ruling narrowly, in 2000 it was forced to reach an agreement with Canada and the US that allowed in their uncooked salmon.

Growing high-income country unease about global trade

After many decades of relative acceptance of increased global trade, at the start of the twenty-first century there were increasing signs of growing unease amongst a large proportion of the population of high-income countries about the costs of global trade. This unease was particularly pronounced in Western Europe and the United States. By 2005 many, if not most, Western Europeans, particularly in Britain, Holland and France, were anxious about the proposed new European Union constitution – which would increase trade with Eastern Europe – and about the proposed deregulation of the trade in services amongst European Union countries. While in the United States the increasing trade deficit with China was a source of growing angst.

Trade fights between high- and low-income countries

High-income countries also of course have fights with low-income countries. Often the fights involve the few export products that low-income countries have a competitive advantage in, particularly agriculture and textiles. Recently the list has also included outsourced services. Low-income countries are resentful that high-income countries subsidise their farm products and are also resentful about the protectionism high-income countries use against agricultural imports from low-income countries. High-income countries defend their subsidies by arguing that farming is integral to their cultures and is an important part of their overall economic make-up. High-income country farm subsidisation goes back to the depression years of the 1930s, in the case of the US, and post-Second World War reconstruction in the case of the EU. The US subsidisation of its cotton industry has been a particularly sore point with low-income countries. The US$3 billion annual subsidies the US pays to its 25,000 cotton farmers played a major part in the collapse of the Cancún WTO talks in September 2003. In September 2002 the Brazilian government challenged the US cotton subsidies at the WTO claiming they violated a Uruguay Round agreement that subsidies should not exceed their 1992 levels. In 2004 the WTO ruled against the US, finding their cotton subsidies did, in fact, violate the Uruguay Round agreement. A similar

WTO finding was made against EU sugar subsidies in August 2004.

As WTO agreements have driven tariff levels ever lower, the number of anti-dumping actions between high- and low-income countries has increased. Dumping is deemed to have taken place when a product is exported at a very low price – generally defined as a price lower than that of an equivalent product sold in the exporting country.[14] Traditionally, high-income countries have used anti-dumping actions to curtail low-income-country exports of products such as clothing and textiles, but increasingly low-income countries are using such actions to curtail high-income-country exports of subsidised farm produce. Anti-dumping actions have become very contentious.

A new area in which some low-income countries, such as India, are increasingly developing a competitive edge is the outsourcing (or 'off-shoring') of technology-enabled services such as accounting, billing, transcription, call centre operation, medical transcription and diagnosis, and general administration. In 2002 alone, the US spent US$450 billion on services outsourced to India and other countries that have educated English-speaking people such as the Philippines and Ireland as well as high-speed data transmission facilities.[15] But the growing scale of the outsourcing is fuelling much anxiety in high-income countries. So concerned has the US become that in January 2004 its government imposed a ban on the overseas outsourcing of government contracts. India called the move hypocritical given that the US is always urging low-income countries to open up their trade markets. Another recent attack on outsourcing to low-income countries has taken the form of claims that these low-income countries cannot offer the same standards of privacy and data protection that is normally expected in high-income countries.

Another sensitive trade issue between high- and low-income countries is the application of the Uruguay Round agreement on Trade-Related Aspects of Intellectual Property Rights (TRIPS). As mentioned in Chapter 2, low-income countries are concerned that the TRIPS agreement could impact on their access to affordable essential medicines and could also limit their access to elements of biodiversity, like seeds, that they have long considered public property. High-income countries are concerned about slack enforcement of intellectual property rights in low-income countries and do not want to lose market share to generic copies. The fight over the application of the TRIPS agreement to essential medicines has been a particularly nasty one which was only resolved in 2003 through a complicated arrangement that involves low-income countries with no generic drug manufacturing capacity applying, in the first instance, to a non-generic drug manufacturer for a voluntary licence to import a generic copy of their drug. If that fails, the low-income country has to prove that it lacks the capacity to manufacture generic drugs of its own, and then must notify the WTO of its intent to import a generic copy. If they manage that they then must issue a compulsory licence to an overseas generic drug manufacturer who can import into the licence-issuing country so long as measures are taken to make sure the generic drugs are not re-exported.[16] The arrangement is very complicated and does not make it easy for low-income countries to access affordable medicines. This unwieldy agreement came after strenuous unsuccessful attempts by the US to limit the relaxation of the application of the TRIPS agreement to a few key diseases such as tuberculosis, malaria and Aids.

High-income countries' 'client state' relationships with low-income countries

One of the most profound changes over the past two decades in the trade relationship between high- and low-income countries has taken place as a result of unprecedented levels of investment by high-income countries in nearby low-income countries in order to take advantage of their low wages (and, in some cases, low taxes). Since the early 1980s Western Europe, Japan and the United States have all poured huge volumes of money into the countries of the former Eastern European bloc, Eastern Asia and Mexico (respectively) where they have established thousands of low-wage factories that carry out the labour-intensive parts of their production processes while leaving the less labour-intensive and more value-added part in their home countries. This has created a tight and potentially nasty 'client state' relationship between these high-income countries and their neigh-bouring low-income countries, a relationship in which the low-income countries become dependent on the high-income-country investment while the high-income countries keep most of the value-adding in their home countries (see Chapter 4). For Western Europe investment in low-wage eastern European countries was stimulated by the fall of the Berlin Wall in 1989 and the democratisation of Eastern Europe that followed shortly thereafter. Japanese investment in low-wage East Asian countries was stimulated by the large appreciation in the value of the Japanese yen in the mid-1980s which made exports from Japan less competitive and provided a strong incentive to shift export investment to neighbouring Asian mainland countries. Japan sweetened its new offshore investment with large increases in its foreign aid to East Asian countries. The big stimulus for the large United States investments in low-wage Mexico came with the signing of the North American Free Trade Agreement in 1994; like Japan, their investment was partly induced by large increases in the value of the dollar in the second half of the 1990s. Low-income countries outside of Eastern Europe, East Asia and Mexico have largely missed out on this new 'client state' investment, while low-income countries valued in these relationships have become tightly bound to the economic whims of their high-income-country investors.

The trade power of transnational corporations

The trade reach of transnational corporations

Increased global trade has meant increased possibilities for transna-tional corporations (TNCs) nearly all of which are based in high-income countries. Of the largest 100 TNCs in the world, 38 have their headquarters in Western Europe, 29 in the United States and 16 in Japan.[17] Of the largest 500 TNCs in the world only 29 are headquar-tered in low-income countries.[18] TNCs have experienced huge growth in recent decades. In the early 1990s the United Nations

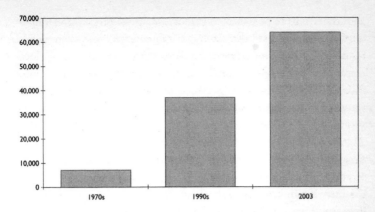

Figure 3.1 Total number of transnational corporations in the world

Source: *Economist*, 31 January 2004, p. 66 and Oswaldo de Rivero, *The Myth of Development: The Non-viable Economies of the 21st Century*, Zed Books, London, 2001, p. 46.

Conference on Trade and Development (UNCTAD) estimates there were 37,000 TNCs with 175,000 foreign subsidiaries but by 2003 they estimate there were 64,000 with 870,000 subsidiaries.[19] Back in the 1970s there were a mere 7,000 TNCs in existence.[20] This expansion has created a symbiotic relationship between TNCs and global trade. Global trade has given TNCs the ability to expand and as a result they have increasingly dominated and driven the direction of global trade. Today TNCs have enormous power over global trade – the largest 500 TNCs control nearly 70 per cent of all the world's trade.[21] About a third of global trade is conducted within individual TNCs – between different arms of the very same TNC.[22] In Delhi the Fashun Wears company, for instance, manufactures children's corduroy dresses for the chainstore Gap using synthetic lining and buttons made in China, zips made in South Korea and linen collars made by another supplier in India.[23] In 1988, US-based subsidiaries of Japanese companies purchased over 80 per cent of their inputs from their parent company in Japan then exported more than 60 per cent of their output back to the same company.[24] When Otis Elevators introduced a new elevator system recently it had the design of the motor drives done in Japan, the door systems were produced in France, the electronics were manufactured in Germany and the small gear components were assembled in Spain.[25] The age of Henry Ford's production line using local employees producing products for local demand made from local materials is fast disappearing. Much of the politics of global trade therefore now pivots around TNCs.

The trade policy influence of transnational corporations

Transnational corporations had enormous influence over the writing of some of the most contentious agreements struck during the Uruguay Round including the Trade Related Aspects of Intellectual Property Rights (TRIPS) agreement and the General Agreement on Trade in Services (GATS). Agitation for the TRIPS agreement followed lobbying of the Reagan administration by a number of large US software, pharmaceutical and chemical companies who wanted the administration to quantify the amount of revenue they claimed they were losing around the world through patent piracy.[26] Companies like Pfizer, Merck, Monsanto and Du Pont succeeded in getting the US government to force the TRIPS agreement into the Uruguay Round. A former Chief Executive of Pfizer, Edmund Pratt, even admitted 'our combined strength enabled us to establish a global private sector/government network which laid the ground for what became TRIPS'.[27] In its assessment of the Uruguay Round, Credit First Suisse Boston described the pharmaceutical industry as the 'greatest beneficiary' of the TRIPS agreement.[28] A major organising force behind the TRIPS agreement was the Intellectual Property Committee (IPC) of industry associations based in the US, Japan and the EU that was originally formed by Pfizer and IBM to ensure the TRIPS agreement said what they wanted it to say. They were subsequently joined by Monsanto, Merck, General Electric, Du Pont, Warner Communications, Hewlett-Packard, Bristol-Meyers, FMC Corporation, General Motors, Johnson and Johnson and Rockwell International.[29] James Enyart, director of international affairs at Monsanto, went so far as to say the following about the role of the IPC in formulating the TRIPS agreement:

Industry has identified a major problem for international trade. It crafted a solution, reduced it to a concrete proposal and sold it to our own and other governments. The industries and traders of world commerce have played simultaneously the role of patients, the diagnosticians and the prescribing physicians.[30]

Large TNC finance companies including American Express, Credit First Suisse Boston and the American International Group were similarly involved in the writing of the GATS agreement. They even formed themselves into the Coalition for Service Industries sometimes also known as the 'AMEX coalition'.[31] TNCs also have a history of affecting trade decisions through political donations. The Clinton administration lodged (an ultimately successful) case with the WTO against the EU for giving preferential access to bananas from various low-income countries days after the US banana TNC Chiquita, gave a US$500,000 donation to Clinton's Democratic Party.[32]

TNC transfer pricing

TNCs don't always get their way with governments. One area in which there is increasing tension between the two is that of TNC profit reporting. Where TNCs report their profits as having been generated determines where they pay tax on those profits. Trade arrangements can have a large bearing on where profits are reported, and as its volume increases, trade is becoming ever more significant in the issue of corporate profit-reporting. The reporting of company profits is largely driven by the prices TNCs ascribe to their goods and services when they cross borders. Increasingly the governments of high-income countries, and to a lesser extent those of low-income countries, are becoming suspicious of the methodology TNCs use for determining their transfer prices and therefore where their profits are generated. They often fear that transfer prices are manipulated to minimise tax. In January 2004 the US Internal Revenue Service slapped a US$5.2 billion tax bill on the UK pharmaceutical TNC GlaxoSmithKline, claiming its predecessor, Glaxo Welcome, under-paid tax on profits it made in the US between 1989 and 1996.[33] Increasingly complex rules are being developed to regulate transfer pricing, the guiding principle being that they should be set at the price an independent party would pay for the same good or service.[34] This is a simple theoretical principle that can be difficult to apply in practice and the issue shows no promise of losing its heat any time soon. In 2001 a US Senate report claimed that in 2000 alone TNCs evaded US$45 billion in US corporate taxes; the Senate even found an instance where one firm sold toothbrushes between its subsidiaries for US$5,655 each in order to minimise tax.[35]

The protectionist history of high-income countries

These days high-income countries are at the vanguard of a global push for free trade. Going by the noises they make one would think they had always pursued free trade themselves. But the reality is that high-income countries generally have economic histories more characterised by protectionism than by free trade. When they were at the stage of economic development that many low-income countries are at today they generally doggedly stuck to protectionism to build up their 'infant industries'. The hesitation that many low-income countries have today about free trade is no different to the hesitation that high-income countries had when they were at similar stages of development.

The protectionist history of Britain and the United States

Historically, Britain and the United States are generally thought of as the champions of free trade but a discerning review of their economic histories reveals that most of their economic development has been built on protectionism. The Tudor monarchs, especially Henry VII (1485–1509), were responsible for transforming Britain from an exporter of raw wool into one of the most significant manufacturers of woollen garments in the world.[36] But they were only able to do so through using decidedly protectionist measures such as increasing the duties on, and even temporarily banning, the export of raw wool. Protectionist British navigation laws introduced in the 1650s restricted the entry of foreign ships into UK ports and gave the country a near-monopoly in its colonial trade. The first prime minister under George I, Robert Walpole, in 1721 broadened the manufacturing base of the country but again used protectionist measures to do so including the raising of tariffs on imported manufactured goods and the granting of export subsidies to manufactured export goods such as silk products and gunpowder. Britain continued these measures until the early nineteenth century when, after the Napoleonic Wars, there was agitation for free trade measures. This agitation culminated in the 1846 repeal of its laws that imposed tariffs on a range of food items (the Corn Laws) and many manufactured imports.[37] It is crucial to note, however, that the United Kingdom only lowered those tariffs once it had established a large and confident manufacturing base, and that it lowered them in part to thwart the establishment of similar manufacturing industries in continental Europe. By 1860 Britain had eliminated most of its tariffs, but its period of free trade proved short-lived. By the First World War the United Kingdom realised it was losing its competitive edge in manufacturing and in 1915 it introduced its protectionist McKenna tariff act; this was augmented in 1932 it with the Import Duties Act.[38]

Although Britain was the first country to pursue a full-blooded protectionist infant industry strategy, the United States was probably the most enthusiastic practitioner. Economic historian Paul Bairoch once described the US as 'the mother country and bastion of modern protectionism'.[39] Britain did not want its US colonies to industrialise but after independence from Britain the US was determined to. It started to establish a manufacturing base through protectionist measures such as the introduction in 1789 of a flat 5 per cent import tariff which between 1792 and 1812 was increased to an average of 12.5 per cent.[40] The first Treasury Secretary of the United States, Alexander Hamilton, wrote what is considered the definitive text on infant industry protectionism. George Washington even insisted on wearing lower quality US clothes – instead of higher-quality British ones – to his inauguration.[41] After war with Britain in 1812 the US significantly increased its long-term tariffs, especially for cotton, woollen and iron goods; between 1816 and the end of the Second World War it had one of the highest average tariff rates for manufactured imports in the world.[42] After the Civil War in particular the US experienced a period of rapid industrial growth enhanced by high tariff walls erected by the Republican governments of the time.[43] The use of tariffs was much debated within the US during the nineteenth century with manufacturers generally in favour of them but farmers generally opposed.[44] Even the infamous Smoot–Hawley tariff increases of 1930 – often viewed as extreme US protectionism – fell within the range of tariff rates that had prevailed in the US since the Civil War. Ulysses Grant, hero of the Civil War and president from 1868 to 1876, said when Britain was adopting free trade in the mid-nineteenth century, 'England has found it convenient to adopt free trade because it thinks that protection can no longer offer it anything. Very well then, gentlemen, my knowledge of our country leads me to believe that within 200 years, when America has gotten out of protection all it can offer, it too will adopt free trade.'[45] It was only after the Second World War – when the US had an industrial base that no other country could challenge – that it started to adopt free trade, but even then it continued to pursue many indirect forms of protectionism.

Protectionism in other high-income countries

Germany and France are often thought of as having unambiguously pursued protectionist policies throughout much of their history and it is generally no secret that they have historically been dubious about free trade. Although this reputation is somewhat exaggerated, the two countries have none the less taken a lot of protectionist initiatives. In the eighteenth century, under Frederick William and Frederick the Great, the state of Prussia erected high import tariffs to establish new industries much as Henry VII had done three centuries before in Britain. In 1879, after the creation of Germany, Otto von Bismarck, chancellor of the new country, significantly increased tariffs, particularly those applied to industries such as the iron and steel industries.[46] In the 1660s and 1670s the finance minister of Louis XIV of France, Jean-Baptiste Colbert, introduced a broad raft of protectionist tariffs.[47] Three centuries later, in the 1960s, France used a lot of interventionist government strategies, including the establishment of many government-owned businesses, to develop further its industrial base.[48] In Asia, until the early twentieth century Japan had a number of 'unequal treaties' that barred it from erecting tariff barriers but once they expired in 1911 it introduced a range of tariff reforms aimed at protecting infant industries; the reforms were generally targeted against the importation of luxury goods. After the Second World War Japan introduced a system of export subsidies and tariff rebates for imports used in re-exported goods.[49]

In short, almost all today's high-income-country advocates of free trade have a history of protected trade and are therefore very hypocritical in pushing free trade assertively today. Economic historian Ha-Joon Chang, of Cambridge University, argues 'when they were developing countries themselves, virtually all of today's developed countries did not practice free trade. ... rather, they promoted their national interests through tariffs, subsidies and other measures'.[50] This does not mean that all high-income countries were always protectionist before the twentieth century (Switzerland and the Netherlands definitely were not), or that they all used the same protectionist devices, but it does mean it is hypocritical for them to deny similar protectionist opportunities to today's low-income countries.

The downsides of trade liberalisation in high-income countries

It is misleading to pretend that high-income countries always win from free trade. Some sectors in high-income countries certainly do win from free trade – transnational corporations in particular – but other sectors do not. One fairly consistent high-income-country loser from free trade is labour-intensive manufacturing. Many jobs in this sector have left high-income countries for lower-wage countries and those that have stayed have often had the threat of relocation used to lower the conditions attached to them. Since the WTO was established, the industrial base of the United States has been significantly hollowed out – with the loss of 2 million manufacturing jobs.[51] A recent survey of 10,000 industrial companies by the German Chamber of Commerce found that nearly a quarter planned to relocate at least part of their operations abroad, with lower wages being the most popular reason for moving.[52] Many German companies move to the countries of the former Eastern Europe where wages are 85 to 90 per cent lower than German wages – if the companies don't move they use the threat of moving to get more out of their workers. The German company Siemens recently managed to persuade its employees to increase their hours from 35 to 40 hours per week – without extra pay – in return for promising not to relocate to Hungary.[53] A factory located in France, run by German car part maker Robert Bosch, recently got its employees to work extra hours by promising not to move their jobs to the Czech Republic.[54] Champions of free trade argue that more exports from service industries in high-income countries make up for the loss of manufacturing jobs, but that all depends on whether a high-income country is competitive in services, and many manufacturing workers can't easily re-skill for service industry jobs even if they are. Another major problem is that the loss of manufacturing jobs narrows the economic base of high-income countries making them less able to weather global economic down-turns when they come along.

In 2003 the Carnegie Endowment for International Peace assessed the ten-year impact of the North American Free Trade Agreement on its participating countries: the US, Canada and Mexico. In the US it found that the job creation that the agreement had been responsible for was somewhere between none and a few hundred thousand despite the prediction of Bill Clinton, when the agreement was signed, that it would create 200,000 US jobs in its first two years of operation alone.[55] In Canada – where free trade with the US began with the 1988 Canada–United States Free Trade Agreement – the Carnegie Endowment found that in those sectors that had previously enjoyed some tariff protection from US imports employment fell by 12 per cent, but in those export-based sectors that were well placed to increase exports to the US there was no overall increase in employment.[56] It also found there had been an increase in inequality in Canada during the life of the NAFTA agreement; this was probably not particularly due to the agreement but it could have been indirectly affected by the downward pressure NAFTA put on government spending which influenced the welfare spending of the Canadian government.[57]

A more subtle and complex trade problem for high-income countries is that trade has come to make up such a large part of their economic activity that policies that relate to other parts of their economy end up intersecting with their trade performance, often in unforeseen and undesirable ways. Germany once had one of the most dynamic economies in Western Europe with growth rates and per capita gross domestic product levels that outstripped most of its neighbours. By 2004, however, its per capita gross domestic product was only higher than four of the other fourteen (pre-expansion) members of the European Union; its rate of economic growth during the 1990s was only half that of the EU.[58] In the past it could have used both domestic interest rate and exchange rate policies to change this – a lower exchange rate would have made Germany's considerable volume of exports more competitive. But in January 1999 Germany joined the European single currency system and lost the ability to set its own interest rates or exchange rates. Germany joined the Euro because it thought the Euro would make the European Union more competitive and attractive to investment, but many Germans now regret their country's loss of economic autonomy. If trade didn't make up such a large part of the German economy the loss of exchange rate autonomy wouldn't matter so much but in 2000 Germany's exports equalled 30 per cent of its gross domestic product[59] and its loss of exchange rate autonomy has had a profound effect on its overall economic performance. The other European countries that use the Euro face a similar problem to Germany. From late 2001 the Euro began a long-term rise against the US dollar as the dollar continued to experience a sustained fall because of structural problems in the US economy (which are discussed in Chapter 8). But the rise in the value of the Euro is punishing the exports from those countries that use the currency; like Germany, exports generally make up a large part of the economic activity of those countries, so reduced exports mean reduced economic growth for them. Relying on exports too heavily opens an economy up to forces way beyond its control.

Like Germany, the United States is increasingly facing deep structural problems in its economy, in its case mainly to do with a large and deteriorating balance-of-payments situation which includes an ever-worsening trade balance. US balance-of-payments problems began in the 1980s: high US interest rates in the late 1970s had attracted a lot of overseas capital into the US economy which pushed up the value of the US dollar and made its exports less competitive. High US interest rates again played havoc with the value of the US dollar – and with its export competitiveness – in 1987 before the stockmarket crash of that year. Since then every time that US interest rates have started to get high its balance of payments and balance of trade have come under pressure. The US can't separate its interest rate policy from its trade performance. Like Germany, when trade was a smaller part of the US economy the detrimental effect that high interest rates could have on its trade performance did not matter so much. But now that trade accounts for a large part of its economic activity its intersection with interest rate policy does matter but the two can't easily be unscrambled.

Probably the most profound economic impact of increased global trade is that it has left all the countries of the world with much less choice about economic growth strategies. If a country pursues a high-growth strategy it is likely to experience increased inflation which will make its traded goods and services less competitive in the global marketplace; most countries these days therefore have little choice other than to pursue fairly low-growth/low-inflation strategies that will keep their exports competitive. But low growth often means high unemployment so jobless people often pay the price for export competitiveness. One of the first leaders to face this dilemma was US president Jimmy Carter who wanted to pursue fairly high economic growth during the second half of the 1970s but realised that he wouldn't be able to without eroding US trade competitiveness, unless the European Economic Community and Japan also pursued high-growth strategies. They refused to cooperate with Carter so he was left with little option other than to contain the economic growth of the US economy.

Trade is now such a large part of most high-income countries' economic activity that a loss of exports can have much the same economic effect as a major slowdown in domestic economic growth. But high-income countries have much less control over their trade performance than they have over their domestic economic growth and, as Germany and the US are now discovering, what is good for their domestic economy isn't always good for their trading relationship with the rest of the world.

High-income countries continue to call most of the shots in global trade politics at the expense of low-income countries, but invariably those that have the final say are not the governments of high-income countries but the large transnational corporations that stand over them. Free trade may yet prove a monster that could devour some high-income countries as many of them come to feel frustrated by their inability to pursue economic policies that will benefit their domestic economies because the policies may not necessarily benefit their trade performance. The two keep colliding.

Notes

1   United Nations Conference on Trade and Development, *UNCTAD Handbook of Statistics 2002*, United Nations, New York and Geneva, 2002, pp. 14–15.
2   'Byrd-brained', *Economist*, 4 September 2004, p. 73.
3   Lori Wallach and Patrick Woodall/Public Citizen, *Whose Trade Organisation?: A Comprehensive Guide to the WTO*, The New Press, New York, 2004, pp. 236–237.
4   Michael Woodin and Carolin Lucas, *Green Alternatives to Globalisation: A Manifesto*, Pluto Press, London, 2004, p. 39.
5   'Enough is enough', *Economist*, 24 July, 2004, p. 15.
6   Wallach and Woodall, *Whose Trade Organisation?*, p. 69.
7   Ibid., pp. 70–71.
8   *Financial Times*, 'EU complies with WTO over beef hormone ban', published by Deb Foskey via WTO Watch email list (debf@webone.com.au), 19 October 2003 (No. 215), p. 1 and Thomas Buck/*Financial Times* 'US 'will not lift' sanctions on EU over beef', published by Deb Foskey via

WTO Watch email list (debf@webone.com.au), 24 October 2003 (No. 217), p. 1. (For archive copy see www.nwjc.org.au/avcwl/lists/archives. html).

9   Wallach and Woodall, *Whose Trade Organisation?*, p. 79.

10 Bhagirath Lal Das, *The WTO and the Multilateral Trading System: Past Present and Future*, Zed Books, London, 2003, p. 21.

11 Ibid.

12 Wallach and Woodall, *Whose Trade Organisation?*, p. 73.

13 Ibid.

14 Lal Das, *The WTO and the Multilateral Trading System*, p. 45.

15 Ranjit Devraj 'US Ban on Outsourcing Smacks of Unfair Policies – India', published by Deb Foskey via WTO Watch email list (debf@webone.com.au), 2 February 2004 (No. 238), p. 1. (For archive copy see www.nwjc.org.au/avcwl/lists/archives.html).

16 Cecilia Oh, *The new 'deal' on TRIPS and drugs: What does it mean for access to medicines?*, Third World Network, Penang, Malaysia, 2003, pp. 2–3, downloaded from www.twnside.org.sg in 2003.

17 Robert Went, *Globalisation: Neoliberal Challenge, Radical Responses*, Pluto Press, London, 2000, pp. 44, 45.

18 George Monbiot, *The Age of Consent: A Manifesto for a New World Order*, Flamingo, London, 2003, p. 195.

19 'A Taxing Battle', *Economist*, 31 January 2004, p. 66.

20 Oswaldo de Rivero, *The Myth of Development: The Non-Viable Economies of the 21st Century*, Zed Books, London, 2001, p. 46.

21 Colin Hines, *Localization: A Global Manifesto*, Earthscan, London, 2000, p. 14.

22 John Madeley, *Hungry for Trade: How the Poor Pay for Free Trade*, Zed Books, London, 2000, p. 91.

23 Kevin Watkins et al., *Rigged Rules and Double Standards: Trade, Globalisation and the Fight Against Global Poverty*, Oxfam International, Washington DC, 2002, p. 41.

24 A. G. Kenwood and A. L. Lougheed, *Growth of the International Economy, 1820–1990: An Introductory Text*, Routledge, London, 1992, p.290.

25 Woodin and Lucas, *Green Alternatives to Globalisation*, p. 41.

26 Vandana Shiva, *Protect or Plunder?*, London, Zed Books, 2001, p. 19.

27 Hines, *Localization*, p. 213.

28 Watkins, *Rigged Rules*, p. 212.

29 Michael P. Ryan, *Knowledge Diplomacy: Global Competition and the Politics of International Property*, Brookings Institution Press, Washington, 1998, p. 69 and Wallach and Woodall, *Whose Trade Organisation?*, pp. 201, 351.

30 Mark Lynas, 'The World Trade Organisation and GMOs', *Consumer Policy Review*, 1 November 1999, and Wallach and Woodall, *Whose Trade*

Organisation?, p. 202.

31   Ann Capling, *Australia and the Global Trade System*, Cambridge, Cambridge University Press, 2001, p. 149.

32   Woodin and Lucas, *Green Alternatives to Globalisation*, p. 20.

33   'A Taxing Battle', p. 65.

34   Ibid., p. 66.

35   Ibid.

36   Ha-Joon Chang, *Kicking Away the Ladder: The 'Real' History of Free Trade*, Foreign Policy in Focus, Silver City (New Mexico), 2003, p. 6, downloaded from www.fpif.org in 2004.

37   Ibid.

38   Kenwood and Lougheed, *Growth of the International Economy 1820–1990*, pp. 176, 202.

39   Paul Bairoch, quoted in Chang, *Kicking Away the Ladder*, p. 7.

40   Ibid., p. 8.

41   Ibid., p. 16.

42   Ibid., p. 8.

43   Peter Hugill, *World Trade since 1431: Geography, Technology and Capitalism*, Johns Hopkins University Press, Baltimore, 1995, p. 153.

44   Roger E. Backhouse, *The Penguin History of Economics*, Penguin Books, London, 2002, p. 186.

45   A. G. Frank, *Capitalism and Underdevelopment in Latin America*, Monthly Review Press, New York, 1967, p. 164.

46   Ibid.

47   Chris Rohmann, *The Dictionary of Important Ideas and Thinkers*, Arrow, London, 2002, p. 258.

48   Chang, *Kicking Away the Ladder*, p. 12.

49   Ibid., p. 14.

50   Ibid., p. 1.

51   Wallach and Woodall, *Whose Trade Organisation?*, p. 10.

52   'Tax Wars', *Economist*, 24 July 2004, p. 55.

53   'Europe's workplace revolution', *Economist*, 31 July 2004, p. 49.

54   Ibid.

55   John J. Audley et al., *NAFTA's Promise and Reality: Lessons from Mexico for the Hemisphere*, Carnegie Endowment for International Peace, Washington, 2003, p. 28, downloaded from www.ceip.org in 2004.

56   Ibid., p. 30.

57   Ibid., p. 31.

58   'How to pep up Germany's economy', *Economist*, 8 May 2004, p. 65.

59   Based on figures in World Bank, *World Development Report 2002*, Oxford University Press, New York, 2002, pp. 236, 238.

4

Low-income countries and trade

Low-income countries have traditionally been the underdogs of global trade negotiations but in recent years they have managed to take the fight to high-income countries. This has made trade negotiations less predictable than they once were. Many complex trade issues face low-income countries, and different groups of low-income countries face vastly different issues.

The emergence of Third and Fourth World low-income countries

One of the most fundamental economic issues facing low-income countries is that increasingly they are diverging; they can no longer be considered one 'job lot'. When it comes to trade and development there is no longer a conglomerate Third World but rather two very different Third and Fourth worlds. Trade statistics reveal the extent of the economic divergence. For the world as a whole the total value of exports trebled during the 1980s and 1990s with developing countries recording an increase slightly better than that of developed countries.[1] But behind the developing country figure were two vastly different stories. Over those two decades East and South Asia enjoyed an extra-ordinary export growth that resulted in a seven-fold increase, with

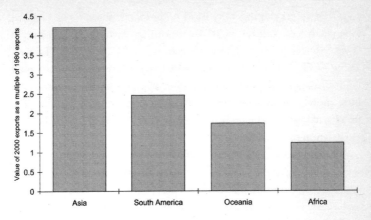

**Figure 4.1 Growth of low-income country regional exports,
1980 to 2000**

Source: 'UNCTAD Handbook of Statistics 2002', United Nations Conference on Trade and
Development, United Nations, New York and Geneva, 2002, pp. 2–8.

some countries doing spectacularly well such as Vietnam (a 42-fold
increase) and China (a 13-fold increase).[2] The developing countries of
Central America and the Caribbean also enjoyed export growth above
the developing-country average though much of it was due to
Mexico's export growth. Other parts of the developing world
performed much less spectacularly, however. South America only
recorded a 1.5-fold increase while the countries of Oceania only experienced a 74 per cent growth.[3] African exports only increased by 24
per cent; exports from West Asia, including the Middle East, increased
by the same amount.[4] Basically when it comes to running the export
race, Eastern and Southern Asia, along with Central America and the
Caribbean, are a long way in front while Africa and the Middle East
are falling way behind, with the other developing countries coming in
somewhere in between.

Another similarly lop-sided picture is revealed by the relative trade
shares of specific low-income countries. A handful of low-income
countries dominate developing country exports. UNCTAD classes 162

countries as 'developing' but just 11 of them accounted for 62 per cent
– or nearly two-thirds – of all the exports by developing countries in
2001.[5] Brazil, Mexico, China, Argentina, India, Indonesia, Taiwan,
Hong Kong, Malaysia, Singapore and Thailand are the 11 developing
country exporting giants; all the other 151 developing countries are
little more than pygmies by comparison. Unsurprisingly, today the
politics of low-income trade negotiations are heavily influenced by the
polarisation of trade shares.

Throughout the 1960s and 1970s, however, low-income countries
were relatively united in their approach to trade politics. The many
low-income countries that achieved independence between the 1940s
and 1960s banded together in 1963 to make a joint declaration on
trade to the United Nations. This was the catalyst for the creation of
the Group of Seventy-seven (G77) low-income countries – named
after the number of signatories to the original declaration. Amongst
other things the 1963 declaration said:

> The existing principles and patterns of world trade still mainly favour the
> advanced parts of the world. Instead of helping the developing countries to
> promote the development and diversification of their economies, the
> present tendencies in world trade frustrate their efforts to attain more rapid
> growth. These trends must be reversed.[6]

The year after the declaration, low-income countries established their
own trade forum – UNCTAD – which they saw as something of a
counterweight to the high-income country organisation, the Organisation for Economic Cooperation and Development. Despite the
objections of high-income countries low-income countries were able
to get UNCTAD made into a permanent United Nations body, and
after threatening to replace the General Agreement on Tariffs and
Trade (GATT) with their own global trade body low-income countries
were also able to get some commitments from high-income countries
about access to their import markets and extending exemptions from
GATT rules to them.[7] These changes ended up having little lasting
effect, however, and by the 1980s a major cleavage in the trade
direction of low-income countries was starting to open up. The so-

called East Asian 'tiger' economies of Taiwan, South Korea, Hong Kong and Singapore were starting to achieve major increases in trade, largely because of their use of decidedly non-free trade devices such as both government subsidisation of exporters and the application of local-content and technology-transfer rules to foreign investors (rules since outlawed by Uruguay Round agreements). During the 1990s the original four 'tiger' economies were joined by other East Asian 'mini tiger' economies such as Thailand and Malaysia, and in 1994 Mexico started significantly expanding its exports after it joined the North American Free Trade Agreement. Also in the 1990s China began a major export expansion after economic changes ushered in by leader Deng Xiaoping; other hitherto fairly protectionist countries, such as India and Brazil, also began to significantly liberalise their trade policies. In the 1980s UNCTAD's influence began to wane, particularly after it failed to get agreement to global raw material price support schemes. Also during the 1980s a large number of low-income countries started actively participating in global trade talks, namely the Uruguay Round conducted between 1986 and 1993.

At the WTO trade negotiations held in Cancún in September 2003 it appeared, despite the divergences of the past two decades, that low-income countries had refound some of the unity on trade policy they had had during the 1960s and 1970s: the G22 group of low-income countries, led by Brazil, India and South Africa, were able to derail the Cancún talks after high-income countries attempted to push the Singapore issues into the round and were obstinate about reviewing their cotton subsidies (see Chapter 2). The Brazilian trade minister, Clodualdo Huguenuy, even boldly claimed that 'the G22 broke the monopoly over trade negotiations by the EU and US'.[8] By 2004, however, it was clear that the trade divergence amongst low-income countries had not gone away and that the G22 unity was something of an aberration.

After Cancún many low-income countries, such as Indonesia, became worried that the G22 (which eventually became the G20) was mainly concerned about securing greater market share for low-income-country agricultural exports and was relatively unconcerned about the ongoing protection of low-income country markets. In response another low-income-country grouping, the G33, continued pushing for various forms of insulation from WTO free trade rules for vulnerable low-income country industries.[9] Other groups of low-income countries were also concerned that the G22 was an inadequate defender of their interests and they grouped around a coalition known as the G90 which was mainly made up of African, Caribbean, Pacific and least-developed countries.[10]

Trade policy unity amongst low-income countries was severely tested during negotiations about the 2004 framework agreement for the Doha Round. The agreement was negotiated by a 'Five Interested Parties' group that included the European Union, the US, Australia (representing the Cairns Group of free trade agricultural export nations), India and Brazil. Although India and Brazil consulted extensively with other low-income countries, the agreement delivered few tangible gains for low-income countries, and it locked India and Brazil – hitherto two of the loudest low-income-country critics of WTO agreements – into the final outcome. As Walden Bello and Aileen Kwa, from the Focus on the Global South organisation, argued, 'the reality is that the G20, and in particular Brazil and India, have been accommodated into the ranks of the key global trading powers, but it is increasingly becoming clear that the price for this has been their diluting the strength of the negotiating position of the South'.[11] In September 2004 there were even rumours that India was contemplating a free trade agreement with the United States.[12]

By about 2015, China is likely to become the largest exporter and importer in the world.[13] It will almost certainly be impossible for it to achieve that status without it having a favourable attitude towards free trade, much as the United States did after it achieved the same status after the Second World War. Indeed Jonathan Anderson, an economist with the UBS company, claims China is currently one of the most rapidly liberalising economies in the world and is opening up its markets much more than other large low-income economies like India or Brazil are.[14] Increasingly, low-income countries are separating into competitive low-income countries – which want to play a limited form of the free trade game of high-income countries – and other low-income countries that want to have as little as possible to do with it. The upshot of this fracturing is that there are now vastly different trade agendas and priorities amongst low-income countries – priorities that can't necessarily be reconciled with each other. Commenting on the 2004 Doha Round framework agreement Robert Wade, professor of political economy at the London School of Economics, gave this summary of the divergence:

> ... the developing countries do not have a united front. Some, including Malaysia and China, are prepared to accept such [tariff] cuts in return for equally radical tariff cuts by developed countries in those industrial sectors with tariff spikes intended to keep out imports from developing countries, such as textiles. Other developing countries, like Kenya and Zambia, insist on retaining substantial tariffs on some industrial imports so as to encourage the development of their weak industrial base.[15]

The issue of differing trade agendas amongst low-income countries looks like coming to a head in 2005 over the liberalisation of the global textile trade. At the time of writing many low-income countries such as Turkey, Mexico, Bangladesh, Mauritius and Lesotho – who currently export a lot of textiles – are fearful that once global textile trade is fully liberalised they will lose global market share to China and India.[16] China has already made major inroads into the textile exports of many low-income countries to the United States. Fearing that this will be repeated around the world, many low-income countries have lobbied the WTO to establish safety mechanisms such as lower tariffs for countries adversely affected by the textile trade liberalisation as well as changes in the way textile exports are classified and/or special assistance funds for countries who lose out. In a similar vein during the 2004 negotiation of the Doha Round framework agreement many low-income countries argued that there should be a special sub-category of low-income countries that would be separate from more advanced low-income countries; the members of this sub-category would be eligible for 'special and different' trade treatment. Although such a call was also made by the then European Union trade commissioner, Pascal Lamy, high-income countries were not supportive of

such low-income country differentiation. As the Doha Round pro-
gresses the tensions between different low-income countries will only
become more acute particularly when the really hard bargaining
begins. This may see some large low-income countries, like Brazil,
that have competitive export agricultural sectors, being prepared to
make concessions on the protection of their service and industrial
sectors in return for high-income countries' concessions on access to
their agricultural markets; other low-income countries may be much
less prepared to make such trade-offs.

Future trade relations between low-income countries

The seemingly permanent divergence amongst low-income countries
poses a great challenge for them. At a time when they are starting to
exercise some real clout in global trade talks, deep divisions are setting
in amidst their ranks. At best these mean that no single trade prescrip-
tion can any longer hope to accommodate all low-income countries –
if it ever could. At worst it means that the day may not be far away
when smaller, less competitive low-income countries have nasty
public arguments over trade policy with larger, more competitive low-
income countries. The day may not be too far away when trade
relations between low-income countries dominate global trade
relations in much the same way that trade relations between high-
income countries currently do. In 1994 the *Economist* magazine
predicted that by 2020 the proportion of global output that low-
income countries are responsible for could reach 60 per cent and that
by the same year nine of the largest fifteen economies in the world will
be (what are currently) low-income countries.[17] Even though this prediction was made before the 1997 East Asian 'meltdown' it still largely
holds. Such a change will return the world to the economic power
balance that existed before the mid-nineteenth century, when China
and India were the largest economies in the world.[18] Several (but by no
means all) large low-income countries, particularly those in Eastern
and Southern Asia, are growing very quickly. China is growing so fast

that it has the official goal of quadrupling its 2002 gross domestic product by 2020.[19] East Asian low-income countries in particular are growing at a rate unprecedented in economic history. After the Industrial Revolution took off in the late eighteenth century, it took Britain 58 years to double its gross domestic product per head; from 1839 it took the US 47 years to do the same, from 1885 it took Japan 34 years to do something similar; but South Korea managed to do it in just 11 years starting in 1966; and China did it in fewer than ten years starting in the mid-1980s.[20]

As well as changes in global trade shares there will also be an enormous shift of overall global earnings towards low-income countries, powered by the sheer weight of their population increases. This too will have enormous implications for the future of global trade. By 2050 there will be about 9 billion people in the world, up from 6.3 billion people today. Nearly all the worldwide increase will take place in low-income countries. The only high-income country that will experience any significant population increase over the next half-century is the United States but its overall increase, of about 120 million, will be almost balanced out by falls in Europe and Japan, which between them are expected to lose 90 million people.[21]

These big shifts cannot help but have an enormous impact on global trade flows and therefore on global trade politics over the next few decades. Indeed they are already having a major impact. The share of exports from developing countries going to other developing countries rose from a little over 20 per cent in 1975 to just under 40 per cent in 1999.[22]

Today one group of low-income countries – including India, Brazil, China and South Africa – is interested in pursuing a limited version of the free trade agenda of today's high-income countries, while another group of low-income countries – including many African countries – is interested in a more protectionist agenda. In future there may be a lot of friction between the two camps. Low-income countries will need to be very careful about what trade choices they make over the coming decades. Trading relations between large, competitive low-income countries and smaller, less competitive low-income countries could, in future, be as bad as they currently are between high-income and low-income countries.

Current trade relations between low-income countries

These days public trade fights are not as common between low-income countries as they are between high-income countries but nevertheless significant wariness exists between low-income countries, and some have been prepared to have public fights over trade. Between January 1995 and January 2003 some 66 of the 279 trade disputes brought to the WTO (24 per cent) were between low-income countries.[23] Brazil and India were the fourth- and fifth-largest plaintiffs respectively (behind the United States, the EU and Canada) during that time.[24] At the other end of the low-income country spectrum, however, as of January 2003 not one of the fifty-two least developed countries in the world had brought a trade dispute to the WTO.[25] This statistic reinforces the reality of increasingly different trade agendas opening up amongst low-income countries.

A major expression of the different trade agendas of low-income countries occurred when China joined the WTO in 2001. This caused significant tensions amongst many low-income countries. Several, especially Mexico, were worried that many of their low-wage manu-facturing jobs would be lost to China once it joined, and Mexico held out on allowing China to join for some time before succumbing to US pressure. Another expression of different low-income country trade agendas is found within the South American Mercosur trade grouping. There is a lot of tension within the group, particularly between Brazil and Argentina. Argentina feels that Brazil doesn't embrace the trade grouping enough while Brazil feels that Argentina doesn't embrace trade with high-income countries enough.[26] Other sources of tension are China and India and the perception of them by other low-income countries. Both China and India are rapidly expanding low-income economies which, eventually, will probably be the largest and second largest economies in the world. As they grow they are increasingly vying with each other for natural resources, foreign capital and export markets which makes them increasingly uneasy with each other.[27] But other low-income countries are becoming uneasy with the increasing dominance of China and India – evidenced by the very justified fears that China and India will end up taking a lot of textile market share from other low-income countries following the deregulation of global textile trade in 2005.

Growing low-income country unease about global trade

As in high-income countries, there is increasing wide-spread unease amongst low-income country societies about the costs of global trade. The unease has a longer history than in high-income countries and is more deep-seated; by 2005 it had come to be very publicly expressed. Large numbers of low-income country peasant farmers regularly protest outside World Trade Organisation meetings. Bolivians protest about the export of cheap gas from their country, Africans protest about low cotton prices, Indian farmers protest about opening their country up to more foreign competition while many societies throughout the Pacific protest about the export of timber from their local regions.

Trade fights between low- and high-income countries

Many of the large number of trade disputes between low and high-income countries are dealt with elsewhere in this book, but several general clusters of issues that such disputes often cover are worth briefly touching on. One is the view amongst many low-income countries that although they have relatively few goods and services that can compete with high-income countries, when they do develop such exports high-income countries always restrict their market access. This particularly applies to the trade of agricultural products, textiles and outsourced services. Many low-income countries are cynical about the likelihood of high-income countries ever really opening their agricultural markets, and a lot of trust has been destroyed over the high-income country Uruguay Round promise to progressively open up their trade in textiles. There is a lot of suspicion that global textile trade will not really be fully liberalised after 2005 as planned. Services tell a similar story. Countries like India have become competitive in computer and communications-related services but already the US has imposed a ban on government outsourcing of services to India. Many low-income countries would like greater freedom of movement of services-related workers between their countries and high-income countries, but high-income countries dismiss this as an immigration issue not a trade issue.

A second cluster of issues concerns the vulnerability of low-income countries. They often feel they simply can't compete with high-income country exports and shouldn't be expected to. They should be able to protect their local industries as high-income countries did for so long in the past, they feel. This particularly applies to agricultural and industrial liberalisation. A huge proportion of people in low-income countries are employed in agriculture – as many as 70 per cent in very poor low-income countries and 30 per cent in moderately poor low-income countries.[28] Not all these people produce traded agricultural produce but a significant proportion do, and the consequences of the forced opening of low-income-country farm markets to subsidised high-income-country farm exports could be very dire. Mexican corn farmers have already been devastated by the flood of cheap US corn that accompanied Mexico's joining the North American Free Trade Agreement in 1994. If that experience is repeated throughout the rest of the world, global poverty could sharply increase. It simply is unfair to wipe out by means of farm trade liberalisation the limited means of survival of hundreds of millions of low-income farm workers.

There is a similar risk of devastation of manufacturing jobs in low-income countries. The Uruguay Round agreement mandated that low-income countries had to end their import substitution subsidies by the end of 1999[29] while the 2004 Doha Round framework agreement said that the industrial goods with the highest tariffs would be subject to the steepest cuts – this could hit low-income countries in

a big way because they often use high tariffs to protect their fledgling manufacturing industries. In addition, the agreement on Trade-related Investment Measures (TRIMS agreement) stipulated that low-income countries could not use local content rules to stimulate local industrial development. These measures come on top of liberalisation already forced on low-income countries by the IMF and World Bank and destroy a lot of the hope that low-income countries might have had of establishing secure domestic manufacturing sectors. So far during the Doha Round, low-income countries have been reluctant to make further concessions on lowering their tariffs on industrial goods although some (like India and Brazil) may be prepared to give ground if high-income countries make concessions on access to their agricultural markets.

Professor Edward Buffie, in his book *Trade Policy in Developing Countries*, gives the following examples of the destruction of African manufacturing after trade liberalisation:[30]

- In Senegal, one third of manufacturing jobs were lost in the early 1990s following liberalisation in the late 1980s;

- In Côte d'Ivoire the chemical, textile, shoe and car-assembly manufacturing sectors nearly completely collapsed after sudden tariff reductions in 1986;

- In Uganda the utilisation of local manufacturing industry capacity dropped to as low as 22 per cent after liberalisation in the 1980s while the importation of consumer goods swallowed nearly half Uganda's foreign exchange;

- In Kenya major contractions occurred in the tobacco, textile, beverage, sugar, leather, cement and glass product industries after trade liberalisation in 1993.

Similarly a 2002 report jointly prepared by the World Bank, non-governmental organisations and various low-income country governments – the Structural Adjustment Participatory Review Initiative – found that in Zimbabwe manufacturing output declined by more than

20 per cent after trade liberalisation, in Bangladesh the manufacturing share of gross domestic product increased only marginally after similar liberalisation, and in Ghana the manufacturing sector showed unimpressive long-term growth after its trade was freed up.[31] The report also said:

> The failure of many local manufacturing firms, particularly innovative, small and medium-sized ones that generate a great deal of employment, is one of the key findings of this study. In several cases, leading manufacturing activities have suffered from indiscriminate import liberalisation, provoking a reduction in output, bankruptcy of enterprises and loss of employment. The decline in domestic manufacturing has followed the flooding of local markets with cheap imports that have displaced local production and goods, and has been exacerbated by the absence of an industrial policy to support domestic firms in dealing with new conditions or with shocks in international markets.[32]

Another cluster of trade issues of concern to low-income countries involves the abuse by high-income countries of WTO measures designed to stop unfair trade practices. These include anti-dumping and special safeguard measures. Low-income countries are often plagued with anti-dumping actions initiated by high-income countries who accuse them of exporting products at marked-down prices but who in reality are using the measures as another form of protectionism. Between 1995 and 1999, anti-dumping investigations by the WTO increased significantly with most of the cases initiated by high-income countries against low-income ones.[33] A recent anti-dumping action involved shrimps imported into the US. All shrimps brought into the US have tariffs applied to them but in February 2004 the US International Trade Commission found that shrimp fishermen in Thailand, China, Vietnam, India, Ecuador and Brazil were unfairly injuring the US shrimp industry through dumping and backed a move for increased tariffs.[34] But while high-income countries complain about low-income country dumping they are all too happy to indulge in dumping themselves. The United States currently spends nearly US$5 billion per year on the subsidisation of its cotton exports which

has seen its share of the world cotton export market rise from 24 per cent in 1996 to 42 per cent in 2004 and which has driven down the price of cotton from USc93 per pound in 1995 to USc37 per pound today.[35] Oxfam estimates this US dumping resulted in trade losses of US$400 million between 2001 and 2003.[36]

Anti-dumping issues aren't confined to agriculture: they often involve base metals (principally steelmaking), chemicals, machinery and electrical equipment and plastics.[37] Anti-dumping measures were the most popular issue of dispute taken to the WTO by low-income countries between January 1996 and September 2002.[38] Similarly, a trade device called special safeguard measures – designed for the protection of domestic farm producers – has also been designed in a way that makes these measures much more available to high-income countries, with the result that by mid-2004 some 38 high-income countries had used them but only 22 low-income countries had done so.[39]

A final cluster of low-income-country trade grievances about high-income countries concerns the ability of low-income countries to participate effectively in WTO disputes and negotiations. WTO trade disputes are very expensive to mount, often taking over two years and involving the engagement of expensive trade lawyers. The cost of these challenges is frequently beyond the reach of many low-income countries with the result, as previously mentioned, that no least-developed country has ever mounted a WTO dispute challenge. Many low-income countries cannot afford to maintain permanent representatives at the WTO headquarters in Geneva, let alone to send large delegations to major WTO meetings as high-income countries always do. In 2000 some 26 low-income countries were unable to afford to have any permanent staff at the WTO headquarters in Geneva and serviced it from other missions or embassies throughout Europe while a further seven periodically sent representatives from their home capitals.[40] Of the 29 least-developed countries that are WTO members, only 12 had permanent staff at the headquarters.[41] This means that many very poor low-income countries simply can not exercise all their rights as WTO members.

The myth of low-income country manufacturing export growth

Trade statistics suggest that low-income countries have recently enjoyed huge growth in manufacturing exports. In 1980 low-income countries had only a 11 per cent share of the world export market for manufactured goods but by 2000 they had 27 per cent.[42] In 1980 manufactured goods accounted for just 29 per cent of all low-income-country exports but by 2000 they accounted for 73 per cent – a fraction not that dissimilar to that of high-income countries.[43] The big problem with these statistics, however, is that while the low-income country share of world manufactured exports increased by 145 per cent over the twenty-year period, between 1980 and 1997 the low-income country share of world manufacturing value-adding increased by only 41 per cent (from 17 per cent to 24 per cent).[44] This means that low-income countries are doing the labour-intensive/low-skill end of global manufacturing while the less-labour-intensive/high-skill end is being kept in high-income countries. This echoes the eighteenth-century move by the British to relocate the value-adding end of cotton production from India to Britain – nothing has changed. Much of the low-value-adding manufacturing in low-income countries is the result of new 'client state' investment made by Western Europe, Japan and the United States over the past two decades to take advantage of the low wages in the neighbouring countries of Eastern Europe, Eastern Asia and Mexico (see Chapter 3). This new client state relationship is now a powerful driver of global trade relations between many high- and low-income countries. Some low-income countries have even experienced a decline in their share of export manufacturing value-adding despite large increases in their share of the overall export manufacturing market. Between 1980 and 1997, Mexico's share of world manufactured exports rose tenfold but its share of manufacturing value-adding fell by more than a third.[45] The only region of low-income countries that has managed to increase significantly its share of global export manufacturing value-adding is Eastern Asia. Most low-income countries have a comparative trade advantage in low-cost raw

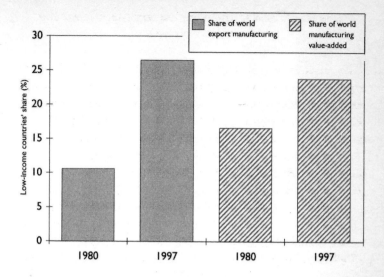

Figure 4.2 Low-income countries' share of world export manufacturing compared with their world manufacturing value-added, 1980 and 1997

Source: Yilmaz Ayuz, *Developing Countries and World Trade: Performance and Prospects*, Zed Books, London, 2003, p. 45.

materials and low-cost labour – if trade is to help them grow richer they need to trade beyond these narrow areas of advantage but the patterns of modern-day export manufacturing do not suggest that many will be able to soon.

Historically today's low-income countries have not always existed on the margins of global manufacturing as they do today. Economic historian Paul Bairoch claims that in 1750 today's low-income countries (mainly China and India) accounted for 73 per cent of world manufacturing (both traded and non-traded) and by 1830 they were still accounting for over 60 per cent but by the start of the First World War their share had fallen to just 8 per cent.[46]

Transnational corporations (TNCs) must shoulder much of the responsibility for low-income countries getting such a bad deal in

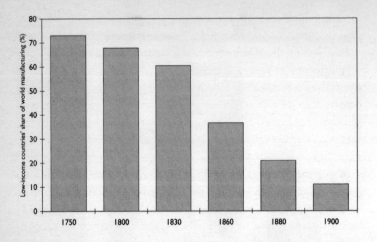

Figure 4.3 Low-income countries' share of world manufacturing output, 1750 to 1900

Source: P. Bairoch, 'International Industrialisation Levels from 1750 to 1980', *Journal of European Economic History*, No. 11, 1982, pp. 294 and 296.

today's global manufacturing. A large proportion of the trade in manufactured goods is controlled by TNCs, particularly those products with the most consistent export growth. TNCs like to site the labour-intensive part of their manufacturing networks in low-income countries that have low wages and low infrastructure costs and that are located close to high-income markets. But they like to keep the less-labour-intensive/high-value-adding part of their networks in high-income countries and they like to keep the knowledge and understanding of their processes to themselves (which the TRIMS agreement allows them to do). This means the labour-intensive part of the manufacture of goods consumed in the European Union is done in Eastern Europe while the value-adding is done in Western Europe and manufactured goods bought in the United States have the labour-intensive parts done in Mexico while the value-adding is done in the US itself etcetera. Low-income countries act as cheap, outlying manufacturing 'feeder' locations for TNCs while the real economic activity continues to be done in high-income countries.

Another significant influence on the manufacturing trading patterns of low-income countries is high-income country preferential trade agreements whereby high-income countries extend special trade access to selected low-income countries. These include the Cotonou agreement between the EU and some African, Caribbean and Pacific countries. The net effect of such agreements is that the low-income countries involved are able to gain significant shares of EU markets, like the clothing market, at the expense of other low-income countries that don't have preferential trade agreements but which have a more competitive edge in clothing.[47] When it comes to penetrating the US market, however, because those countries don't have preferential trade agreements with the US they are unable to gain much market access.

There are two major concerns associated with the concentration of low-income-country export manufacturing at the low-value-added end of the production chain. One is that low-income countries compete amongst themselves for shares of that type of manufacturing and often try and undercut each other, thereby collectively lowering their wage levels etcetera. There is intense competition amongst low-income countries for clothing exports, for instance, with countries such as China, Mexico and Turkey significantly increasing their market share since the 1980s at the expense of Southern Asian countries such as Bangladesh, Pakistan and Sri Lanka.[48] The other major concern is that, as happened with raw materials, low-income countries could end up flooding the global market with low-value-added/labour-intensive manufactured products which could drive down their price (a phenomenon known as 'the fallacy of composition', meaning that what is in an individual's interest isn't necessarily in a group's interest). There is evidence that this is already happening. A study of the (relatively early) period of 1970 to 1987 found that the terms of trade of manufactured exports from low-income countries fell by an average of 1 per cent per year relative to the price of high-income country manufactured exports.[49] Some argue that if you take non-ferrous metals out of the definition of low-income country manufactured exports there is no evidence of declining prices, but other studies have shown clear evidence of a decline since 1975 even when they are excluded.[50] An UNCTAD study into China's net barter terms of trade in manufactures found a decline of more than 10 per cent over the period 1993 to 2000.[51]

The high-income country policy of keeping most value-adding to themselves applies also to raw materials. Many high-income countries have a policy of 'tariff escalation' that imposes ever-increasing tariffs on raw materials from low-income countries according to how much refinement or value-adding they have had before landing in the relevant high-income country. This creates a significant disincentive against low-income countries processing and value-adding their raw material exports. The EU tariff imposed on imported cocoa beans, for instance, is zero but the tariff for cocoa butter or paste is 9.6 per cent.[52]

Another major concern is that low-income manufactured exports often have high levels of imported componentry and don't necessarily yield significant net balance-of-trade gains. The import content of manufactured exports from low-income countries is high and has been increasing in recent years, particularly in those low-income countries that have significantly liberalised their trade and have become heavily involved in the labour-intensive end of the manufacturing production chain.[53]

Much of the labour-intensive manufacturing performed in low-income countries is performed in export processing zones. These are special zones within low-income countries where government con-cessions like company tax holidays, the free supply of infrastructure and minimal labour regulation are extended to attract foreign indus-tries. In the past three decades their popularity has exploded – in 1970 export processing zones only existed in ten low-income countries but they hugely increased in number throughout the 1980s with the result that by 1990 at least 63 low-income countries had them.[54]

The problem of low-value-added labour-intensive manufacturing is particularly significant for China. Labour-intensive manufactured exports account for 90 per cent of China's total exports.[55] Although China is currently experiencing high economic growth it has a vulnerable economy. China has a dualistic economy made up of a highly competitive labour-intensive export sector and a relatively uncompetitive government-supported state-owned enterprises sector (which mainly undertakes heavy industrial manufacturing) as well as a large government-subsidised agricultural sector which is also relatively uncompetitive with the rest of the world.[56] Membership of the WTO, and the obligation it brings with it to observe Uruguay and Doha Round agreements, is putting a lot of pressure on China to scale back the subsidies and protection extended to its farming and state-owned enterprise sectors; this could significantly add to the country's unemployment. China's labour-intensive export manufacturing sector won't necessarily absorb the unemployed from those sectors, however, because it is not experiencing any increase in its value-adding and is becoming increasingly focused on areas such as electronics and machinery exports that aren't particularly labour-intensive. About 24 million workers, or approximately 10 per cent of China's urban workforce, lost their jobs in state-owned enterprises and collectives that closed between 1998 and 2002.[57] China has cheap labour costs but it suffers from relatively low productivity which means the country is not necessarily able to develop a competitive edge in a wide range of exported manufactured products, particularly those further up the value-adding chain.[58] Chinese unemployment is already being fed by a large exodus of people from its countryside – exposing itself to the harsh winds of global trade could, eventually, bring a lot of social disruption to China. Income inequality in China is already worse than in India or Indonesia and is nearing the levels of South America.[59]

The free trade experience of Mexico

Mexico is an interesting case study on the effect of free trade on low-income countries. In 1994 it became the first low-income country in the world to enter a free trade pact with a high-income country when it became part of the North American Free Trade Agreement (NAFTA) with the United States and Canada. Given that it signed

NAFTA more than a decade ago, enough time has passed for long-term effects to become apparent.

Before the early 1980s Mexico pursued a policy of import substitution supported by a large public service which for several decades enabled it to significantly reduce poverty[60] but which also left it with a high foreign debt on which it defaulted in 1982 (sparking the start of the Third World debt crisis). The response by the then president, Miguel de la Madrid Hurtado, was to refocus Mexico as an export economy[61]– a strategy that was deepened in the 1990s with the signing of NAFTA. The results of this strategy have been mixed and were comprehensively reviewed by the (US) Carnegie Endowment for International Peace in a report released in 2003.

The Carnegie Endowment found that far from reducing Mexican inequality NAFTA increased it to high levels (in common with much of Latin America) thereby undoing many of the gains of previous decades.[62] While Mexico's inequality increased, its poverty levels have experienced a slight decline during the life of NAFTA, however, but at 31 per cent they remain no lower than they were in the early 1990s immediately before the start of NAFTA (although it should be stressed that the start of NAFTA coincided with a major Mexican currency crisis which significantly increased national poverty).[63] Part of the reason for the lack of any significant progress on inequality or poverty has been the mixed Mexican performance on employment since the start of NAFTA. In overall terms NAFTA has managed to generate no or very few extra jobs in Mexico. About 550,000 more Mexicans now have jobs in the export manufacturing sector (mainly in the so-called *Maquiladora* assembly plants) and a roughly equivalent number of new jobs have been created in the service sector (often low-paid informal-sector jobs) but these gains have been offset by the loss of about 100,000 jobs in the non-export manufacturing sector, which faced stiff competition from US manufactured imports, and by more than a million jobs lost in agriculture, which struggled to survive the competition from cheap subsidised US farm products that flooded on to the Mexican market after NAFTA began.[64] This massive loss of farming jobs defies the conventional wisdom that low-income countries necessarily do well out of farm trade liberalisation and is a salient warning to other low-income countries (and some groups in the global justice/anti-globalisation movement) that put faith in that strategy. Crucially for inequality and poverty performance, the after-inflation value of Mexican wages has actually fallen since the start of NAFTA despite significant increases in national productivity.[65] Much of the fall in real wages was originally a consequence of the currency crisis in the early 1990s but NAFTA has not enabled Mexican workers to convert productivity gains into higher after-inflation wages. The net effect of falling wages and the huge decline in rural employment has been that rural-based Mexicans in particular are now more reliant than ever on remittances from relatives who have moved to other parts of Mexico or the United States and the level of these remittances has reached record levels in the past few years.[66] Unsurprisingly, immigration to the US from Mexico has also increased dramatically in recent years.[67]

Mexico's post-NAFTA overall trade performance also shows mixed results. On the positive side, Mexico has been able to convert a net trade deficit with the US before NAFTA into a net surplus, although most of this is probably not due to NAFTA but to the 1994–95 currency crisis. The overall Mexican trade surplus masks a growing net deficit in agricultural trade with the US, however, which is offset by a surplus in manufactured exports to the US.[68] On the negative side much of Mexico's export manufacturing has become focused on low-skill assembly line manufacturing in which components are imported then assembled then re-exported without a lot of value-adding or high-skilled employment.[69] Another major concern for Mexico relates to increased competition from China for labour-intensive manufactured exports, particularly since China joined the WTO in 2001. In 2003 China took Mexico's spot as the second-largest exporter to the US (after Japan).[70] Yet another significant concern is that while Mexico's trade balance with the US has improved significantly, its overall trade balance has not. In 1992–93 its overall trade deficit was US$17.7 billion but by 1999–2001 its annual trade deficit was scarcely better at US$14.5 billion.[71]

From an environmental point of view the Carnegie Endowment feels that Mexico's membership of NAFTA has not necessarily led to a 'race to the bottom' in its environmental standards but it does believe that the cost of the pollution damage done to the Mexican environment since NAFTA began exceeds the benefits of the developments that caused it and that Mexico's diverse ecosystem is now more at risk than ever from concentrations of nitrogen and other chemicals associated with industrial farming.[72]

Challenges confronting low-income countries' trade

Several trends in world trade patterns pose serious challenges for low-income countries. One is that their share of the world's exports has not increased very much over the past two decades while their share of imports has. In 1980, developing countries were responsible for 29 per cent of the world's exports, and by 2001 that share had only climbed to 32 per cent, but over the same period their share of global imports rose from 23 per cent to 29 per cent.[73] Part of the problem for low-income country exports is that a massive amount of the trade of high-income countries is confined to other high-income countries that are partners in regional free trade agreements – in 2001 some 61 per cent of the total exports of the European Union were exported between different EU countries while in the same year 55 per cent of the exports from the NAFTA countries were to each other.[74] The faster growth of low-income country imports over exports affects their overall trade balance. During the 1970s – when export raw material prices were high – developing countries enjoyed a large trade surplus equal to about 16 per cent of their imports but throughout most of the 1990s developing countries had an overall trade deficit generally equal to between 2 and 7 per cent of their imports.[75] Between 1999 and 2001 developing countries began to enjoy an overall trade surplus again but more than 90 per cent was accounted for by Eastern and Southern Asian developing countries whose combined trade surpluses nearly doubled between 1997–98 and 1998–2001.[76]

Another big problem for low-income countries is that over time they have tended to experience deteriorating terms of trade. The terms of trade of a country is the unit value of its exports compared to the unit value of its imports – improving terms of trade mean a country's unit export prices are improving compared to its import prices (and/or its unit import prices are declining compared to its export prices) and deteriorating terms of trade mean that a country's unit export prices are declining compared to its import prices (and/or its import prices are rising compared to its export prices). Between 1980 and 2000 the terms-of-trade for developed countries improved by 12 per cent while those for developing countries deteriorated by 33 per cent.[77] The developing-country regions that suffered the greatest declines were: North Africa (decline of 34 per cent), West Asia (26 per cent) and South America (33 per cent).[78] The worsening terms of trade for developing countries are partly a consequence of declining unit export prices experienced by low-income countries and partly a result of rising unit import prices. Between 1980 and 2000 the unit export prices of developed economies rose by 13 per cent but for developing countries they fell by 10 per cent.[79] Between 1980 and 2000 the unit prices of imports into developed countries were unchanged but for developing countries they rose by a massive 35 per cent.[80] The developing-country regions that suffered the greatest decline in unit export prices were: North Africa (decline of 15 per cent), Asia-outside-West-Asia (decline of 11 per cent) and America (decline of 21 per cent).[81]

The reasons for the worsening terms-of-trade for developing countries are complex but are largely to do with the ongoing dependence of many low-income countries on raw materials for most of their export income. Over time the export prices of raw materials have declined (the reasons for this are explained in Chapter 8). As the prices of low-income country raw material exports decline their currencies come under strain, often resulting in falling values. Lower currency values mean rising import prices. Amongst other things, worsening terms of trade mean that low-income countries have to export more and more commodities (often raw materials) to pay for the same amount of imports which can have a devastating effect on the environment (see Chapter 6). Quite apart from the politics of global trade the very foundation of global trade is fundamentally flawed and is structurally and systemically tilted against low-income countries.

Some low-income countries have benefited from global trade but most have not. At best low-income countries have gleaned little, if any, benefit from free trade deals like NAFTA, at worst many are falling further and further behind because of free trade and are badly positioned to survive the onslaught of more liberalised global trade.

Notes

1   United Nations Conference on Trade and Development, *UNCTAD Handbook of Statistics 2002*, United Nations, New York and Geneva, 2002, p. 2.
2   Ibid., p. 6.
3   Ibid., pp. 2 and 8.
4   Ibid., pp. 4 and 6.
5   Ibid., pp. 2 to 8.
6   Joan E. Spero and Jeffrey A. Hart, *The Politics of International Economic Relations: Fifth Edition*, Routledge, London, 1997, p. 222.
7   Ibid., p. 223.
8   Walden Bello and Aileen Kwa, 'How Washington Triumphed in WTO Geneva Talks', published by Deb Foskey via WTO Watch email list (debf@webone.com.au), 16 August 2004 (No. 269), p. 1. (For archive copy see www.nwjc.org.au/avcwl/lists/archives.html).
9   Ibid., p. 2.
10 Ibid.
11 Ibid., p. 5.
12 Shefali Sharma, 'An India-US FTA: Free Trade for America?', published by Deb Foskey via WTO Watch email list (debf@webone.com.au), 5 September 2004 (No. 271), p. 1. (For archive copy see www.nwjc.org.au/avcwl/lists/archives.html).
13 Pam Woodall, 'The Dragon and the Eagle – A Survey of the World Economy', *Economist*, 2 October 2004, survey p. 4.
14 Ibid., p. 9.
15 Robert Hunter Wade, 'The WTO still has a long way to go', *International*

Herald Tribune, 3rd August 2004.

16 Evelyn Iritani, 'Textile Quota Phaseout Gives WTO a Headache', *Calcutta Telegraph* (Calcutta, India) 3 October 2004, published by Deb Foskey via WTO Watch email list (debf@webone.com.au), 14 October 2004 (No. 274), p. 1. (For archive copy see www.nwjc.org.au/avcwl/lists/archives.html.)

17 Pam Woodall, 'War of the Worlds: A Survey of the Global Economy', *Economist*, 1st October 1994, p. 4.

18 Robert Gilpin, *The Challenge of Global Capitalism: The World Economy in the 21st Century*, Princeton University Press, Princeton, 2002, p. 36.

19 'A Great Wall of Waste', *Economist*, 21 August 2004, p. 58.

20 Woodall, 'War of the Worlds: A Survey of the Global Economy', p. 8.

21 John Vidal, 'World population in full swing', *Guardian Weekly*, 27 August 2004, p. 28.

22 Yilmaz Akyüs (ed), *Developing Countries and World Trade: Performance and Prospects*, United Nations Conference on Trade and Development, Geneva and New York, Third World Trade Network, Penang and Zed Books, London, 2003, p. 2.

23 Lori Wallach and Patrick Woodall/Public Citizen, *Whose Trade Organisation?: A Comprehensive Guide to the WTO*, The New Press, New York, 2004, p. 244.

24 Ibid., p. 245.

25 Ibid., p. 244.

26 'A Free-trade Tug-of-war', *Economist*, 11 December 2004, p. 35.

27 'Clash of the Titans', *Economist*, 6 November 2004, p. 38.

28 Kamal Malhotra (ed), *Making Global Trade Work for People*, Earthscan, London, 2003, p. 109.

29 Bhagirath Lal Das, *The WTO and the Multilateral Trading System: Past, Present and Future*, Zed Books, London, 2003, p. 69.

30 Edward Buffie, *Trade Policies in Developing Countries*, Cambridge University Press, Cambridge, 2001, pp. 190–191.

31 The Structural Adjustment Participatory Review International Network, *The Policy Roots of Economic Crisis and Poverty: A Multi-Country Participatory Assessment of Structural Adjustment*, SAPRIN Secretariat, Washington, 2002, pp. 42–43, downloaded from www.saprin.org in 2003.

32 Ibid., p. 4.

33 Akyüs, *Developing Countries and World Trade*, p. 17.

34 'Shrimp Wars', *Economist*, 10 July 2004, p. 34.

35 Emad Mekay, 'US appeals WTO ruling on cotton subsidies', published by Deb Foskey via WTO Watch email list (debf@webone.com.au), 25

October 2004 (No. 275), pp. 1–2. (For archive copy see www.nwjc.org.au/avcwl/lists/archives.html.)

36   Ibid., p. 2.

37   Akyüs, *Developing Countries and World Trade*, p. 17.

38   Malhotra, *Making Global Trade Work for People*, p. 84.

39   Devinder Sharma, 'WTO accord: Faulty frame, crude reality', published by Deb Foskey via WTO Watch email list (debf@webone.com.au), 13 August 2004 (No. 268), p. 2. (For archive copy see www.nwjc.org.au/avcwl/lists/archives.html.)

40   Malhotra, *Making Global Trade Work for People*, p. 87.

41   Ibid.

42   Akyüs, *Developing Countries and World Trade*, p. 45.

43   United Nations Conference on Trade and Development, *UNCTAD Handbook of Statistics 2002*, p. 112.

44   Akyüs, *Developing Countries and World Trade*, p. 45.

45   Ibid., p. 46.

46   Paul Bairoch, 'International Industrialization Levels from 1750 to 1980', *Journal of European Economic History*, 11, 1982, quoted in 'A Game of International Leapfrog' in 'A Survey of the Global Economy: War of the Worlds', *Economist*, 1 October 1994, p. 10.

47   Akyüs, *Developing Countries and World Trade*, p.113.

48   Ibid., p. 97.

49   Ibid., p. 89.

50   Ibid.

51   Ibid., p. 92.

52   William Sutcliffe, 'Counting beans', *Guardian Weekly*, 20 August 2004, p. 16.

53   Akyüs, *Developing Countries and World Trade*, p. 84.

54   John Madeley, *Hungry for Trade: How the Poor Pay for Free Trade*, Zed Books, London, 2000, p. 269.

55   Akyüs, *Developing Countries and World Trade*, p. 123.

56   Ibid., p. 126.

57   'No Right to Work', *Economist*, 11 September 2004, p. 27.

58   Akyüs, *Developing Countries and World Trade*, p. 146.

59   Hamish McDonald, 'Class, Religion Spark Riots Across China', *The Age*, 3 November 2004, p. 15.

60   John J. Audley et al., *NAFTA's Promise and Reality: Lessons from Mexico for the Hemisphere*, Carnegie Endowment for International Peace, Washington, 2003, p. 26, downloaded from www.ceip.org in 2004.

61   Ibid., p. 4.

62   Ibid., p. 26.

63   Ibid.
64   Ibid., pp, 15 and 20.
65   Ibid., p. 12.
66   Ibid., p. 21.
67   Ibid., p. 6.
68   Ibid., p. 14.
69   Ibid., pp. 16 –17.
70   Ibid., p. 17.
71   United Nations Conference on Trade and Development, *UNCTAD Handbook of Statistics 2002*, p. 28.
72   Audley, *NAFTA's Promise and Reality*, p. 6.
73   United Nations Conference on Trade and Development, *UNCTAD Handbook of Statistics 2002*, pp. 14, 15.
74   Ibid., p. 35.
75   Ibid., p. 42.
76   Ibid., pp. 26, 27 and 30.
77   Ibid., p. 42.
78   Ibid.
79   Ibid., p. 40.
80   Ibid., p. 41.
81   Ibid., p. 40.

5

Trade, poverty and inequality

Trade is a means to an end. Nations trade with each other to increase their national incomes and to increase the prosperity of their citizens – they don't trade for the sake of it. In recent years champions of global trade have become obsessed with the volume of trade around the world and have lost sight of whether it is having the effect it is meant to have. They have lost sight of whether it is necessarily making peoples' lives better. There's no doubt the world is now handling an unprecedented volume of global trade but until the extra trade is squared against the higher or lower incomes it might (or might not) have delivered to people on the ground it is impossible to say whether all the extra trade is necessarily a good or bad thing.

The connection between trade and inequality

During the past decade in particular, the relationship between trade, globalisation, world poverty and global inequality has become an issue of growing importance to public finance institutions like the World Bank, the International Monetary Fund (IMF), the World Trade Organisation (WTO) and the Organisation for Economic Cooperation and Development (OECD) as well as academics and activists. Unfortunately they reach very different conclusions and the whole issue of whether trade and globalisation necessarily benefit people is often bogged down in debates about methodologies rather than about tangible results.

The most influential report prepared in recent years on the issue of the possible link between trade and global inequality or poverty was *Trade, Growth and Poverty* by two World Bank economists, David Dollar and Aart Kraay, released in 2000. Dollar and Kray have no doubt that greater trade delivers higher economic growth which lowers poverty. To reach their conclusions they separated a large number of low-income countries into 'globaliser' and 'non-globaliser' categories depending on their trade volumes and trade policies (especially their openness to imports). They then examined the relationship between national trade volumes and national rates of economic growth, and concluded that 'the evidence from individual cases and from cross-country analysis supports the view that open trade regimes lead to faster growth and poverty reduction in poor countries'.[1] Dollar and Kraay said the globalisers experienced an increase in economic growth rates from 2.9 per cent per year in the 1970s to 3.5 per cent in the 1980s and 5.0 per cent in the 1990s while the non-globalisers experienced a decline in growth rates from 3.3 per cent per year in the 1970s to 0.8 per cent in the 1980s then up to 1.4 per cent in the 1990s.[2] Although they found isolated examples of increased inequality in globalising countries they said 'there is no systemic relationship between changes in trade and changes in household inequality'[3] and concluded that 'the evidence from individual cases and from cross-country analysis supports the view that open trade regimes lead to faster growth and poverty reduction in poor countries'.[4] They went on to make the sweeping generalisation that 'while rich country growth rates have slowed down over the past several decades, the growth rates of the globalisers have shown exactly the opposite pattern, accelerating from the 1970s to the 1980s to the 1990s ... thus, the globalisers are catching up with rich countries while the non-globalisers fall further and further behind'.[5] The Dollar and Kraay study echoed a 1995 study by the academics Jeffrey Sachs and Andrew Warner (*Economic Reform and the Process of Global Integration* published by Brookings Papers on Economic Activity) that found there is 'strong evidence that protectionist trade policies reduce overall growth'.[6]

The Dollar and Kraay study in particular, and their methodology in general, have become widely quoted and are often used as the standard proof of the mantra that more trade – more exposure to the global marketplace – is necessarily good for economic growth and therefore for poverty reduction. The OECD says 'more open and outward-orientated economies consistently outperform countries with restrictive trade and (foreign) investment regimes'[7] while the IMF proclaims that 'policies toward foreign trade are among the more important factors promoting economic growth and convergence in emerging countries'.[8] The IMF has also separately argued that 'globalisation leads to economic growth and higher incomes. No country has benefited for any length of time from closed-door policies and the countries that have achieved most prosperity have embraced globalisation, together with the policies that make it work.'[9] In 2002 the World Bank issued a report entitled *Globalisation, Growth and Poverty* which drew heavily on Dollar and Kraay's findings and methodology (Dollar and Kraay were not necessarily expressing the World Bank's views) and concluded, like them, that the more globalised countries 'have made very significant gains in basic education' and that 'the less globalised had made less progress and now lag behind in primary attainment'.[10]

So no end of people and institutions are saying free trade is good for economic growth. But a number of dubious assumptions and devices behind Dollar and Kraay's confident pronouncements make their conclusions highly questionable. There are at least six major flaws in the analysis of Dollar and Kraay, three have to do with their conclusions and three have to do with their methodology.

The major flaws in Dollar and Kraay's conclusions are as follows:

Many academics disagree with Dollar and Kraay

A large number of academics have reached conclusions about the link between trade and economic growth that are fundamentally different to those of Dollar and Kraay. Francisco Rodriguez (from the

University of Maryland) and Dani Rodrik (from Ha~~r~~
claim, for instance, that there is in fact very scant rigoro
a link between lower barriers to trade and higher econo~
They say 'we find little evidence that open trade policies – i~
of lower tariff and non-tariff barriers to trade – are significantly
ated with economic growth'.[11] Rodriguez and Rodrik argue that
many indicators of trade openness used by the champions of free trade
are linked to other factors that can influence economic growth. They
say that simply linking economic growth with coincidentally increased
trade is 'simplistic, failing to address important questions such as the
exact mechanism through which export expansion affects GDP
growth'.[12] Like many observers they feel a mix of influences affect a
country's rate of economic growth and that the relationship between
trade and growth 'is a contingent one, dependent on a host of country
and external characteristics'.[13] Rodriguez and Rodrik say their
bottom line is 'that the nature of the relationship between trade policy
and economic growth remains very much an open question … we are
in fact sceptical that there is a general, unambiguous relationship
between trade openness and growth waiting to be discovered.'[14]

In 1992 a definitive and exhaustive study on the possible link
between a range of political and institutional influences in different
economies around the world and their long-term rates of economic
growth was completed by US academics Ross Levine and David
Renelt. They found that the links between almost all influences they
looked at and economic growth were 'fragile'; they only found a
strong link between economic growth and investment as well as
between investment and trade.[15] Dollar and Kraay admit that Levine
and Renelt's study is 'influential' and that they concluded 'that trade
volumes were not robustly correlated with growth'.[16]

Academics Ann Harrison (from the Columbia Business School) and
Gordon Hanson (from the University of Michigan) believe that part of
the reason why a link is sometimes found between trade and growth is
that not enough data about trade policies are pursued by a large
enough group of countries over time[17] and that many of the measures
of trade 'openness' that are used touch on other areas of economic

globalisation apart from trade policy.[18] Like Harrison and Hanson, Rodriguez and Rodrik believe that the trade-equals-growth school often gets trade policies and trade volumes confused, frequently taking one to be a proxy for the other.[19]

Economic growth rates are influenced by many variables, not just trade

The main problem with Dollar and Kraay's analysis is oversimplification. It just is impossible to isolate a single influence that determines a country's rate of economic growth. Economic growth is the product of many influences. Dollar and Kraay even acknowledge this – in *Trade, Growth and Poverty* they admit that 'differences in economic growth reflect a confluence of many factors other than trade'[20] and 'the available data on trade, growth and other policies may not be sufficiently informative to enable us to isolate the precise partial effect of trade on growth'.[21] Several specific country examples confound Dollar and Kraay's analysis. China began to experience high economic growth in the late 1970s but did not start seriously reducing its trade barriers until the second half of the 1980s.[22] Similarly India's economic growth rate started to increase significantly in the early 1980s but it did not undertake substantial trade reform until 1991–93.[23] For every country that did start to experience high economic growth at much the same time as it reduced its trade barriers – like, say, Vietnam, whose growth took off in the mid-1980s when it cut its tariffs – there is always another country whose experience has been different – like, say Haiti, which liberalised its trade barriers in the mid-1990s but which has since experienced no pick-up in economic growth.[24] A 2003 report by the United Nations Development Programme, the Heinrich Böll Foundation, the Rockefeller Brothers Fund and the Wallace Global Fund, *Making Global Trade Work for People*, found no link between trade and economic growth, concluding that there is 'no systemic relationship between countries' average levels of tariffs and non-tariff barriers and their subsequent economic growth'; if anything they found a very slight (statistically insignificant) positive relationship between a lack of reduction in tariff barriers and economic growth through the 1990s.[25] The report argued the only safe conclusion one could reach was that as countries become richer they tend to dismantle their tariff barriers.[26] In a similar vein Dani Rodrik argues that the size of a country's trade relative to its gross domestic product is something that governments only have limited influence over. Trade volumes say as much about a country's size and position in relation to other countries (particularly large high-income countries) as they do about its trade policies. Rodrik also argues that trade-to-GDP figures should not be mixed up with tariff levels to decide who is a 'globaliser' and who is not.[27] Dollar and Kraay claimed their analysis eliminated 'time-invariant' factors that influence a country's rate of economic growth as well as 'time-varying factors' that can be found in all countries but this still left a large number of unelimated factors – to believe that any formula could eliminate all the factors that Dollar and Kraay claim theirs did is very hard to believe.

Dollar and Kraay make a tenuous link between trade and inequality

The crux of Dollar and Kraay's analysis is that trade is good for growth and – because they found no link between increased trade and increased inequality – trade must, therefore, be good for inequality too. But like the factors behind economic growth the factors behind inequality are complex and Dollar and Kraay attempt to grossly over-simplify them. There are just too many specific countries whose experiences confound Dollar and Kraay's conclusions. Research by UNCTAD supports the competing conclusions of Rodriguez and Rodrik. Between 1995 and 1999 half the people living in the world's 49 least developed countries lived on less than US$1 per day while 80 per cent lived on less than US$2 per day, but in 22 of the 39 countries for which data is available amongst these 49 countries, international trade significantly expanded between 1987 and 1999 becoming equal to more than half their gross domestic products – higher than in most high-income countries.[28] If the trade-equals-growth mantra held, one would expect per capita gross domestic products to have increased and poverty to have decreased. But in 8 of the 22 countries per capita gross domestic product declined, or stagnated, and in 10 of the countries poverty significantly increased.[29] By contrast, between 1960 and 1973 at least 42 low-income countries experienced high rates of growth in per capita gross domestic product even though most had pursued import substitution policies behind high tariff barriers.[30]

Dollar and Kraay also fail to recognise that as a country develops, many people who may have subsisted outside the monetarised part of the economy switch to paid jobs that bring them into the regular, cash-based parts of the economy. But the switch may not make them better off even though figures for the gross domestic product per head suggest they are.[31]

The major flaws in Dollar and Kraay's methodology are as follows:

Dollar and Kraay's use of the terms 'globaliser' and 'non-globaliser' is very arbitrary

Dollar and Kraay took an arbitrary point in time, 1980, then applied equally arbitrary criteria to decide whether certain countries were 'globalisers' or 'non-globalisers' after that point. They used simple and inconsistent rules to categorise a complex situation and as a result their analysis is shallow. Their categorisation of many countries is highly debatable. Both China and India are categorised as 'globalisers' but both still maintain significant trade restrictions so their qualification for the term is arguable, to say the least. Dollar and Kraay even admit that 'there cannot be a definitive list of recent globalisers'.[32]

Dollar and Kraay use trade volumes as a proxy for trade policies

Much, but not all, of Dollar and Kraay's analysis uses changes in a country's trade volume as an indicator of changes in its trade policies. Even Dollar and Kraay admit 'we use decade-over-decade changes in the volume of trade as an imperfect proxy for changes in trade policy'.[33] As Dollar and Kraay concede, however, changes in trade volumes may have nothing to do with changes in trade policy (as Rodrik argues) and they are therefore a very imperfect proxy for trade policy: 'we recognise that growth in trade volumes may also reflect many factors other than trade liberalisation'.[34] They claim they tempered their use of trade volumes with some analysis of tariff rates but concede that tariff data before 1985 is scarce and that they mainly had to rely on tariff data from the short period between 1985–89 and 1995–97.[35]

Dollar and Kraay weighted country results according to population

Dollar and Kraay weighted their results according to the populations of different countries which meant their questionable categorisation of China – which has 20 per cent of the world's population – had a large bearing on their final results. If they were really interested in making generalisations about all the world's economies there should have been no need to weight the results.

Per capita gross domestic product as an indicator of wealth

All the studies quoted above used per capita gross domestic products (GDPs) as their indicator of economic prosperity. It is a very common economic indicator and is frequently used as a measure of whether a country is getting richer or poorer. Per capita GDPs are a crude indicator of increasing or decreasing economic prosperity but can none the less give a very rough indication of whether a country's inhabitants are going forwards or backwards.

Throughout the 1980s and 1990s even though global per capita GDP (the sum of all the world's GDPs divided by global population) increased, both saw major regions of the world slide backwards in per capita GDP terms (casting further doubt on the trade-equals-growth theory). Between 1981 and 1990 global per capita GDP increased by 12 per cent with developed countries increasing by 23 per cent over the period and developing countries increasing by 12 per cent.[36] But for parts of the developing world the decade wasn't as kind as these statistics suggest. Per capita GDPs in Latin America fell by 6 per cent over the period, they fell in Africa by 8 per cent and in West Asia by 35 per cent.[37] The 1980s is sometimes referred to as the 'lost decade' of many low-income countries. Some developing countries performed quite well during the 1980s, however, with East Asia increasing its per capita GDP by a huge 46 per cent.[38]

The 1990s were kinder to low-income countries but, again, not all parts of the world went forward during the decade. Global per capita

Table 5.1 Global changes in per capita incomes, 1980s and 1990s (%)

Region	1981 to 1990*	1991 to 1999*
Developed countries	22.6%	9.8%
Developing countries	12.0%	30.1%
Latin America	−6.4%	13.1%
Africa	−8.4%	−5.4%
East Asia	46.2%	29.1%
West Asia	−35.4%	0%
South Asia	28.6%	27.1%
Transition economies	12.2%	−29.1%

* Figures are based on per capita changes in gross domestic product measured on a purchasing power parity basis.
Source: United Nations Department of Economic and Social Affairs, *World Economic and Social Survey 2000: Trends and Policies in the World Economy*, United Nations, New York, 2000, p. 245.

GDP increased by 12 per cent between 1991 and 1999 while the per capita GDP of developed countries increased by 10 per cent and that of developing countries increased by 30 per cent.[39] Africa lost out in the 1990s once again with its per capita GDP falling by another 5 per cent. West Asia did scarcely better.[40] East Asia surged ahead again, its per capita GDP increasing by 29 per cent during the period, but 'transition' economies (mostly former communist Eastern European ones) saw their per capita GDPs fall by 29 per cent (after increasing by 12 per cent during the 1980s).[41] During the 1980s and 1990s about one-third of all countries saw a decline in their per capita incomes each year – up from about one-fifth in the 1960s and 1970s.[42]

Although widely quoted, per capita GDPs are a rough measure of economic prosperity and have major limitations. One significant limitation is that they are an average across a country's entire population and tell you nothing about possible deviations from the average. They tell you nothing about possible inequality and poverty within a country because they basically assume that everyone is the same. A second major limitation is that they treat all countries the same and assume they all have the same population size. Obviously different countries don't all have the same population size, and a rigorous analysis of changes in global economic prosperity needs to take account of that fact because otherwise every person in the world would not be given the same consideration and weighting. Basically, per capita GDP figures are a useful 'United Nations General Assembly' type approach to income analysis, in which each country has the same weighting, but one cannot read too much into them (which is another reason to treat trade-equals-growth statistics with a generous measure of scepticism). To analyse properly whether the world community is going forwards or backwards during this age of unprecedented global trade one has to look at international poverty and inequality data.

Global poverty

Poverty is an intrinsically different measure to inequality and the two should not be confused. A country can have growing poverty without necessarily experiencing growing inequality and it can have growing inequality without necessarily experiencing increasing poverty. Poverty is a measure of a standard of living that no one should have to live below. It is a line in the sand. Poverty lines are a financial benchmark above which everyone should be able to live. Poverty lines can be determined in a relative or an absolute way. Governments or public financial institutions can draw poverty lines relative to the incomes of all the people who live in the society for which poverty is being measured or they can determine an absolute poverty line that isn't influenced by the incomes of all the people it is drawn up for.

The World Bank has developed two global poverty lines. One is the number of people in the world who live on less than US$1 per day, and another is the number of people in the world who live on less than US$2 per day (neither poverty line is affected by the incomes of the societies in which it is used). In 1981 the bank claims there were 1,482 million people living on less than $US1 per day which equalled 40 per cent of the global population at the time.[43] By 2001 the bank claims there were 1,093 million people living on less than US$1 per day which equalled 21 per cent of the then global population.[44] On the higher US$2 per day poverty benchmark the World Bank's data indicates that in 1981 2,450 million people lived on less than US$2 per day which then equalled 67 per cent of the world's population and by 2001 the number had risen to 2,736 million although the proportion by then had fallen to 53 per cent of the global population.[45] On the basis of these reductions the bank claims the global war on poverty is (slowly) being won. Whether the bank is right or not about the trend in world poverty, their statistics are chilling. It is nothing short of a global disgrace that a fifth of the world's population live on less than US$1 per day and just over half live on less than US$2 per day. Few people in high-income countries could conceive what it would be like to live in grinding poverty of the sort suggested by these figures. These numbers are a sad indictment of humanity's compassion and egalitarianism. All 191 members of the United Nations have signed up to the 'Millennium Development Goals' that include a halving by 2015 of the proportion of people in the world living on less than US$1 per day (from 1990 levels). The World Bank thinks there is a reasonable chance of meeting this goal, particularly because of the high growth being experienced throughout Asia, but many observers are dubious. Even the World Bank admits that it is extremely unlikely that sub-Saharan Africa will lower its proportion of population living on less than US$1 per day (which increased during the 1990s) and they also admit it is likely that the proportion of people in South America living in poverty will remain high as well.

Inevitably the World Bank's poverty data are controversial and attract their share of critics. Some say the bank's numbers for the world's poor are too high, others that they are too low. Those who say their numbers are too high criticise the fact that the bank's figures are based on household surveys and not on government-compiled national accounts which nearly always produce a rosier picture of poverty. They argue that household surveys can be badly designed, can have fluctuations in sample sizes and can be poorly executed.[46] But national accounts data can be flawed as well, one of their most common problems being a failure to include non-market income and consumption.[47]

Those that claim the bank's data understate the extent of global poverty argue that a new methodology the bank introduced into its poverty 'head count' in the late 1990s makes the data less reliable than it used to be and that in most countries the change resulted in a lower national poverty line.[48] Because the incomes of poor people are often concentrated close to the poverty line small changes in the exact level that a poverty line is drawn at can make a big difference in the numbers said to be living in poverty. The World Bank's data are also criticised because it doesn't disclose which standard goods and services in different countries it uses to calculate the relative purchasing power of different national currencies (which recognises that US$1 can buy, amongst other things, many more loaves of bread, say, in China, and in low-income countries in general, than it can in the United States and other high-income countries).[49] Those who claim the World Bank data are too conservative also criticise the household expenditure survey methodology. They claim household surveys often exclude the benefit of publicly provided goods and services and that they are very sensitive to changes in the period of spending/earning that is being asked about – other periods could include times of better crop harvests or more generous government spending, etcetera, that could considerably boost reported incomes.[50] In short, the study of global poverty is riddled with argument and systemic flaws that mean you can't place too much store in precise numbers or trends. One can, however, get a general picture of global poverty from them and that picture shows a lot of people missing out on the claimed benefits of global trade.

Global poverty has a very uneven spread around the world and has a much greater impact on some parts of the world than on others. Different parts of the world are also experiencing vastly different trends in poverty. In 1981 the two largest regional concentrations of poverty were East Asia and the Pacific (which then accounted for 54 per cent of people in the world living on less than US$1 per day and where 58 per cent of the population lived below US$1 per day) and South Asia (which accounted for a further 32 per cent of the global total living below US$1 per day and where 52 per cent of the population lived below the US$1 per day poverty line).[51] By 2001, however, East Asia and the Pacific only accounted for 25 per cent of all the people in the world living on less than US$1 per day (with 15 per cent of its regional population living below that poverty line); South Asia made more modest inroads into poverty over the twenty-year period and by 2001 had come to account for 39 per cent of the global total living below US$1 per day (although the proportion of its regional population living below that poverty line had fallen to 31 per cent).[52] The region that is making no inroads into poverty whatsoever is sub-Saharan Africa. Between 1981 and 2001 the number of people in that region living on less than US$1 per day nearly doubled while the proportion of its regional population living below that poverty line increased from 42 to 47 per cent.[53] By 2001 sub-Saharan Africa accounted for 29 per cent of all the people in the world living below US$1 per day – more than double its 11 per cent proportion in 1981.[54] Latin America and the Caribbean are also making no real inroads into poverty. By 2001 they had added to their 1981 poverty total, and in that year they had the same proportion living below US$1 per day (10 per cent) as they had in 1981.[55]

Although the World Bank's figures are encouraging for regions outside sub-Saharan Africa and Latin America and the Caribbean, in general terms they need to be treated with caution. The bank's 1981 to 2001 poverty statistics cover a period before and after it changed its methodology in the late 1990s which, as mentioned earlier, made its data less reliable after that date. More fundamentally the World Bank conducted two large global price-setting exercises in 1985 and 1993 to arrive at the exchange rates on which its calculations are based. These exchange rates can have a crucial influence on the number of people under the US$1 poverty line. But the Chinese government refused to take part in either of the exercises and the Indian government declined to take part in the 1993 exercise.[56] This makes the poverty statistics for China (home to 19 per cent of those living below US$1 per day in 2001), somewhat unreliable because the final exchange rate used was based on guestimates from small, *ad hoc* surveys in a few Chinese cities roughly adjusted for price differences throughout the country.[57] Basically, estimating global poverty is a very inexact science and the World Bank's data can only give a general idea of its trends.

Table 5.2 Global poverty headcount, 1981 and 2001

	Percentage of population living below US$1 per day		Percentage of population living below US$2 per day	
	1981	2001	1981	2001
East Asia and the Pacific	57.7%	14.9%	84.8%	47.4%
South Asia	51.5%	31.3%	89.1%	77.2%
Europe and Central Asia	0.7%	3.7%	4.7%	19.7%
Latin America and the Caribbean	9.7%	9.5%	26.9%	24.5%
Middle East and North Africa	5.1%	2.4%	28.9%	23.2%
Sub-Saharan Africa	41.6%	46.9%	73.3%	76.6%
World	40.4%	21.1%	66.7%	52.9%

Source: 'Global Poverty Monitoring' by the World Bank, downloaded from www.worldbank.org in 2004.

Global inequality

Inequality is a fundamentally different concept to poverty. It is a measure of the spread of incomes within a society. It is an indicator of how unequal income distribution is rather than how many, or what proportion, of people live below a minimum standard of living. Global inequality is more complex to measure than global poverty and has been exposed to more debate about how best to measure it. Three of the most fundamental choices that have to be made when measuring world income inequality are as follows:

- whether you use market exchange rates or purchasing power parity when converting currency values

- whether you weight the results of each country according to their different population levels

- whether you incorporate changes in income distribution within countries as well as changes that take place between countries.

Today it is a well-known and accepted fact that global income is very unequally distributed between developed and developing countries, but the full extent of this maldistribution has only been known since the 1940s. It has only been since the Second World War that the income difference between the rich and poor parts of the world has been quantified and therefore the exact extent of the income difference has been known. The quantification was first done by economists Colin Clark and Simon Kuznets.[58]

Exchange rates measures of inequality

An examination of the per capita GDPs of different countries, such as the one earlier in this chapter, needs to use a common currency. You can arrive at this common currency by either converting different national per capita GDPs using market exchange rates or you can convert them using purchasing power parity exchange rates (which, as earlier explained, try to recognise that you can buy different amounts of goods and services in different countries with the same amount of money). If you take the world's different per capita GDPs, then convert them to a common currency using market exchange rates you find that the world has become much more unequal over the past two or three decades.[59] Even if you weight countries according to their different population sizes, you find that global income distribution has become a fair bit more unequal.[60] On the face of it this suggests that many people in the world have not shared in the benefits of expanded global trade or in globalisation in general. Many argue this statistic doesn't mean much, however, because any legitimate attempt to measure global inequality should necessarily take account of the different purchasing powers of money in different countries and should not rely on market exchange rates. For this reason most inequality studies use purchasing power parity exchange rates and not market exchange rates. Although the argument for using purchasing power parity rates is generally accepted, using market exchange rates can sometimes, none the less, be legitimate. If you are interested in changes in the ability of different countries to repay their foreign debts or to import or export goods and services to the world, the use of market exchange rates in those instances can be legitimate.

Purchasing power parity measures of inequality

If you use purchasing power parity exchange rates you get a very different view of changes in global inequality than if you use market exchange rates. If you don't take account of the different population sizes of different countries, but do use purchasing power parity exchange rates, you find that global inequality did not change very much between 1950 and 1978 but from 1978 to 1998 it grew much worse at a fairly significant rate.[61] Between 1960 and 1980 the slow growth of African per capita incomes was balanced out, in inequality terms, by the fact that many poorer high-income countries caught up, to some extent, with richer high-income countries – this meant that overall global inequality did not change much during that twenty-year period.[62] In the 1980s and 1990s, however, three major sources of increased inequality around the world opened up:

1 in the 1980s the incomes of Latin American countries stagnated, and in some cases fell;[63]

2 in the 1990s the incomes of Eastern European economies (including former Soviet countries) stagnated or declined;[64]

3 overlaying the influences mentioned above, there was an increasing divergence between the per capita incomes of high-income countries and those of Africa and the (mainly Eastern European) 'transition economies' which was a large source of the overall rise in global inequality between 1960 and 1998. By 1998 the relative difference between the incomes of high-income countries and those of Asia and Latin America was roughly at the same level as in 1960 but the difference between the incomes of high-income countries and those of Africa and the transition economies was much greater than in 1960; this drove much of the overall increase in global inequality during the 1980s and 1990s.[65]

The measure of global inequality based on purchasing power parity exchange rates that does not take account of different population levels is often quoted by the global justice movement (sometimes known as the antiglobalisation movement) as evidence that economic globalisation is necessarily making the world less equal. Supporters of economic globalisation argue, however, that measures of inequality must take account of the different population sizes of different countries. Like the use of market exchange rates to compare different country levels of per capita GDP, the use of inequality statistics that do not recognise different population sizes has its place only if you are interested in a United Nations General Assembly type analysis where all countries have equal importance.

Supporters of economic globalisation invariably claim that an examination of the per capita incomes of all the world's countries using purchasing power parity exchange rates and weighted according to different population sizes is the only indicator that really tells you about changes in the economic fortunes of individuals around the world and therefore about the real impact of globalisation. But it doesn't. It only tells you about the population-adjusted changes in inequality *between* countries – it tells you nothing about inequality changes *within* countries. The reason supporters of globalisation like this measure of global inequality is that it shows a decline in global income inequality from about 1968 right through to the end of the twentieth century.[66] The changing fortunes of China and India are the main reason why this measure shows *decreasing* inequality from 1968 while the apparently contradictory non-population-weighted measure shows *increasing* inequality from 1978 onwards. A fifth of the world's population lives in China so changes in their economic fortunes are sure to have a major effect on a measure that is weighted according to population levels. China's per capita GDP doubled between 1965 and 1980, then quadrupled between 1980 and 1998 (using a purchasing power parity exchange rate).[67] In this measure of global inequality China has an enormous influence – in fact if you take China out of the measure there is no clear trend of decreasing world inequality from 1968 onwards.[68] If you go further and take out both India and China

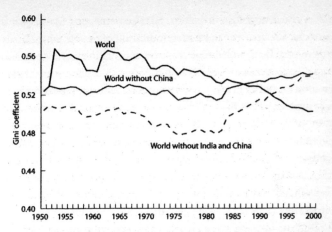

Figure 5.1 Between-country inequality weighted according to population, 1950–1998 (using purchasing power parity)

Source: Branko Milanovic, *Worlds Apart: Measuring Global and International Inequality*, Princeton University Press, Princeton, 2005, p. 87.

(whose combined population equalled 37 per cent of the world total by the end of the twentieth century) global inequality got worse throughout the second half of the twentieth century, not better.[69] So the relative economic fortunes of China and India carry a lot of weight in this measure. This population-adjusted measure is far from perfect and is sometimes erroneously taken to reflect changes in inequality within countries – as well as between countries – which it definitely does not do.

Changes in global inequality both within and between countries

Changes in the global economy can affect income distribution *within* countries as well as affecting income distribution *between* countries. Measuring the changes in the distribution of income within countries, as well as the distribution of income between countries, is essential if one is to get a really clear and honest indication of exactly what impact globalisation and expanded trade are having on all the world's citizens. Such a comprehensive overview only became possible in the 1980s when most countries began to conduct household income and expenditure surveys. The first person to calculate this comprehensive measure of world inequality using household surveys alone (and also employing purchasing power parity exchange rates and population weightings), instead of using proxies for the surveys, was Branko Milanovic, an economist with the World Bank in the late 1990s. Based on household surveys covering 101 countries for 1988 and 117 countries for 1993[70] he calculated that global inequality increased between those two years. Inequality is generally measured through an index known as the 'gini coefficient'. This index ranges between 0 and 100 where 0 is a perfectly equal distribution of income and 100 is a perfectly unequal distribution. Most high-income countries have a gini coefficient somewhere between 25 and 50. Milanovic found that between 1988 and 1993 world inequality rose from a gini coefficient of 62.5 to 65.9.[71] In other words he found that world inequality was high and got slightly worse during the five-year period. He concluded that no more than 25 per cent of the change was due to changes in inequality within countries while no less than 75 per cent was due to changes in inequality between countries.[72] Like the previously mentioned population-weighted per capita GDP measure, this measure is heavily influenced by countries with large populations, especially China and India. Milanovic ascribed most of the increase in inequality over the period to three forces: increasing divergence between the incomes of high-income countries and the incomes of rural-based Indians and Chinese; increasing divergence between the incomes of urban-based Indians and Chinese and rural-based Indians and Chinese; and the falling relative incomes of many middle-income countries, especially those of Latin America and Eastern Europe.[73] Milanovic has recently updated his research to take his analysis through to 1998. By 1998 he found world inequality was still high but had fallen slightly from the 1993 level of 65.9 to 64.[74] The three forces that increased global inequality between 1988 and 1993 reversed, to some extent, over the following five years: many people left rural India and China for the wealthier cities, and the incomes of Eastern European countries began to pick up again. Milanovic does not consider the differences between the indexes for 1988, 1993 and 1998 to be statistically significant, however, and generally does not consider there to have been an obvious trend of either increasing or decreasing world inequality over the ten-year period.[75] Milanovic feels that by the early twenty-first century the three main determinants of global inequality were: the income of the world's high-income countries, the incomes of city dwellers in India and China, and the incomes of country dwellers in India and China.[76] Other economists, using other methods to calculate world inequality, agree with Milanovic that it is high although there is no consensus about whether it is increasing, decreasing or staying the same.[77]

So, basically, it is clear that world inequality is high and remains high but it is not clear that the expansion of world trade, and of world economic engagement in general, over the last ten years of the twentieth century necessarily made it worse or better. One thing we can be clear about, however, is that economic globalisation shows no unambiguous evidence of decreasing world inequality despite what its champions might have you believe.

Income gaps

If the average income of one country is growing faster than the average income of a country that is richer than it then the average inequality between those two countries is decreasing. This observation can mask, however, the absolute gaps that can continue to exist between the incomes of the two countries. The average income of China is growing faster than the average income of the United States but their absolute income levels are still a very long way apart. In 2001 the average per capita income of China (measured in purchasing power parity terms) was US$4,260 while that of the United States was US$34,870[78] – this means China had an average income level of just 12 per cent of that of the United States. If China experiences twenty years of economic growth, averaging 8 per cent per year after 2001, and the United States experiences twenty years of growth at 4 per cent per year, the income of China will become US$19,856 and that of the United States will become US$76,404 after the twenty-year period. But this means that the average Chinese income is still only equal to 26 per cent of that of the United States after two decades of double their economic growth. This means that even when low-income countries are able to record high rates of growth it takes a long time for them to claw back a meaningful amount of the absolute gap between their earnings and those of high-income countries. More sobering still are the income levels of very poor countries, like Uganda, which in 2001 had an average income (again measured in purchasing power parity terms) of US$1,250 compared with Britain which had an average income of US$24,460 in the same year.[79] Uganda's income was just 5 per cent of that of Great Britain.

Long term changes in global inequality

Given the high current levels of global inequality it is tempting to think the world has always been a fairly unequal place. An oft-quoted indicator of global inequality is the ratio between the average incomes of the world's poorest and richest countries. This statistic needs to be treated with caution because it tells nothing about the distribution of income amongst countries between the extremes of global income distribution but it does none the less give an idea of the spread of global income. The UNDP estimates that the ratio of the per capita incomes of the world's richest and poorest countries was 35:1 in 1950, rose to 44:1 in 1973, and by 1992 had blown out to an alarming 72:1.[80] It is tempting to think that the extremes of global income distribution have always been of this order but in fact they haven't. In 1820, during the early years of the Industrial Revolution, the ratio was only 3:1.[81] This doesn't mean that everyone was universally well off before the Industrial Revolution – in fact most of the world's population (apart from a select few) was then universally fairly poor – but it does point to the fact that the benefits of the Industrial Revolution have been very unevenly distributed and have largely gone to a select few countries – a fact underscored by Milanovic's statistics.

In contrast to the debate currently raging about whether globalisation in general, and global trade in particular, has worsened or improved global inequality over the last two or three decades, no one disputes the fact that before the Industrial Revolution world income was much more equally distributed. David Lendes, Professor Emeritus of History and Economics at Harvard University, argues:

> the difference in income per head between the richest industrial nation, say Switzerland, and the poorest non-industrial country, Mozambique, is about 400 to 1. Two hundred and fifty years ago, this gap between richest and poorest was perhaps five to one, and the difference between Europe, and, say, East or South Asia (India or China) was around 1.5 or 2 to 1'.[82]

Even the pro-trade, pro-globalisation Centre for International Economics in Australia admits that 'for nearly two centuries, productivity improvements did not spread quickly, and international inequality widened'.[83]

So today we have a global economy that is much more unequal than it was two hundred years ago. We also have vocal supporters of globalisation arguing that it is making the world a more equal place and opponents of globalisation arguing the opposite. There are lies, damn lies and statistics but the most comprehensive measures of changes in global inequality – that take into account changes in income both between and within countries – indicate that in a sense both camps are wrong and that the data indicates that so far the expansion of global trade and globalisation in general is not managing to make our very unequal world much more or less equal.

Notes

1 David Dollar and Aart Kraay, *Trade, Growth and Poverty*, p. 27, downloaded from www.worldbank.org in 2004.
2 Ibid., p. 2.

3 Ibid., p. 27.

4 Ibid.

5 Ibid.

6 Quoted in Anne Harrison and Gordon Hanson, *Who Gains from Trade Reform?: Some Remaining Puzzles*, National Bureau of Economic Research, Cambridge (USA), 1999, p. 6, downloaded from www.nber.org/papers in 2003.

7 Organisation for Economic Cooperation and Development, *Open Markets Matter: The Benefits of Trade and Investment Liberalisation*, OECD, Paris, 1998, p. 36.

8 International Monetary Fund, *World Economic Outlook*, IMF, Washington, 1997, p. 84.

9 International Monetary Fund, *Debt Relief, Globalisation, and IMF Reform: Some Questions and Answers*, IMF Issues Brief, IMF, New York, 2000. See: www.imf.org/external/np/exr/ib/2000/041200b.htm. Quoted in Michael Woodin and Caroline Lucas, *Green Alternatives to Globalisation: A Manifesto,* Pluto Press, London, 2004, p. 17.

10 World Bank, *Globalisation, Growth and Poverty*, World Bank, Washington, 2002, p. 35, downloaded from www.worldbank.org in 2003.

11 Francisco Rodriguez and Dani Rodrik, *Trade Policy and Economic Growth: A Skeptic's Guide to the Cross-National Evidence*, National Bureau of Economic Research, Cambridge (USA), 1999, abstract, downloaded from www.nber.org/papers in 2003.

12 Ibid., p. 3.

13 Ibid., p. 4.

14 Ibid.

15 The World Bank, *A Sensitivity Analysis of Cross-Country Growth Regressions by Ross Levine and David Renelt: Abstract*, p.1, downloaded from www.worldbank.org/research/growth/aer92lr.htm in 2004.

16 Dollar and Kraay, *Trade, Growth and Poverty*, p. 15.

17 Harrison and Hanson, *Who Gains from Trade Reform?*

18 Ibid., p. 7.

19 Rodriguez and Rodrik, *Trade Policy and Economic Growth*, p. 3.

20 Dollar and Kraay, *Trade, Growth and Poverty*, p. 14.

21 Ibid., p. 20.

22 Kamal Malhotra et al., *Making Global Trade Work for People*, Earthscan, London, 2003, p. 31.

23 Ibid.

24 Ibid., p. 28.

25 Ibid., p. 29.

26 Ibid.

27 Rodrik, quoted in Woodin and Lucas, *Green Alternatives to Globalisation*, Pluto Press, London, 2004, p. 53.

28 Malhotra, *Making Global Trade Work for People*, p. 34.

29 Ibid.

30 Ibid., p. 37.

31 Woodin and Lucas, *Green Alternatives to Globalisation*, p. 50.

32 Dollar and Kraay, *Trade, Growth and Poverty*, p. 8.

33 Ibid, p. 3.

34 Ibid., p. 7.

35 Ibid., p. 8.

36 Based on: United Nations Department of Economic and Social Affairs, *World Economic and Social Survey 2000: Trends and Policies in the World Economy*, United Nations, New York, 2000, p. 245.

37 Ibid.

38 Ibid.

39 Ibid.

40 Ibid.

41 Ibid.

42 Branko Milanovic, *Worlds Apart: Measuring Global and International Inequality*, Princeton University Press, Princeton, 2005, p. 87.

43 World Bank, *Global Poverty Monitoring*, World Bank, Washington, 2004, downloaded from www.worldbank.org/research/povmonitor/index.htm in 2004.

44 Ibid.

45 Ibid.

46 'Special report: Global economic inequality', *Economist*, 13 March 2004, p. 68.

47 Ibid.

48 Robert Hunter Wade, *The Disturbing Rise in Poverty and Inequality: Is it All a 'Big Lie'?* in David Held and Mathias Koenig-Archibugi (eds), *Taming Globalisation: Frontiers of Governance*, Polity Press, Cambridge, 2003, pp. 19, 20.

49 Ibid., p. 21.

50 Ibid., p. 22.

51 World Bank, *Global Poverty Monitoring*.

52 Ibid.

53 Ibid.

54 Ibid.

55 Ibid.

56 Wade, *The Disturbing Rise in Poverty and Inequality*, p. 22.

57 Ibid., p. 22.

58   Roger E. Backhouse, *The Penguin History of Economics*, Penguin Books, London, 2002, p. 301.

59   Wade, *The Disturbing Rise in Poverty and Inequality*, p. 24.

60   Robert Wade, *Winners and Losers*, in Kate Galbraith (ed), *Globalisation: Making Sense of an Integrating World*, Profile Books/*Economist*, London, 2001, p. 217.

61   Branko Milanovic *Worlds Apart: Measuring Global and International Inequality*, Princeton University Press, Princeton, 2005 as detailed in: Branko Milanovic, *Worlds Apart: International and World Inequality 1950–2000*, World Bank, Research Department, Washington, 2002, p. 27, downloaded from www.worldbank.org in 2003.

62   Ibid. p. 32.

63   Ibid.

64   Ibid.

65   Ibid., pp. 34–35.

66   Ibid., p. 69.

67   Ibid., p. 73.

68   Ibid., p. 71.

69   Ibid., p. 71.

70   Ibid., p. 82.

71   Ibid.

72   Ibid., p. 84.

73   Ibid., p. 86.

74   Personal email correspondence with Branko Milanovic, 1.11.03.

75   Ibid.

76   Milanovic, *Worlds Apart: Measuring International and Global Inequality*, p. 115.

77   Ibid., p. 119.

78   World Bank, *World Development Report 2003: Sustainable Development in a Dynamic World*, Oxford University Press, New York, 2003, pp. 234–235.

79   Ibid., p. 235.

80   Ankie Hoogvelt, *Globalisation and the Postcolonial World: The New Political Economy of Development*, Palgrave, London, 2001, p. 90.

81   Ibid., p. 90.

82   David Lendes, *The Wealth and Poverty of Nations*, Abacus, London, 1998, p. xx.

83   Centre for International Economics, *Globalisation and Poverty: Turning the Corner*, Commonwealth of Australia, Canberra, 2001, p. 9.

6

Trade and the environment

The rapid growth in global trade has put enormous stress on the world's environment. The use of energy required to move ever greater quantities of goods around the world has put stress on the environment. The global competitive pressures induced by trade have put stress on the environment. The World Trade Organisation (WTO) has put stress on the environment, and the opening up of access to all the world's farms, forests, rivers and wildlife by ever more powerful transnational corporations (TNCs) has put stress on the environment. In no small way the world's ecosystem has subsidised the expansion of global trade. But the environment cannot subsidise global trade forever. We all ultimately depend on nature, and one day our impact on the environment will reach its limit.

The environmental impact of moving goods around the world

The pollution effect of global trade

Most trade depends on oil. Because the burning of oil produces pollution, trade produces pollution. Today the global use of oil is more than seven times its level immediately after the Second World War.[1] Of all the oil consumed around the world today, global trade uses about one-eighth[2] while transport in general uses more than half. The transport systems that are mainly responsible for the movement of global trade are currently experiencing huge growth so their appetite for oil is also experiencing huge growth.

Shipping moves about 80 per cent of all global trade while air transport moves most of the rest.[3] Shipping is expected to expand by about 85 per cent between 1997 and 2010.[4] Ports like Los Angeles are anticipating a doubling of cargo throughput over the next twenty-five years while major shipping arteries such as the Panama Canal are increasingly unable to handle the ever-larger ships. Air transport is growing even faster than shipping: world air cargo traffic tripled between 1983 and 1997, and Boeing is even forecasting a further tripling by 2017.[5] Air transport is a very inefficient user of energy compared to shipping: freight moved by aeroplane uses as much as 49 times as much energy as freight moved by ship.[6] Other forms of trade-related transport have also experienced sharp growth. Rail freight in the United States has doubled since 1960.[7] In the EU the number of kilometre/tonnes that trade has been responsible for doubled between 1970 and 1999 and the amount of road freight nearly trebled over the same period.[8]

The pollution effect of all this oil-powered trade and transport growth has been staggering. Carbon, the major global warming agent, is the main pollutant emitted by the burning of oil. Since the Second World War the world's emissions of carbon have more than quadrupled while the global concentration of carbon dioxide in the atmosphere has increased by 18 per cent over the same period.[9] Trade and transport have been major contributors to the steep growth in carbon emissions. A study conducted in 1997 by the Organisation for Economic Cooperation and Development (OECD) and the International Energy Agency (IEA) found the transport sector accounted for between 20 and 25 per cent of all the world's carbon emissions.[10] Within the transport sector freight accounted for 55 per cent of all emissions.[11]

The greenhouse effect that carbon emissions contribute to may eventually see world temperatures rise by up to four degrees Celsius by the end of the twenty-first century. This is only one or two degrees less

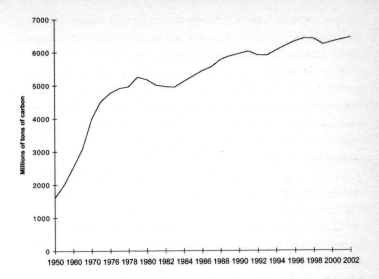

Figure 6.1 Global carbon emission, 1950 to 2002

Source: Worldwatch Institute, *Vital Signs 2003–2004: The Trends That Are Shaping Our Future*,
Earthscan, London, 2004, p. 41.

than the total increase in global temperatures that has taken place since
the end of the last ice age. Global average temperatures are already 0.6
degress Celsius above their pre-industrial average, and the 1990s were
the warmest decade recorded since 1861 (see Chapter 7).[11]

The non-carbon pollution effects of aircraft and shipping are also
alarming. As well as carbon dioxide, aeroplanes produce large quantities of nitrogen oxides. Like carbon dioxide, nitrous oxide is a significant greenhouse gas, while nitrogen dioxide causes acid rain. Aircraft
emissions of nitrogen oxides are predicted to double between 1996
and 2010.[13] A major problem with aircraft pollution is that at least 60
per cent of it enters the atmosphere more than nine kilometres above
sea level where it has fewer molecules to react with than at ground
level, which means that the polluting molecules live up to a hundred
times longer than if the pollution was released at ground level.

Shipping uses a low-grade type of fuel that produces nitric oxide and nitrogen dioxide, which can cause acid rain and photochemical smog. Global shipping's emissions of nitric oxide and nitrogen dioxide are equal to about half of all the land-based emissions of these gases generated by the United States.[14] Shipping also produces nitrous oxide, another potent greenhouse gas, as well as sulphur oxides, which cause acid rain. Almost incredibly, however, pollution from global freight is exempt from the Kyoto protocol on greenhouse gas emissions.

The energy requirements of global trade

It is easy to see why trade accounts for so much pollution. According to the United States Food and Drug Administration, the food ingredients of a typical plate of food on an American dinner table are estimated to have travelled an average 1,500 miles from their source to the dinner plate.[15] Flying a kiwi fruit from New Zealand to Europe results in carbon emissions equal to five times the weight of the fruit.[16] Flying a kilogram of apples from New Zealand to Britain results in the release of a kilogram of carbon dioxide which is more than 20 times the emissions that the transport of locally sourced apples is responsible for.[17] Most orange juice consumed in Europe is produced in Brazil; to move all the juice from Brazil to Europe requires a consumption of fuel equal to 10 per cent of the weight of the juice.[18] The German Wuppertal Institute once researched the distance travelled by the ingredients of a 150-gram container of strawberry yoghurt and found they had travelled 1,005 kilometres before being put together – the strawberries came from Poland, the corn and wheat flour came from the Netherlands, the jam was from western Germany, the sugar beet was from eastern Germany and the yoghurt itself came from northern Germany while the aluminium used for the cover came from 300 kilometres away.[19]

Species invasion associated with global trade

Another devastating environmental impact of global trade results from the invasion of species held in the ballast water of ships. Ships regularly take in ballast water at their port of departure then release the water in their destination port they are going to. Many marine species are taken on board with the ballast water. Most of these species die but those that live can have a devastating impact in the port of arrival. In the San Francisco Bay area – one of the busiest ports in the world – at least 234 non-native marine species have entrenched themselves. One of these species, the Asian clam – which was first spotted in the area in 1986 – quickly overwhelmed the area's ecosystem. The clams not only crowd out native shellfish, they also poison native fish and the birds that feed on them.[20] Likewise zebra mussels have invaded the Great Lakes of North America, North American comb jellies have invaded the Black Sea, and Japanese starfish have overwhelmed Port Phillip Bay in Australia. It is not just ballast water that can carry invasive species, – the goods being transported can also be hosts. African bees once arrived in the San Francisco Bay area in a shipload of unrefined sugar that came from Guatemala. California's US$4 million abalone farming industry has been threatened by a parasite carried on South African abalone.[21] It is difficult to understate how much devastation this sort of bio-invasion can result in. Bio-invasion is now the second largest cause of native species extinction in the world and is implicated in the decline of over 40 per cent of all species listed as threatened or endangered in the United States.[22]

The spread of global transport infrastructure

More trade also means more pressure on the infrastructure it requires to operate, such as roads, ports and airports. Increased trade also inevitably means increased spending on transport infrastructure. These days nearly every country in the world has plans to increase its transport infrastructure. To facilitate the new trade brought about by the North American Free Trade Agreement between Mexico, Canada and the United States major highway expansions and high-speed rail links are being planned and built. In Western Europe 12,000 kilometres of new highway construction is being planned for Greece, Bulgaria, Portugal, Spain, Ireland, Britain and the Scandinavian countries.[23] The EU plans to spend a massive €400 billion on its Trans-European Networks transport infrastructure projects.[24] The road networks of Poland,

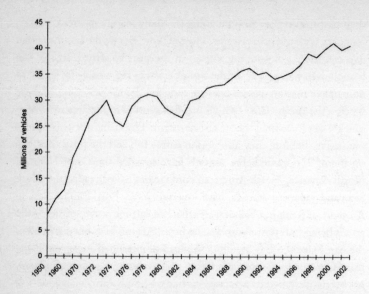

Figure 6.2 Global automobile production, 1950 to 2002

Source: Worldwatch Institute, *Vital Signs 2003–2004: The Trends That are Shaping our Future*, Earthscan, London, 2004, p. 57.

Slovakia, Hungary and the Czech Republic are expected to triple in size over the next ten to twenty years.[25] China also plans to increase significantly its transport infrastructure with a recent US$400 million World Bank loan to be used to build the Jinzhu highway to 'improve long distance transport and promote trade'.[26] In Brazil a trans-Amazonian highway, the BR-163, is being planned to help bring more timber and minerals to world markets; similarly a Japanese-funded highway in Sarawak, Malaysia, is being planned to give Japanese and Malaysian timber corporations more access to the timber of the area.[27] And the governments of Brazil, Argentina, Paraguay, Uruguay and Bolivia are currently putting the finishing touches to a massive water infrastructure project that will deepen, straighten and widen 2,100 miles of four Amazonian rivers to make them navigable all year round.[28]

Basically there are no free lunches with trade: it inevitably has an impact on the environment somehow. Trade has an enormous pollution cost and an enormous infrastructure cost. These costs are rarely considered when people talk about the benefits of global trade but they are real and they must be given the same weight as the financial merits (or demerits) of ever-expanding global trade.

The environmental impact of the WTO

Anti-environment rulings of the WTO

There is no neater encapsulation of the assumption that the rights of trade should always trump the rights of the environment than the agenda of the WTO. No multilateral organisation has ever provided any check or balance on the influence of the WTO. It has never been part of the United Nations, and it is a law unto itself. As a result the WTO has assumed enormous power, a power that unquestioningly puts trade first and any influence that might reduce the power of global trade a distant second. This philosophy has found a clear expression in the trade rulings that the WTO (and its predecessor, the GATT) has delivered on issues concerning the environment.

One of the very first rulings of the WTO, in 1996, involved a challenge by Venezula and Brazil to 1994 regulations by the US Environment Protection Agency that required the cleanliness of petrol sold in the most polluted cities of the US to improve by 15 per cent over their 1990 levels. The US saw this initiative as a health measure designed to reduce the risk of asthma, inflammation and damage to people's lungs as well as potential impairment of people's general ability to fight bacterial respiratory infections.[29] Venezula and Brazil, however, saw the measure as unfair trade discrimination against their petrol imports into the US. The WTO sided with Venezula and Brazil and dismissed a US appeal, agreeing that the measure did, in fact, discriminate against petrol trade with those two countries.

Two of the most famous anti-environment decisions of the GATT/WTO involved measures designed to save dolphins and sea turtles. In 1991, and again in 1994, the WTO (and the GATT) ruled against a 1988 United States law that banned the sale of domestic or foreign tuna caught with encirclement nets – which often drown or crush dolphins. Over thirty years more than 7 million dolphins have been unnecessarily killed by encirclement nets and two of the four affected dolphin species have been severely depleted as a result.[30] But the GATT ruled that its laws prohibit member countries from discriminating between products according to either where they are produced, or how they are produced and therefore the dolphin laws were deemed to be anti-trade (even though other GATT laws allowed exemptions for the protection of human, animal or plant life). Similarly in 1998 the WTO struck down another US law designed to protect sea turtles. This law was a provision of the US Endangered Species Act that said that only shrimp caught with turtle excluder devices could be sold in the United States. The worldwide population of sea turtles is plummeting with shrimp nets killing and dismembering as many as 150,00 of them every year. The scale of the shrimp netting threat is underscored by the fact that industrial-scale shrimp netting kills more sea turtles each year than all other human impacts combined.[31] But, yet again, the WTO argued that all the shrimp that came on to the US market was 'like product' and couldn't be discriminated against in terms of how it was caught and the US provision was struck down.

Sometimes the mere threat of taking action through the WTO can be enough to scuttle environmental initiatives. In 1995 the EU banned the importation of pelts from 13 species of animals caught through the use of steel-jaw leg-hold traps. But it wasn't long before North American and Russian trappers and furriers began objecting to the measure claiming it amounted to an unfair trade barrier. They also argued that few of the species affected were native to Europe and that the traps were allowed in many US states as well as in Canada and Russia.[32] The EU offered to delay introduction of the measure but the US and Canada were not satisfied and kept threatening WTO action. In the end a compromise was struck whereby the traps would be phased out over a long period during which pelts caught by the traps could still be imported into the EU. But the US still wasn't completely satisfied and only gave a limited commitment to the compromise, arguing the final say on the issue rested with its states. By 2002 only eight US states had banned the use of the traps.[33] Yet again a progressive and far-sighted measure to protect the environment was scuttled by the supremacy of global trade.

It is not just the health of the natural environment that is undermined by trade – human health is also frequently compromised by WTO decisions. Throughout the world artificial breast-milk substitutes contribute to the deaths of large numbers of babies – recent United Nations figures claim as many as 1.5 million babies die each year through its use. Often fatal infant diarrhoea is contracted when mothers mix the formula with unsafe water.[34] In the 1970s a public campaign against the infant formula manufactured by Nestlé resulted in new public health rules on the marketing of breast-milk substitutes. A WHO/UNICEF code on the marketing of the substitutes was agreed to by many countries. The government of Guatemala enacted laws to give national effect to the code – which, amongst other things, required breast-milk substitutes to make clear the superiority of natural milk – and the government also disallowed the use of images that suggested the formula necessarily produced healthy babies. The US-incorporated Gerber Products Company – which operates in Guatemala – refused to comply with these two measures, however, and in 1995 threatened to take the case to the WTO.[35] Guatemala lacked either the legal expertise or the money to fight the challenge so it backed down and changed its laws to exempt imported baby products from the measure. Again, global trade won out.

Like the WTO the North American Free Trade Agreement has also been responsible for a string of anti-environment decisions. In 1997 the US Ethyl Corporation forced Canada to repeal a law banning MMT – a petrol additive and suspected neurotoxin (see page 174).[36] Similarly Canada's Methanex Corporation has filed a case against the state of California which banned another fuel additive, MTBE, known to be carcinogenic to animals (and which may also be carcinogenic for humans).[37]

Basically measures that help the environment run up against two fundamental WTO brick walls time and time again. One is that governments are not allowed to discriminate between foreign producers, or between foreign and domestic producers, of a 'like' product – discrimination based on how a product is produced falls into this category. The second brick wall is that no environmental measure can be deemed to be legitimate unless it is both 'necessary' and the 'least trade restrictive' means of achieving the desired environmental outcome.[38] Very few environmental measures can possibly get around these two barriers, and as things stand the WTO will oppose nearly all environmental initiatives brought before it.

WTO supremacy over multilateral environmental agreements

The consistent anti-environment bias of the WTO inevitably throws up the question of whether, in fact, its rulings and its authority necessarily hold more weight than global multilateral environment agreements (MEAs) such as the Convention on Biological Diversity, the Kyoto protocol on greenhouse gases and the Basel Convention on the Trade in Hazardous Waste. The WTO assumes, of course, that its rulings and laws always necessarily have the upper hand if there is any conflict. The WTO attempted to clarify the issue in a declaration from its 2001 Doha ministerial meeting but despite this the issue remains confused. The Doha declaration set up a negotiation process on the relationship between trade agreements and MEAs but it also said the negotiations would not be subject to any 'prejudged outcomes' (such as those promulgated in multilateral environmental agreements) and further stipulated that the outcomes of the negotiations 'shall not add to or diminish the rights and obligations of members under existing WTO agreements'[39] – in other words it tried to prejudge the results of the negotiations. The Doha declaration also said the negotiations 'shall be limited in scope to the applicability of such existing WTO rules as among parties to the MEA in question' – in other words it further prejudged the negotiations by exempting in advance any countries that are not signatories to MEAs including the United States which is not a signatory to most MEAs.[40]

To try and put the issue beyond doubt attempts have been made since 1999 to insert clauses into MEAs that make it clear they are ultimately subservient to WTO rules. At the World Summit on Sustainable Development held in Johannesburg in August 2002, high-income countries, fronted by Australia, tried to insert text into the final summit declaration that said the role of the summit was to 'continue to enhance the mutual supportiveness of trade, environment and development in a manner consistent with WTO rights and obligations'.[41] Non-government organisations in particular found the language offensive and asked the EU and low-income countries to fight the text, particularly the words 'consistent with WTO rights and obligations'. Secret negotiations were held and in the end a compromise was struck that used ambiguous wording calling for 'mutual supportiveness' between the United Nations and the WTO systems.[42] High-income countries (particularly Japan, the US, Canada, Australia and New Zealand) also wanted text that said that economic growth through trade and globalisation was the best hope for the environment.

High-income countries had a similar WTO-comes-first approach to the final negotiations of the Basel Convention on the Trade in Hazardous Waste in 2000. The US insisted that the agreement should contain explicit text that made it clear the WTO had precedence over the agreement. Such wording would have destroyed much of the purpose of the agreement so other countries insisted on opposite wording. In the end the agreement contained text that embraced both conflicting sentiments.[43] Similarly in 1999 and 2000 during the final negotiation of a global Biosafety Protocol that was to include regulations governing genetically modified organisms (GMOs), the US-led 'Miami group' of GMO-exporting countries wanted to insert text that would make the protocol subject to WTO constraints that would mean, in effect, that if countries wanted to prohibit or restrict access to GMOs they would first have to satisfy the WTO. In the end, like the text for the World Summit on Sustainable Development and the Basel Convention on the Trade in Hazardous Waste, the protocol had conflicting wording that gave no clear guidance on the issue and left it as muddy as ever.[44]

Part of the reason why high-income countries have been keen to insert clarifying statements about the supremacy of WTO rules into recent MEAs is that under the Vienna Convention on the Interpretation of Treaties more recent international treaties always have more authority than older treaties unless the older ones have specific 'savings' clauses that say otherwise.[45] But the conflicting wordings that have ended up in recent MEAs have only made the issue more confusing than it has ever been. So, despite the best efforts of high-income countries, the issue of whether the WTO always dominates over MEAs remains unresolved. But as far as the WTO is concerned, it is not even an issue.

The WTO limits the spread of environmental technologies

Another pernicious way in which the WTO works against the environment is through the Trade Related Intellectual Property Rights (TRIPS) agreement. The TRIPS agreement is a global copyright agreement that was developed during the Uruguay Round. It introduced strict new rules that enhanced the intellectual property rights of transnational corporations, which were concerned they were losing global sales to generic and pirated copies of their products. As well as protecting the markets of large drug and finance companies the TRIPS agreement also protects the markets of companies that produce environment-friendly technologies, with the result that low-income countries are often unable to use new technologies that could improve their environmental performance. One example involves ozone-depleting chemicals. In the 1970s it was discovered that chorofluorocarbons (CFCs), which were frequently used in spray cans, refrigerators and air conditioners, were destroying the earth's ozone layer. Growing concern over the thinning of the ozone layer and its ever-larger holes opening up over Antarctica led to the 1987 signing of the Montreal Protocol which regulated the production, use and trade in ozone-depleting chemicals such as CFCs. The protocol made it illegal for low-income countries to produce or import CFCs except for limited essential services but it left a giant loophole that allowed low-income countries to manufacture unlimited quantities of CFCs until 2010.[46] Many corporations have used this loophole to continue their unbridled production of CFCs by moving their factories to low-income countries, their ability to do so having been made easier through the limiting of the transfer of green technologies to low-income countries under the TRIPS agreement. Low-income countries would generally prefer to use CFC substitutes but their ability to use them is constrained by their limited availability and the inability of low-income countries to promote local production of substitutes through fear of breaching the TRIPS agreement. In India companies that manufacture CFCs have been unable to use substitutes because of patent rights held by a select few transnational corporations. Several Indian companies expressed interest in purchasing a patent at market rates but were rebuffed by the patent holder who said it would only give access to the technology if it could have majority ownership of the local production company.[47] The patent holder has preserved its profits but the ozone hole has grown larger as a result.

The WTO blocks measures against global warming

The long arm of the WTO also reaches into crucial attempts to stop global warming. The most proactive global warming initiative to date was the 1997 Kyoto Protocol which committed signatory high-income countries to reductions (averaging 5.2 per cent) on their 1990 levels of greenhouse gas emissions. Japan committed to a 6 per cent reduction. Japan's emissions have long been increasing, however, largely because of increased car use. So as part of its Kyoto undertakings Japan introduced new fuel efficiency standards for cars which were particularly targeted at middle-range cars. They used as their benchmark an engine manufactured by Mitsubishi that was the most non-polluting engine in that category available in Japan. The government said all engines had to achieve at least the performance of the Mitsubishi engine.[48] By 1999, however, both the EU and the US were crying foul and threatening WTO action over the measure. They claimed their cars were being unfairly discriminated against because they did not use the Mitsubishi engine. Now, however, the EU has introduced its own set of new vehicle emission standards as part of its commitment to reduce its greenhouses gases by 8 per cent. The EU developed a voluntary agreement with the European Automobile Manufacturers Association under which carbon dioxide emissions from new cars had to be reduced by 25 per cent by 2008.[49] In their case the new standards were based on fleet averages rather than the performance of a specific engine, but that didn't stop the Japanese challenging the standards on the same basis that the EU challenged theirs. We now have the truly absurd situation where two major car manufacturing regions of the world want to reduce greenhouse emissions but don't want to lose trade market share and as a result both may make sure that no one is able to reduce greenhouse emissions through fear of inhibiting free trade.

The fear that initiatives that will reduce greenhouse emissions could undermine a country's trade competitiveness threatens seriously to undermine international efforts to stop global warming. Fear of losing a competitive edge could end up being the greatest single barrier, in fact, along the road towards achieving lower global greenhouse emissions. Western Europe has traditionally been a global leader in introducing taxes designed to change environmental behaviour: Scandinavian countries were the first to introduce (modest) environment taxes later followed by Austria, Belgium, Finland, France, Germany, Italy, the Netherlands and the United Kingdom.[50] The European green taxes included emissions taxes that have had some success in reducing greenhouse gas emissions in those countries. In 1992 an attempt was made to introduce a universal European Union carbon tax, but fear of losing trade competitiveness killed it off. Opponents argued that because the tax would not apply to the EU's trade rivals it allowed them to gain a competitive edge, and the tax never got off the ground.[51] A similar theme runs through opposition in the United States to ratifying the Kyoto Protocol. Senators Byrd and Hagel, the co-authors of the Senate resolution that originally blocked US endorsement of the protocol, as well as President George W. Bush, have all argued that signing the protocol would result in hundreds of manufacturing plants being relocated to low-income countries that are not bound by the Kyoto protocol.[52] In no small way global trade is threatening the very survival of our planet.

The environmental impact of foreign investment

Using relocation for lower environmental standards

Foreign investment is a huge driver of global trade. The global production of goods and services is more mobile, and more fluid, today than it has ever been before. Today's open financial borders make it all too easy for factories or call centres etcetera to relocate to another country to take advantage of major profit-influencing factors such as lower wages. Unfortunately the mobility of global investment has also made it all too easy for businesses to relocate to new countries to take advantage of looser environmental controls. Foreign direct investment is the largest single source of capital flow into low-income countries but the United Nations estimates that between 20 and 50 per cent of all the foreign investment that goes into low-income countries is invested in what it calls 'pollution intensive industries'.[53] The most infamous example of this opportunistic type of investment was the pesticide factory built by the Union Carbide corporation in Bhopal, India, which in 1984 released over 40 tons of lethal gas into the town of Bhopal that killed more than 6,000 people and injured another 70,000.[54] Like India, Mexico has become a haven for foreign investors – particularly US investors – who seek slack environmental regulations. In the Mexican border town of Mexicali, foreign factory owners freely admit that Mexico's lax environmental law enforcement influenced their decision to locate there.[55] Similarly three-quarters of surveyed furniture manufacturers that relocated from Los Angeles to Mexico between 1988 and 1990 cited California's more stringent air pollution laws as a major influence in their decision to relocate.[56] There is little doubt that Mexican environmental regulation is more relaxed than that in the US. One study revealed that three-quarters of surveyed *maquiladora* plants in the border area of Mexico dumped their toxic waste directly into waterways thereby seriously polluting nearby soils, rivers and groundwater.[57]

Sometimes just the threat of relocation can be sufficient to force looser environmental control. In 1995, for example, the transnational timber corporation Boise Cascade threatened to relocate some of its operations to Mexico as a lever to get looser environmental control in the US. It had earlier demonstrated it was prepared to deliver on its threats when it closed mills in Oregon and Idaho and set new ones up in Guerro, to exploit Mexico's looser regulations.[58]

Investor lawsuits over environmental measures

Because trade is inextricably linked to foreign investment, trade agreements are giving more and more rights to foreign investors. The Uruguay Round gave foreign investors new intellectual property and service industry rights, while regional trade agreements like the NAFTA have given foreign investors the right to sue national governments if they feel their investor rights have been restricted by host governments. This right to resort to legal action extends to environmental measures. Under NAFTA rules if an investor feels its rights are compromised by environmental measures it can seek redress in the courts – and there's no shortage of investors who have done so.

In Mexico the US Metalclad Corporation applied to the municipal council of Guadalcazar to expand a hazardous waste site the corporation operated in the municipality into a toxic landfill. The council refused – even though Metalclad had obtained permission from the state and national governments – because the site was designated by local authorities as an ecological protected zone. Metalclad claimed the council's actions amounted to expropriation of investor rights without compensation which is forbidden under Article 1110 of the NAFTA agreement. In 2000 they successfully sued the Mexican government and were awarded compensation of US$16,685,000.[59]

In 1997 the Canadian government imposed a ban on the import and transportation of MMT – a fuel additive that contains manganese that can harm human health and can also cause air pollution including the release of greenhouse gases. A US corporation, Ethyl Corporation, which manufactures MMT, took legal action against the Canadian government claiming (like Metalclad) that the government had breached NAFTA investor rights. Ethyl Corporation claimed US$175 million in damages and eventually got a settlement from the Canadian government that included a reversal of the ban and payment of US$9 million to cover legal fees.[60] Similarly in 1995 the Canadian government placed a ban on the export of PCB waste which contains highly toxic coolants used in electricity transformers. A US corporation, SD Meyers, which processes and disposes PCB waste, took exception to the measure and, like Metalclad and Ethyl Corporation, filed a claim that argued Canada was not honouring its NAFTA investor obligations and that the company had been hurt by the measure through lost contracts and business opportunities. A tribunal ruled in favour of SD Meyers and awarded it damages of US$4 million. By the time of the tribunal's decision the Canadian government had already withdrawn its export ban.[61] It seems nothing can stand in the way of free trade investor rights, least of all the environment.

The global spread of trade's environmental impact

The effect of trade on global habitat destruction

Probably the most devastating environmental effect of global trade is the way it makes all the world's natural resources available for potential plunder. Before the nineteenth century if a country, or a region, ran out of a particular natural resource it often had little choice but to go without or find an alternative. Today, however, trade has made all the world's natural resources available to all the world's producers. If Europe runs out of minerals it can import them from Africa, if Japan runs out of fish it can import it from the Pacific, if North America runs out of timber it can import it from South America. No resources are inaccessible any more. Global trade has removed all barriers to the exploitation of the world's natural resources – distance is no longer a problem.

Some of the major impacts of this unbridled ability to exploit all the world's natural resources have been the following:

- every year global forest cover equal to the size of Norway is lost; 13 per cent of the world's forest cover was removed between 1960 and 1990. The world has now lost half of all its original forest cover.[62]

Between 1960 and 1990 the global trade in wood fibre increased fourfold while the global trade in pulp grew fivefold.[63]

- between 1950 and 1996 the world's catch of fish increased from 20 million tons each year to 120 million tons while global fish exports have grown fivefold since 1970 equalling US$52 billion in 1997.[64] By 2000 three-quarters of the world's major marine fish stocks had either been depleted through overfishing or had been fished to their ecological limit.[65]

- global production of minerals has increased two and a half times since the early 1960s while global production of metals is now 2.1 times higher. Global production of copper, to meet increased demand from automobile, electrical and other industries, is now a staggering 22 times higher than it was in 1900.[66]

- in the past twenty-five years alone the world has lost 30 per cent of its biodiversity; it is now losing species at 10,000 times the natural rate of extinction. If current trends continue, by the second half of the twenty-first century the world will have lost between one third and two thirds of all its plant and animal species.[67]

The environmental effects of global farming

Just as global trade has opened up all the world's mineral deposits, fish populations, forests, etcetera for global exploitation it is also increasingly opening up all the world's farms for global exploitation. As it does so, more and more of the world's farms are changing from being family-run farms based around local markets – which invariably take reasonable care of their soils and water supplies etcetera – to globally focused factory farms that are often oblivious to the health of the natural elements on which their farms ultimately depend. In Mexico, for instance, after the North American Free Trade Agreement was introduced the farming of maize – the dominant agricultural crop in the country – was devastated by the flooding of the national market by cheap US-grown corn. According to a report by the Carnegie Endowment Foundation, the cheap corn forced 1.3 million farmers off their land who generally sold out to larger, export-focused farmers. But the larger farmers use farming methods that are much more chemical- and water-intensive than the methods used by the smaller farmers, both gradually devastating the country's scarce water resources and increasing the amount of fertiliser runoff into the Sea of Cortez starving its marine life of oxygen.[68]

The explosion in industrial-scale farming around the world has had the following environmental effects:

- global consumption of water is doubling every twenty years – a major influence behind the growth has been steep worldwide increases in water demand for irrigated crops. The number of large dams in the world has grown from 5,000 in 1950 to 38,000 today; almost 60 per cent of the world's largest rivers are now significantly fragmented by dams, diversions and/or canals.[69] Global agriculture accounts for a staggering 70 per cent of the world's water use.[70]

- farming is exhausting more and more soils around the world. Between 1945 and 1990 a global area equal to twice the size of Canada's farmlands was destroyed because of soil erosion and salinisation. Soil erosion and oxidisation cause a net worldwide loss of 26 billion tons of soil every year.[71]

- farming soils are becoming less and less sensitive to fertiliser use, resulting in ever-increasing quantities of fertiliser being required for the same output. In 1980 the application of a ton of fertiliser resulted in a typical yield of 15 to 20 tons of corn in the United States but by 1997 the same amount of fertiliser yielded only 5 to 10 tons of corn.[72] Fertiliser is also contributing to water contamination. In 1997 the European Environment Agency found that surplus nitrogen applied to farmland (either as fertiliser or manure) in 91 of the 113 EU regions it surveyed was certain or very likely to have contributed to nitrate contamination of water.[73] Around the world the global use of nitrogen fertilisers has risen from 14 million tons in 1950 to 143 million tons in 1989.[74]

The environmental destruction fuelled by falling raw material prices

Despite the growth of international trade and despite the spread of economic liberalisation over the past twenty years many countries remain dependent on the export of raw materials much as they have been since colonial times. This is also a source of major worldwide environmental stress. Of the roughly 150 low-income countries in the world, at least half remain highly dependent on raw materials for most of their export income. In 1996, some 23 low-income countries derived 80 per cent, or more, of their export income from just one 'commodity' (raw material); a further 21 derived between 60 and 80 per cent of their export income from one commodity; and another 23 low-income countries derived between 40 and 60 per cent from one commodity.[75] The big problem with this dependency on raw material exported is that raw materials are a very insecure foundation for a nation's exports because, over time, they have tended to fetch increasingly lower prices. Throughout the twentieth century in particular there was a long-term downward trend in the prices raw materials fetched which saw only occasional interruptions. Today non-fuel raw materials only command, on average, prices about half the level they commanded in the mid-1970s and only a third of their levels of 1900.[76]

None of this makes for good news for these low-income countries, but most alarmingly for the global environment it means that many low-income countries have little alternative but to push more and more raw materials on to the global market earning less and less money as supply exceeds demand. They have got to sell off their natural resources at bargain basement prices because there is simply no other option for them in today's highly integrated global trade market. Yet again, the environment ends up paying the price.

Tariff escalation encouraging raw material exports

The ongoing dependency on raw material exports by many low-income countries is reinforced by the policies of the WTO. The WTO claims to want to help low-income countries out of their raw material export dependency, but the reality is that they do nothing with any real effect to help low-income countries move away from the dependency and often conspicuously work against ending it. One way in which the WTO attempts to continue low-income raw material export dependency is through what is known as 'tariff escalation'. During the Uruguay Round a schedule of tariffs was negotiated for raw materials that linked tariffs to the amount of value-adding applied to a raw material – the more value adding, the higher the tariff. Rough tropical timber imported into the United States, for instance, attracts no import duty, but plywood veneer that includes tropical timber attracts an 8 per cent tariff while almost all furniture above quota limits attracts a 40 per cent import duty.[77] This leaves no incentive for low-income countries to add value to their raw materials exports, pushing them into a corner where 'rip-and-ship' exploitation of their natural resources is the only answer.

Basically free trade is getting a free ride courtesy of the world's environment. Both the structure and the sheer volume of world trade mean the world's environment pays the price every time. But the global environment is finite; expanding global trade is eating away at the earth's natural capital – and it is capital we cannot reinvest in. Once it's gone it's gone forever. Global trade desperately needs to open its eyes and ears to the impact it is having on our global ecosystem.

Notes

1   The Worldwatch Institute, *Vital Signs 2003–2004: The Trends That Are Shaping our Future*, Earthscan, London, 2003, p. 35.
2   Simon Retallack, Jerry Mander and E. Koohan Paik (eds), *Intrinsic Consequences of Economic Globalisation and the Environment: Interim Report*, International Forum on Globalization, San Francisco, 2002, p. 66.
3   Ibid., p. 8.
4   Ibid., p. 66.
5   Ibid., p. 67.
6   Ibid.
7   Ibid., p. 68.
8   European Commission, *White Paper, European Transport Policy for 2010: Time to Decide*, European Commission, Brussels, 2000, available from: http://europa.eu.int/comm/energy_transport/en/lb_en.html, quoted

in Michael Woodin and Caroline Lucas, *Green Alternatives to Globalisation: A Manifesto*, Pluto Press, London, 2004, p. 40.

9   The Worldwatch Institute, *Vital Signs 2003–2004*, p. 41.

10   Andrew Simms, *Collision Course: Free Trade's Free Ride on the Global Climate*, New Economics Foundation, London, 2000, p. 9.

11   Ibid., p. 11.

12   Retallack et al., *Intrinsic Consequences of Economic Globalisation*, p. 64.

13   R.M. Gardner et al, 'A Global Inventory of Aircraft Nox Emissions: A revised inventory (1996) by the European Civil Aircraft Conference/ Abatement of Nuisances Caused by Air Transport and EC Working Group', discussion of this paper can be found at: www.grida.no/climate/ ipcc/aviation/137.htm .

14   James J. Corbett and Paul Fischbeck, 'Emissions from Ships', *Science* 278, October 1997.

15   Retallack et al., *Intrinsic Consequences of Economic Globalisation*, p. 8.

16   Simms, *Collision Course*, p. 8.

17   J. A. Jones, 'The environmental impacts of distributing consumer goods: A case study on dessert apples', unpublished Phd thesis, Centre for Environmental Strategy, University of Surrey, United Kingdom, 1999, cited in Woodin and Lucas, *Green Alternatives to Globalisation*, pp. 149–150.

18   Simms, *Collision Course*, p.8.

19   Retallack et al., *Intrinsic Consequences of Economic Globalisation* , pp. 65, 66.

20   Ibid., p. 150.

21   Ibid.

22   Ibid., p. 51.

23   Ibid.

24   Woodin and Lucas, *Green Alternatives to Globalisation*, p. 203.

25   Retallack et al., *Intrinsic Consequences of Economic Globalisation*, p. 68.

26   Ibid., p. 51.

27   Ibid., p. 52.

28   Ibid.

29   Lorri Wallach and Patrick Woodall/Public Citizen, *Whose Trade Organisation?: A Comprehensive Guide to the WTO*, The New Press, New York, 2004, p. 26.

30   Ibid., p. 28.

31   Ibid., p. 33.

32   Ibid., p. 39.

33   Ibid., p. 40.

34   Ibid., p. 92.

35   Ibid., p. 93.

36   Woodin and Lucas, *Green Alternatives to Globalisation*, p. 43.
37   Ibid.
38   Retallack et al., *Intrinsic Consequences of Economic Globalisation*, p. 55.
39   Ibid., p. 28.
40   Fatoumata Jawara and Aileen Kwa, *Behind the Scenes at the WTO: The Real World of International Trade Negotiations*, Zed Books, London, 2003, p. 127.
41   Wallach and Woodall, *Whose Trade Organisation?*, p. 25.
42   Ibid.
43   Ibid., p. 24.
44   Ibid., p. 212.
45   Wallach and Woodall, *Whose Trade Organisation?*, p. 235.
46   Retallack et al., *Intrinsic Consequences of Economic Globalisation*, p. 76.
47   Ibid., p. 78.
48   Wallach and Woodall, *Whose Trade Organisation?*, p. 41.
49   Retallack et al., *Intrinsic Consequences of Economic Globalisation*, pp. 74, 75.
50   Ibid., p. 73.
51   Ibid.
52   Ibid.
53   Ibid., p. 48.
54   Ibid., p. 49.
55   Ibid., p. 53.
56   Ibid.
57   Ibid.
58   Ibid., p. 54.
59   Wallach and Woodall, *Whose Trade Organisation?*, p. 270.
60   Michael Kerr, *ACF Position on Australia–United States Free Trade Agreement: October 2003*, Australian Conservation Foundation, Melbourne, 2003, p.2.
61   Ibid., p. 3.
62   Retallack et al., *Intrinsic Consequences of Economic Globalisation*, p. 83.
63   Ibid., p. 85.
64   Ibid., pp. 132, 133.
65   Ibid., p. 132.
66   Ibid., p. 121.
67   Ibid., p. 146.
68   Michael Pollan, 'Exporting Cheap Corn and Ruin', published by Deb Foskey via WTO watch email list (debf@webone.com.au), 5 May 2004 (No. 252), p. 1. (For archive copy, see www.nwjc.org.au/avcwl/lists/archives.html)
69   Retallack et al., *Intrinsic Consequences of Economic Globalisation*, p. 83.

70   Ibid., p. 162.
71   Ibid., p. 161.
72   Ibid.
73   Woodin and Lucas, *Green Alternatives to Globalisation*, p. 149, see http://themes.eea.eu.int/Sectors_and_activities/agriculture/indicators/nutrients/index_html
74   Jeremy Rifkin, *The Hydrogen Economy: The Creation of the Worldwide Energy Web and the Redistribution of Power on Earth*, Polity Press, Cambridge (UK), 2002, p. 157.
75   Worldwatch Institute, *Vital Signs 2001–2002: The Trends that Are Shaping Our Future*, Earthscan, London, 2001, p. 122.
76   Ibid.
77   Wallach and Woodall, *Whose Trade Organisation?*, p. 21.

7
The future of oil

The British statesman Ernest Bevin once said, 'The kingdom of heaven may run on righteousness but the kingdom of earth runs on oil.'[1] Within the 'kingdom of earth' there is no 'monarchy' that relies on oil more than trade. Trade is utterly dependent on oil. The way global commerce is arranged today, without oil there would simply be no trade. This dependency is a delicate one and the future of trade's dependency on oil may well determine the future of trade. At the moment transport is responsible for about half the world's oil use and up to a quarter of the world's carbon emissions. These are large fractions; what makes them worse is the fact that transport is the fastest-growing user of oil in the world and the fastest-growing producer of carbon emissions so the fractions will rise over time and the future of the world's oil supplies – and the future of global warming – will necessarily be bound up with the future of transport and trade. Oil and trade haven't always been co-dependant, however. Indeed the world's dependency on oil is relatively new. As recently as the start of the twentieth century oil only supplied 4 per cent of the world's total energy whereas today it supplies about 40 per cent.[2] Our current oil dependency is very much a twentieth-century phenomenon. To understand how we developed this dependency you have to understand the history of global energy use.

A brief history of global energy use

Energy use before oil

Today fossil fuels provide about 85 per cent of the world's energy[3] but up until about 300 years ago wood provided most of the world's energy. Europe had a dense cover of forest after the last age – particularly in northern and western Europe – that provided a then seemingly inexhaustible supply of energy. But the forests often grew on prime agricultural land and were frequently cleared to create farmland to feed Europe's growing population. Europe's population experienced significant growth after the Industrial Revolution but there were also sharp population increases between 1100 and 1350 and between 1450 and 1650.[4] These population surges created extra pressure to clear European forest with the result that between 400 and 1600CE the amount of forest cover in Europe was reduced from 95 per cent of the post-ice-age cover to 20 per cent.[5] By the fifteenth century a lot of European forest was being felled to supply fuel for cottage industries such as glassworks and soap production. Further pressure on British forests came from ship construction for the navy.[6] The net result of all these pressures was that wood shortages became commonplace and pressure mounted to find alternative fuel supplies. Elsewhere in the world the rate of forest clearance was nowhere near as extreme as it was in Europe and local populations had a better record of keeping their forests intact (although a lot of forest was cleared throughout the Saharan region of Africa, which once boasted extensive forest cover, and in parts of Asia).

The European wood shortages became so extreme that by the start of the eighteenth century Britain moved to coal as its primary energy source; it was followed in this by the rest of Europe.[7] Unlike wood coal was not generally locally available throughout Europe and a history began of sourcing energy from remote places – a history that has continued to this very day. Like oil, once the world discovered the energy potential of coal its use took off. In 1800 the world's coal output stood at just 15 million tons but by 1900 it was producing 46 times that amount.[8] In the last two years of the nineteenth century the world used more coal than during the entire eighteenth century.[9] More than a third of the global production of coal took place in Britain which in no small way gave it an early lead in the Industrial Revolution. A large force behind the rapid increases in coal use was, of course, the steam engine which literally drove much of the development of the Industrial Revolution.

Energy use after coal

Unlike the conversion from timber to coal the conversion from coal to oil did not occur because coal supplies were becoming scarce; the change mainly took place because of new demands for a transportable and efficient source of energy. Both continental railways and oceangoing steamships proved that coal-fed engines could operate over long distances, but their fuel was bulky and frequent stops were required to refuel the ships and railway engines. Karl Benz's invention of the motor car in 1885, the invention of the diesel engine in 1897, and the Wright Brothers' first successful flight in 1903 all heralded new sources of demand for the more efficient and transportable energy source that was oil. The first oil well had been sunk in 1859 by one Edwin Drake in Pennsylvania after oil springs were discovered in western Pennsylvania six years before. Drake's discovery did not start an immediate oil boom, however – in the mid-nineteenth century there were few applications for oil and the main demand for it came from kerosene usage. But in the late nineteenth century oil-fed appliances started to become widespread. In 1896 Henry Ford produced the first commercial motor car and in 1912 Britain built its first oil-fired battleship. As new types of oil demand began to spring up so too did new sources of oil supply. In 1873 the Baku region of Russia was opened up for oil development, in 1885 oil was discovered in Sumatra, Indonesia, and in 1901 William D'Arcy acquired the first oil concession in the Middle East – in Persia (Iran).[10] At the same time motor vehicles began to gain popularity, first in North America and then in Europe. In 1914 there were 3.4 million cars in the United States but by 1930 there were 23.1 million.[11] In 1868, the first big oil company in the world, Standard Oil Trust, was created and in 1911 the first petrol station was opened (in the United States).

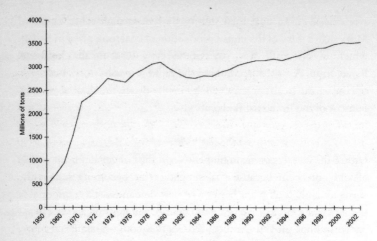

Figure 7.1 Global oil consumption, 1950 to 2000

Source: Worldwatch Institute, *Vital Signs 2003–2004: The Trends That Are Shaping Our Future*, Earthscan, London, 2004, p. 41.

By the late 1930s oil had replaced coal as the major energy source of the United States[12] although it took much longer to become dominant in Europe. For the world as a whole, oil consumption didn't surpass total coal consumption until 1965.[13] Oil demand was kicked along by large-scale highway construction which was well under way in the US by the 1920s and by diesel-powered trucks which began to be commercially produced in the same decade. Transport was not the only consumer of oil, however – the patenting of nylon, whose production also uses a lot of oil, by the Du Pont company in 1938 also added to oil demand.

Global oil production has risen from a few thousand barrels per day in 1859 to more than 70 million barrels per day today. At the end of the Second World War, however, the world was still producing less than 7 million barrels per day, or a tenth of today's production.[14] The really big increases in oil demand that brought it up to today's level were very much a phenomenon of the post-Second World War years.

Global oil demand since the Second World War

The tenfold jump in world oil demand since the Second World War hasn't happened in consistent steps. Global consumption doubled in the 1950s, then more than doubled in the 1960s, then slowed to increase by only about a third in the 1970s in response to major increases in oil prices in 1973 and 1979.[15] After peaking in 1979 world oil demand was flat throughout the 1980s and only surpassed its 1979 level in 1990. For a while it seemed the world had developed a sensible caution in its oil use, but then there was a 12 per cent increase in global demand between 1990 and 2000.[16]

Most of the new increase in demand is coming from rapidly growing low-income countries. In 1970 low-income countries consumed 26 per cent of the world's oil but they are now consuming 40 per cent.[17] One shouldn't infer from this, however, that oil consumption in low-income countries is anything like that of high-income countries. In 2002 per capita oil consumption in the United States was a massive 16 times that of China.[18] Having said that, however, throughout the 1990s growth in low-income country oil consumption was very significant. In several high-income countries oil demand actually fell during the 1990s: in Britain and Germany it fell by about 5 per cent while in France it fell by 2 per cent (the conspicuous exception was the United States where it grew by 16 per cent).[19] By contrast, China's oil consumption doubled during the 1990s while India's grew by 60 per cent, South Korea's by 50 per cent and Brazil's by 40 per cent.[20]

Much of the increase in low-income country oil demand is coming from transport. There is no escaping the fact that the future of global oil is necessarily bound up with the future of global transport. The IMF predicts that transport demand in low-income countries will contribute half of their predicted 56 per cent rise in global oil demand over the next 25 years.[21] There are currently 750 million vehicles on the world's roads and this figure is set to double in the next twenty-five years[22] with most of the extra vehicles being purchased in low-income countries (though it should be emphasised, again, that even after this

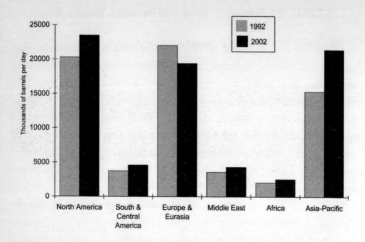

Figure 7.2 Global regional oil consumption, 1992 and 2000

Source: *BP Statistical Review of World Energy June 2003*, BP, London, 2003, p. 9.

doubling the low-income countries' per capita oil use will only still be a fraction of that of high-income countries). In China, alone, about five million vehicles were sold in 2004 making that country a larger market, by volume, than Germany. By 2007 car sales in China will probably surpass those of Japan and will then only be exceeded by those of the United States.[23] China's car sales leapt by 56 per cent in 2002 and by 75 per cent in 2003[24] helping it to become the world's second-largest global importer of oil (and second-largest consumer) by 2004 (although Chinese car sales growth slowed to 15 per cent in 2004). Despite these increases China still has only one car for every seventy people compared to one car for every two people in the US; if China's level of car ownership were to increase to equal that of the US there would be 650 million cars on Chinese roads – or nearly as many as all the cars on all the world's roads today.[25] The IMF estimates China will have about 387 million cars by 2030 – up from 21 million in 2002.[26]

Frustratingly, there is much evidence of increased efficiency in worldwide oil use but growth in the sheer volume of users overrides

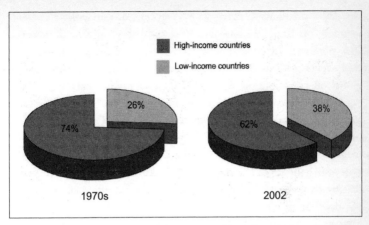

Figure 7.3 Oil use by high-income and low-income countries, 1970s, 2002

Source: Jeremy Rifkin, *The Hydrogen Economy: The Next Great Economic Revolution*, Polity Press, Cambridge, 2002, p. 239, and BP *Statistical Review of World Energy June 2003*, BP, London, 2003, p. 9.

the efficiency gains. The US economy now requires only 60 per cent of the energy it required in the 1950s to earn each dollar of its gross domestic product,[27] and the efficiency of engines has increased by more than a third since the 1970s, but the problem is there are a lot more dollars (or their equivalent) of gross domestic product being earned around the world and there are a lot more engines running as well, and even though each engine is more efficient than it used to be there is an overwhelmingly larger number of them.

Future world oil demand

The statistics of future global oil use are frightening. If just China and India, alone, increase their per capita oil consumption to half the present-day per capita level of Germany – which they have every right to do – and if all other things remain equal (including population levels), global oil consumption will increase by 31 million barrels per day – an increase equal to 40 per cent of the world's current demand.[28] If Brazil, Indonesia, China and India together all increase their per capita oil consumption to two-thirds of the present-day per capita level of Germany – and if all other things again remain equal – global oil consumption will increase by 49 million barrels per day, equal to 64 per cent of the world's current demand.[29] This would take global consumption to 125 million barrels per day. Coincidentally (or perhaps not), this is the same order of increase the Energy Information Administration of the United States Department of Energy Forecasts believes the world will be looking at by 2020. It believes that by then the world will be consuming 120 million barrels of oil per day[30] or nearly double the 1992 level of global consumption.[31] Edward Carr, former business editor of the *Economist*, believes 'the growth in energy consumption in developing countries between 2000 and 2010 will be greater than today's consumption in Western Europe'.[32]

These hugely increased levels of demand would be of less consequence if there was no global warming and if the world had limitless reserves of oil. But we do have global warming and we don't have limitless reserves of oil. If the world discovers no more oil we have about 1,300 billion barrels of it left (see page 193). Global usage of 120 million barrels per day equates to 44 billion barrels per year so unless we quickly start to find vast new oilfields we only have about thirty years of oil left. This figure assumes that oil consumption will immediately jump to 120 million barrels per day, which it won't, and it also assumes that we won't find any new oilfields, which we will, but it is a measure of how acute the world's looming oil shortage really is. Given how utterly dependent trade is on oil, a near-term end to oil availability means a near-term end to the world trading system as we know it unless alternatives are developed soon. The scale of the crisis that world oil supplies are looking at over the next few decades cannot be overstated. Global trade simply cannot keep consuming ever-increasing quantities of oil pretending it will never run out. It will run out – and is running out – and it is stupid to pretend otherwise. In 2004 global oil prices touched US$50 per barrel for the first time in what some termed the world's 'third oil shock'. Some of the price spike was caused by fears of terrorist disruptions of oil supplies and by supply uncertainty in Russia, Venezuela and Nigeria but most of the high price was the result of increased demand – the *Economist* magazine claimed the supply 'risk premium' was worth about US$10 per barrel meaning that the other US$40 per barrel was demand-driven.[33] When the price spike occurred Larry Elliot, correspondent for the *Guardian Weekly*, said 'in the gloomiest scenario, we are getting an early taste of life as the oil wells run dry, which means that while the price may jag around, the long-term trend will be up'.[34]

In 1972 the Club of Rome predicted that 'if the present growth trends continue in world population, industrialisation, pollution, food production, and resource depletion continues unchanged, the limits to growth on this planet will be reached sometime within the next one hundred years'.[35] The Club of Rome's warnings have become somewhat discredited in most economists' eyes because some of their short-term predictions did not come true. But the broad thrust of their projections remains true in many vital areas, especially oil. The world in general, and trade in particular, simply cannot keep ignoring the precarious future of oil.

The world's remaining reserves of oil

Projections about how much longer the world's oil will last would be much easier, and much more certain, if there was clarity about how much we have left. But there is a conspicuous absence of certainty about remaining world oil reserves. There are some fundamentals that most observers can agree on, however. The first is that in stark contrast to past decades the world is now using oil much more quickly than it is discovering it. Discoveries of new oilfields only equal between a third and half of our annual usage (depending on the year in question). Today we are using about 28 billion barrels of oil per year but discovering only about 12 billion new barrels each year. Our oil discovery rate is only about one third of the level of the 1970s[36] but our usage rate is now more than a third higher.[37] There are about 1,500 major oilfields in the world today but only 41 of these have been discovered since 1980.[38] Today about 80 per cent of the world's oil flows from wells that were discovered before 1973.[39]

The other fundamental that most observers agree on is that the vast majority of the world's oil reserves will continue to be located in the Middle East which is likely to account for an increasing share of future global oil production. In 1973 the Middle East accounted for 38 per cent of world oil production but after the OPEC oil price shocks of 1973 and 1979 – which encouraged nations to use less oil and look for it elsewhere – it fell to 18 per cent; today it is back up to 30 per cent and is likely to go higher.[40] This is because the world has not found any alternative large oilfields of the sort found in the Middle East and looks increasingly unlikely to do so. Some minor oilfields have been discovered in recent decades in areas such as the Caspian Sea, Kazakhstan, Iran and Central and Western Africa, but no large oilfields have been discovered for several decades now. There are currently more than 140 new oil and gas fields under development but all of them are small – none are expected to have large peak production capacities.[41]

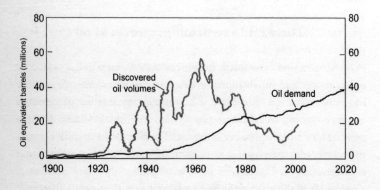

Figure 7.4 Global annual oil discovery and global oil use

Source: Jean Laherrère, *Forecast of Oil and Gas Supply to 2050*, Petrotech, New Delhi, 2003, p. 2, using graph by Exxon-Mobil.

As many of the world's minor oilfields start to run out of oil, the Middle East has yet to exhaust the first half of its reserves. The United States has only 14 per cent of its reserves left, Russia – currently the world's second-largest oil producer – has 39 per cent of its original oil remaining while Saudi Arabia still has a massive 70 per cent left.[42] At current production rates, and without further discoveries, the oil reserves of countries like Iran, Saudi Arabia, the United Arab Emirates and Kuwait will last fifty to a hundred years while the reserves of countries like Norway, Canada and the United States will be lucky to last much longer than ten years.[43]

Most studies estimate the world has discovered reserves whose original capacity was somewhere between 1,800 and 2,200 billion barrels, of which we have used about 875 billion barrels leaving roughly half the original capacity.[44] The quantification of oil reserves is, however, a very slippery science. Some truly bizarre changes sometimes take place in oil reserve estimates. Between the mid-1980s and the 1990s proven global oil reserves increased by a third without any major new oilfields being discovered![45] In January 2004 the oil giant Royal Dutch/Shell admitted to gross overstatement of its reserves and suddenly decreased them by a fifth,[46] prompting other energy companies such as BP and El Paso also to revise their reserve estimates.[47] The problem is that there is no agreed methodology for measuring oil reserves. The United States has a fairly strict and conservative standard, Russia has quite a loose one and the Middle East seemingly has none at all. Middle Eastern countries often boost their reserve figures to help increase their OPEC production entitlements and/or to help qualify for foreign loans. Most of the mysterious increase in global reserves between the mid-1980s and the 1990s came from Middle Eastern reserves that suddenly increased without explanation. What is desperately needed is independent audits of global oil reserves using common, agreed standards.

As well as different definitions of what constitutes an oil reserve another 'swing factor' is changing technology. Oil reserve estimates can change over time because of better drilling methods and better examination of seismic data (which often means that the size of more recently discovered reserves is underestimated compared to older reserves).[48]

Two structural features of the modern global oil industry that don't help the fundamental supply-and-demand equation are recent take-overs between oil companies and the price of oil. Between 1998 and 2001 there was a wave of mergers in the global oil industry which saw Exxon merge with Mobil, Chevron merge with Texaco, BP merge with Amarco and Arco, Conoco merge with Phillips and France's Total merge with PetroFina and Elf.[49] This has made the industry less interested in drilling for new oilfields and more interested in buying out rivals in what is sometimes known as 'drilling for oil on Wall Street'.[50] The other structural issue is price. In 2004 global oil prices broke through US$40 per barrel for the first time since 1990, then went on to break through US$50 per barrel, sending the financial world into a panic. But even at US$40 per barrel – which is roughly double the price it stayed at throughout most of the 1990s – oil is cheap. After adjusting for inflation, oil at US$40 per barrel is still only about two-thirds its 1980 cost.[51] Although we all squeal when the cost of petrol goes up it is still inexpensive, especially when we factor in how much more efficiently a typical engine uses petrol these days. Cheap oil creates little incentive to conserve, and this compounds the uncertain future that global oil supplies face. In the United States – which is the most profligate user of oil in the world and the consumer of a full quarter of the global oil supply – motorists get worried when the price of petrol breaches US55c per litre which is ridiculously cheap compared to, say, Europe. If we want to buy time with global oil consumption we have to use it more sparingly and that means increasing its price. But a major rise in the price of oil will fundamentally affect trade and transport. A significant increase in the price of oil cannot help but reduce the amount of global trade. With the quantity of oil used by transport set to double over the next twenty years there is no doubt that the future of oil will continue to dictate much of the future of trade.

The peaking of global oil supply

In 1956 a geophysicist who worked for the Shell Oil Company, M. King Hubbert, published a landmark paper that predicted oil production in the United States would 'peak' somewhere between 1965 and 1970.[52] When he used the word 'peak' he meant that within his predicted period about half the US oil supply would have been used up and the flow rate would begin to decline as the physical pressure that forces oil up through the earth's surface began to fall off. Gushes would turn into dribbles after that time, he predicted. In the 1950s the US was then pumping a record amount of oil and most fellow geologists therefore scoffed at his prediction.[53] Two decades later, however, Hubbert was taken very seriously as US oil supplies began to do exactly what he had predicted when they peaked in 1970. Today it is universally recognised that US oil is well past its peak of production – in fact the US now has to import half of all its oil consumption and by 2020 it is likely to be importing at least two-thirds.[54] Today most observers are applying Hubbert's methodology to the global supply of oil and are predicting that the world oil supply will also peak soon.

Peaking is a phenomenon that has not been confined to the United States. North Sea oil production probably peaked in late 2002 and production in the Caspian Sea area is likely to peak by about 2010.[55] Hubbert died in 1989 but after his prediction of the US peak he went on to predict the peak of global production. With figures then available he predicted that peak global oil production would occur between 1990 and 2000.[56] That period is now considered to be slightly earlier than the actual time when the peaking will occur, but there is a general consensus that the global peak will occur in the next few decades although there is considerable disagreement about exactly when. Colin Campbell, a geologist who has worked for Texaco and Amoco, and Jean Laherrère, who has worked for Total, predict a global peak by 2010.[57] The Swiss-based company Petroconsultants also believes the peak will occur by 2010.[58] Peaking predictions are very dependent on assessments of current reserves, estimates of future reserves and estimates of global consumption over the next few years.

Craig Hatfield, a geologist at the University of Toledo, agrees with Campbell and Laherrère.[59] Kenneth Deffeyes, from Princeton University, thinks the peak could occur as early as 2003 or possibly as late as 2009.[60] The International Energy Agency of the OECD thinks the peak will occur somewhere between 2010 and 2020.[61] But others think predictions like these are based on estimates of current and future likely reserves that are too conservative. William Fisher, a geologist from the University of Texas, says 'we're thirty, maybe even forty, years before the peak'.[62]

So experts on peaking broadly divide into two camps: those that think the peak will occur somewhere between 2010 and 2020 and those that think it will occur somewhere between 2030 and 2040.[63] No one, however, argues the peak won't occur relatively soon, and the world ignores this at its peril just as the United States ignored Hubbert's original 1956 prediction at its peril. Unless viable substitutes for oil can be found, peaking will mean that declining amounts of oil will be coming out of the ground as world demand increases. This must impact on global trade – there is no way it can't.

Global warming

As if the imminent supply problems associated with oil weren't problematic enough, another fundamental problem with oil, of course, is global warming. Carbon, the major global warming agent, is the main pollutant emitted by the burning of oil. Global carbon emissions from fossil fuel sources have quadrupled since 1950 with trade and transport being the major contributors to the increase.[64] A 1997 study by the OECD and the International Energy Agency found the transport sector accounted for a massive proportion of all the world's carbon emissions – between 20 and 25 per cent of the global total.[65]

Today the world emits about 6.5 billion tons of carbon dioxide every year by burning fossil fuels; on top of that the best part of another two billion tons is released through human-induced changes to land-use, mainly in the form of deforestation taking place in tropical areas.

Of the roughly 8.5 billion tons of carbon dioxide released each year, a little over half is absorbed by the world's oceans and other natural 'sinks', but a little under half ends up being released into the atmosphere which increases the atmospheric concentrations of carbon dioxide. Before the Industrial Revolution global carbon concentrations were about 280 parts per million (by volume) but current levels are about a third higher at 370 parts per million – a level that has not been exceeded in the last 420,000 years, or, most likely, in the past 20 million years.[66] According to the Intergovernmental Panel on Climate Change (IPCC) – a United Nations/World Meteorological Organisation global warming research group that brings together thousands of the world's most pre-eminent climate scientists – by the end of the twenty-first century the world can expect to see atmospheric carbon concentrations running at anywhere between two and five times their pre-Industrial Revolution levels.[67] At the moment about two-thirds of global carbon dioxide emissions come from high-income countries with the balance coming from low-income countries but if current usage trends continue – particularly the rapid increase in low-income country oil consumption – by 2035 the world will be releasing about 12 billion tons of carbon dioxide with about half coming from low-income countries (whose per capita emissions will still only be a fraction of those of high-income countries).[68]

There is little doubt that all these extra emissions are having an effect and that the world is getting warmer. The average global surface temperature in 1998 was 0.66 degrees Celsius above the long-term global average surface temperature (as measured between 1880 and 1997) of 13.8 degrees Celsius.[69] The ten hottest years recorded on accurate instruments (since the late nineteenth century) have all occurred since 1989. The warmest year was 1998 followed by 2002 and 2003 (tied), 2001, 1997, 1995, 1990 and 1999 (tied) and 1991 and 2000 (tied).[70] The IPCC has no doubt that human activity is to blame. Since its establishment in 1988 it has issued three major reports. The most recent one, published in 2001, concluded 'there is new and stronger evidence that most of the warming observed over the past 50 years is attributable to human activities'.[71] This was considerably

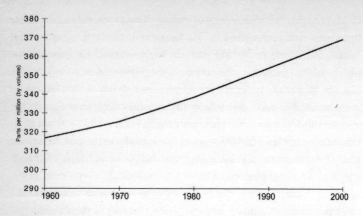

Figure 7.5 Global concentrations of carbon dioxide, 1960 to 2000

Source: Worldwatch Institute, *Vital Signs 2003–2004: The Trends That Are Shaping Our Future*, Earthscan, London, 2004, p. 41.

stronger wording than that used by an earlier IPCC report which said only that 'the balance of evidence suggests a discernable human influence on global warming'.[72]

It is almost impossible to understate the significance and likely consequences of global warming. By the end of the twenty-first century the global average surface temperature is predicted to rise by between 1.4 and 5.8 degrees Celsius. The upper end of this range is equal to the total amount of global warming the earth has experienced since the end of the last ice age some 8,000 years ago. As a result of this warming world sea levels will rise by between 9 and 88 cm by the end of this century (having already risen by about 18 cm over the past hundred years). This will result in more extremes of precipitation (droughts and floods), more heatwaves, fewer frosts and more intense tropical cyclones. Sea ice and snow cover will retreat. Currently 46 million people in the world live in areas at risk from sea storm surges – that number will increase to about 92 million if global sea levels rise by 50 cm.[73] If sea levels rise by a full metre the number increases to about 118 million. Increasing rates of precipitation will result in drier soils in many parts of the world. Deserts will become hotter. The geographical spread of vector-borne diseases such as malaria, dengue fever, yellow fever and encephalitis will increase. To survive climate change, forests may have to migrate up to 500 km to reach cooler zones (if they can). A lot of vegetation will have to migrate to higher elevations (if it can). Water quality will reduce and estuaries and freshwater aquifers will become more saline.[74] Global food production is not expected to change significantly as a result of global warming but crop yields in some areas will increase and in other areas decrease, the latter especially in tropical and sub-tropical areas. The variety of crops that can be grown in many regions is also expected to decrease.[75]

Global warming will radically change the world as we know it unless we act soon. But acting on global warming means addressing fossil fuel use and the use of oil in particular. With transport using about half the world's oil we cannot address global warming without addressing transport and trade.

Alternatives to oil

Once the peak of global oil supply has passed and the world starts seriously contemplating the end of oil, the only way trade will survive in anything like its current form is if commercially and environmentally viable alternatives can be found. If they can't be found, the future of trade does not look good. If alternatives are found but aren't as cheap as oil then global trade will have to be significantly reconfigured. Global trade could survive with a more expensive fuel source but it would have to be a lot more selective than it is today. It simply couldn't be profitably carried on at today's level. More expensive transport fuel would mean traders would have to question seriously the worth of sending massive volumes of goods across borders; local production would become a lot more attractive. To date trade and transport have driven oil demand, but over the next few decades oil demand is going to drive trade and transport; the result may be a major reorganisation of how trade is conducted around the world.

There are several possible transportable alternative fuels to oil but none are both commercially and environmentally viable right now. One popularly mooted alternative is ethanol – a fuel produced from the fermenting of grain, generally corn. Ethanol emits far fewer pollutants than oil when burned, and several countries have toyed with the idea of requiring it to be mixed with petroleum to create cleaner fuel. But the problem with ethanol is that a lot of agricultural pollution is involved in its production and it doesn't yield much, if any, more energy than is consumed in its production. When burned, oil yields about eight times the energy required to produce it. The US Department of Agriculture claims ethanol yields 34 per cent more energy upon burning than it takes to produce it but some commentators, including entomologist David Pimentel, claim that if you factor in the energy cost of absolutely everything involved in the production of corn ethanol it doesn't yield any net energy 'profit' – in fact it incurs a major energy loss.[76] Another major problem is that ethanol is expensive to produce and currently requires a 50 cents per gallon subsidy in the United States to compete with oil.[77] Yet another major problem that ethanol shares with biodiesel – diesel oils made from plants – is that they both require a huge amount of cropland for their production. British author George Monbiot has calculated that to run all of Britain's cars and buses on biodiesel would require an area of arable land equal to four and a half times all the arable land currently available in the entire country.[78]

Natural gas is another popularly suggested alternative to oil. In many high-income country cities it is now commonplace to see gas-powered vehicles. Like oil, however, natural gas is a fossil fuel and emits significant greenhouse gases when burnt (although at a lesser rate than oil).[79] It also suffers from a similar long-term supply shortage. Estimates of the world's discovered and yet-to-be-discovered gas reserves vary enormously but currently proven reserves will only last ten years at present rates of usage.[80] No one seriously suggests the world's natural gas will last for more than a few decades at the very best.

Another alternative is oil made from coal or shale oil. The world still has large reserves of coal, particularly in Australia and China, from which oil can be extracted. But it takes an enormous amount of coal, energy and pollution to do this. The production of synthetic oil from coal results in 72 per cent more carbon dioxide emissions than the production of the same volume of crude oil.[81] A full ton of coal yields only 5.5 barrels of oil.[82] Efforts to extract oil from shale oil (which is actually rock made of organic marlstone) have been going on for ninety years but, like making oil from coal, it involves the use of enormous amounts of energy and results in a large amount of waste. Shale oil has to be mined, transported and heated to 900 degrees Fahrenheit with the addition of hydrogen resulting in a huge amount of waste.[83] Germany tried making oil from shale oil during the Second World War but found it required too much energy and too much shale oil for too little return.

Yet another oil alternative is tar sands which are extensively found in Canada, Venezuela and elsewhere. There is so much tar sand in Canada that industry observers expect it to be responsible for as much as 75 per cent of the country's oil production by 2010.[84] But like coal, tar sands require an enormous throughput of material to produce a small volume of fuel – it takes a full two tons of tar sand to produce one barrel of oil.[85] The extraction of the oil also requires large volumes of heated water and solvents. One recent study has found that by 2010 a quarter of the gas produced in the Canadian state of Alberta will be required to extract oil from tar sands in that state.[86] The net result is that the whole tar sands oil extraction process produces enormous quantities of non-reclaimable waste – it is as much as twelve times more expensive than conventional oil to produce and once produced still has all the greenhouse emission problems that regular oil has.

The big alternative to oil that has many people excited is hydrogen. Hydrogen is the most abundant element in the universe making up about 90 per cent of its molecules.[87] As long ago as the 1930s and 1940s hydrogen was being used as an experimental fuel for cars, trucks, trains and even submarines in the UK and Germany.[88] The really big attraction of hydrogen is that when it is used to produce electricity via a fuel cell the only effluents are heat and distilled water. So exciting is the potential of hydrogen that in 1999 Iceland declared that it wanted to become the first economy in the world to be powered solely by hydrogen.[89] It is hard not to see hydrogen as the sustainable fuel source waiting to replace oil but, like all the other potential alternatives, there are major drawbacks associated with it. A fundamental problem with hydrogen is that it does not naturally occur in a pure state – it has to be extracted. Today about half of all the hydrogen produced in the world comes from natural gas via a steam-reforming process but, as already mentioned, natural gas has an even more finite supply future than oil and simply doesn't present itself as a realistic long term hydrogen source. One hydrogen source that is plentiful, however, is water from which hydrogen can be produced using electrolysis (electrolysis is essentially a reverse fuel cell process). While technically feasible, electrolysis uses an enormous amount of energy with the result that producing hydrogen from water using electrolysis currently costs three to four times as much as extracting it from natural gas using the steam-reforming process.[90] As a result, only about 4 per cent of the world's current production of hydrogen is made via electrolysis.[91]

The production of hydrogen via electrolysis has two fundamental problems associated with it that must be overcome before it has any chance of replacing oil. One is that the process requires a huge amount of electricity and actually consumes more energy than is yielded when the hydrogen is burnt. Like other oil substitutes hydrogen doesn't have any net energy 'profit'. The second fundamental problem is that the sources of the electricity used in the electrolytic process can, potentially, emit as many greenhouse gases as oil does (especially if coal is used to generate the electricity) and therefore, when considered as a whole, the process of hydrogen generation may be as harmful to the environment as the burning of oil is. These problems have not stopped nearly all global car producers working on their own versions of a hydrogen fuel-cell car, Honda being the first to have one ready for the market.[92] But the problems associated with hydrogen fuel cells prompt some commentators to argue that, in the words of Richard Heinberg, author of *The Party's Over: Oil, War and the Fate of Industrial Societies*, 'it is difficult to avoid the conclusion that the hydrogen economy touted by well-meaning visionaries will by necessity be a much lower-energy economy than we are accustomed to'.[93] Jeremy Rifkin, author of *The Hydrogen Economy: The Next Great Economic Revolution*, argues, however, that the pollution problems of electrolysis disappear if renewable sources of energy are used to generate the electricity needed for the electrolytic process. Rifkin also implies that if hydrogen is the only means through which we are ever going to have a sustainable transportable fuel then we basically have no choice but to embrace it and to make the processes associated with it as efficient as possible. Rifkin specifically argues:

> The real question, then, is whether it is possible to use renewable forms of energy that are carbon-free, like photovoltaic, wind, hydro, and geothermal, to generate the electricity that is used in the electrolysis process to split water into hydrogen and oxygen. A growing number of energy experts say yes, but with the qualification that the costs of employing renewable forms of energy will need to come down considerably to make the process competitive with the natural-gas steam-reforming process.[94]

So for trade, and transport in general, the implications from all this are clear. Hydrogen could provide an alternative transportable fuel to oil but it will not come cheaply nor will it come soon. A hydrogen economy will, no doubt, allow global trade still to be carried on but unless the cost of producing hydrogen comes down a long way, trade in a post-oil global economy will be a lot more expensive and by necessity a lot more selective than it is today. In this scenario local production may look very attractive.

Notes

1 Jeremy Rifkin, *The Hydrogen Economy: The Creation of the Worldwide Energy Web and the Redistribution of Power on Earth*, Polity Press, Cambridge (UK), 2002, p. 73.
2 Ibid., pp. 65, 66.
3 Ibid., p. 66.
4 Richard Heinberg, *The Party's Over: Oil, War and the Fate of Industrial Societies*, New Society Publishers, Gabriola Island (Canada), 2003, p. 49.

5 Ibid.

6 Rifkin, *The Hydrogen Economy*, p. 67.

7 Ibid., p. 68.

8 Heinberg, *The Party's Over*, p. 53.

9 Ibid.

10 Daniel Yergin, *The Prize: The Epic Quest for Oil, Money and Power*, Free Press, New York, 1991, p. 789.

11 Rifkin, *The Hydrogen Economy*, p. 72.

12 Ibid.

13 Worldwatch Institute, *Vital Signs 2003–2004: The Trends that Are Shaping Our Future*, Earthscan, London, 2003, p. 35.

14 Yergin, *The Prize*, p. 792.

15 Worldwatch Institute, *Vital Signs 2003–2004*, p. 35.

16 Ibid.

17 Rifkin, *The Hydrogen Economy*, p. 239.

18 Based on figures in: *BP Statistical Review of World Energy: June 2003*, BP, London, 2003, p. 9 and The World Bank, *World Development Report 2003*, Oxford University Press, New York, 2003, pp. 234 and 235.

19 Ibid., p. 9.

20 Ibid.

21 'Chinese gas guzzlers in driver's seat', *The Australian*, 8 April 2005, p. 17.

22 Rifkin, *The Hydrogen Economy*, p. 208.

23 'The Rich hit the Road', *Economist*, 19 June 2004, p. 64.

24 'A billion three, but not for me', *Economist*, 20 March 2004, China business survey p. 6.

25 'Chinese gas guzzlers in driver's seat', *The Australian*, 8 April 2005, p. 17.

26 Pam Woodall, 'The Dragon and the Eagle – A Survey of the World Economy', *Economist*, 2 October 2004, survey p. 12.

27 Heinberg, *The Party's Over*, p. 60.

28 Based on figures in: *BP Statistical Review of World Energy: June 2003*, pp. 234 and 235.

29 Ibid.

30 Rifkin, *The Hydrogen Economy*, p. 23.

31 *BP Statistical Review of World Energy*, p. 9.

32 Edward Carr, 'Energy', *Economist*, 18 June 1994, pp. 3–18.

33 'Unstoppable', *Economist*, 21 August 2004, p. 61.

34 Larry Elliot, 'Oil supply on a knife edge', *Guardian Weekly*, 13 August 2004, p. 11.

35 Donella H. Meadows et al., *The Limits to Growth: A Report for the Club of Rome's Project on the Predicament of Mankind*, Earth Island Limited, London, 1972, p. 23.

36   Heinberg, *The Party's Over*, p. 108.
37   Based on figures in Worldwatch Institute, *Vital Signs 2003– 2004*, p. 35.
38   Rifkin, *The Hydrogen Economy*, p. 20.
39   Heinberg, *The Party's Over*, p. 94.
40   Rifkin, *The Hydrogen Economy*, p. 34.
41   Heinberg, *The Party's Over*, p. 102.
42   Rifkin, *The Hydrogen Economy*, p. 17.
43   Ibid., p. 34.
44   Ibid., p. 24.
45   Ibid., p. 19.
46   'Another Enron', *Economist*, 13 March 2004, p. 59.
47   'Needlessly murky', *Economist*, 10 April 2004, p. 12.
48   Heinberg, *The Party's Over*, p. 113.
49   Peter Coy, 'Why Big Oil is Taking a Back Seat', *Australian Financial Review*, 17 June 2004, p. 69.
50   Ibid.
51   'It's a gas', *Economist*, 22 May 2004, p. 36.
52   Heinberg, *The Party's Over*, p. 25.
53   Ibid.
54   Michael Klare, 'United States Energy and Strategy', *Le Monde Diplomatique*, November 2002, p. 1.
55   Rifkin, *The Hydrogen Economy*, p. 21.
56   Heinberg, *The Party's Over*, p. 90.
57   Rifkin, *The Hydrogen Economy*, p. 27.
58   Heinberg, *The Party's Over*, p. 86.
59   Rifkin, *The Hydrogen Economy*, p. 27.
60   Ibid., p. 28.
61   Ibid.
62   As quoted in Richard A. Kerr, 'The Next Oil Crisis Looms Large – and Perhaps Close', *Science Magazine*, August 1998, pp. 1128–1131.
63   Rifkin, *The Hydrogen Economy*, p. 28.
64   The Worldwatch Institute, *Vital Signs 2003-2004,* p. 41.
65   Andrew Simms, *Collision Course: Free Trade's Free Ride on the Global Climate*, New Economics Foundation, London, 2000, p. 9.
66   National Oceanic and Atmospheric Administration, *Global Warming: Frequently Asked Questions*, p. 2, downloaded from www.ncdc.noaa.gov/oa/climate/globalwarming in 2004.
67   Ibid.
68   The Woods Hole Research Centre, *Environmental Outcome of Global Warming: The Culprits* pp. 1–2, downloaded from whrc.org/resources/online_publications/warming_earth in 2004.

69 Ibid., *Scientific Evidence*, p. 3.
70 Ibid.
71 Leigh Dayton, 'Science warms to the cause', *Weekend Australian*, 19 June 2004, p. 30.
72 The Woods Hole Research Centre, *Environmental Outcome of Global Warming*, p. 2,
73 Ibid., *Potential Outcome*, p. 1.
74 Ibid., p. 3.
75 Ibid., p. 4.
76 'Dirty as well as Dear', *Economist*, 17 January 2004, p. 30.
77 Ibid.
78 George Monbiot, 'Fuel for Thought', *Guardian Weekly*, 3rd December 2004, p. 13.
79 Rifkin, *The Hydrogen Economy*, p. 125.
80 Heinberg, *The Party's Over*, p. 126.
81 Rifkin, *The Hydrogen Economy*, p. 133.
82 Ibid., p. 130.
83 Heinberg, *The Party's Over*, p. 111.
84 Rifkin, *The Hydrogen Economy*, p. 131.
85 Ibid.
86 Ibid., p. 132.
87 Ibid., p. 177.
88 Ibid., p. 182.
89 Ibid., p. 183.
90 Ibid., p. 187.
91 Ibid.
92 Iain Carson, 'Clean Machine', *Economist*, 4 September 2004, Survey p. 14.
93 Heinberg, *The Party's Over*, p. 149.
94 Ibid., p. 187.

8
The future of global balance-of-payments problems

The future of global trade will be dictated not only by the future of oil but also by the future of the large balance-of-payments imbalances that currently plague the global economy. In today's globalised economy it is impossible to separate the global financial flows that are associated with trade from the global financial flows that are associated with the movement of capital around the world (in the form of loans, investment or short-term speculative funds). The two are completely mixed in together these days. Balance-of-payments imbalances are the combined product of trade imbalances – where the money leaving an economy to pay for imports exceeds the money coming in from the sale of exports (or visa versa) – and debt and investment servicing imbalances – where the money leaving an economy as interest or dividends to service foreign investment and/or foreign debt exceeds the money coming in from overseas investment and loans (or visa versa). There is no shortage of acute balance-of-payments imbalances in today's global economy.

For most of the peacetime period of the century between 1870 and 1970s there were various schemes that generally worked against large, persistent balance-of-payments imbalances and which tended to bring the world economy back into balance. But since the early 1970s no such scheme has existed. In balance-of-payments terms the world has largely muddled through the three decades since the early 1970s but there is growing evidence it won't be able to keep muddling through for much longer. Large, persistent balance-of-payments imbalances exist around the world that pose a serious long-term threat to the ongoing viability of the world economy and therefore to the ongoing viability of global trade. Unless the world economy finds a way of dealing with the problem of large ongoing balance-of-payments imbalances soon, the fragile, *ad hoc* arrangements that have been in place since the early 1970s may come horribly unstuck. If they do, the global trading system will come horribly unstuck with them. The ability of the world economy to manage large, persistent imbalances will have a huge bearing on the future of globalisation in general and the future of the global trade network in particular.

The gold standard fixed exchange rate systems

For most of the hundred years between the 1870s and the early 1970s, three successive global economic systems delivered a high degree of predictability of global financial flows. They did this through systems of fixed (or relatively fixed) exchange rates which generally tended to keep balance-of-payments imbalances within reasonable bounds. Because exchange rates were fixed, if a country was experiencing ongoing balance-of-payments difficulties it made internal changes such as reducing its import demand or reducing its export cost pressures to try and correct the imbalances. The system did not neces-sarily allow a lot of financial autonomy for participant countries but it did deliver a large degree of predictability to global financial flows. Today, however, countries with floating exchange rates rely on the exchange rate to fix their balance-of-payments problems. But invari-ably the floating exchange rate fails to deliver the desired fix, and the imbalances persist.

The three fixed exchange rate systems that covered most of the time between the 1870s and the early 1970s were: the gold standard that operated from the 1870s to the start of the First World War, the revived gold standard that operated from the mid 1920s to the early 1930s, and the Bretton Woods system that operated from 1944 to

1971. A brief look at the workings of each of these provides some pointers to the future of today's laissez-faire system.

The gold standard system from the 1870s to the First World War

The gold standard that operated from the 1870s to the First World War was a remarkably efficient global exchange system that was generally good at ensuring that large balance-of-payments imbalances did not persist in the global economy. This early exchange rate system was more efficient than later systems at resolving long-run balance-of-payments imbalances although it was fairly inflexible and didn't allow for a lot of freedom of decision making.

Although a number of countries had had gold, silver or combined gold/silver standards throughout much of the nineteenth century (and as early as the sixteenth century), the universal system that started in the 1870s was largely initiated at an international monetary congress held in Paris in 1867.[1] The system was based on the assumption that all participating currencies could ultimately be converted into gold, but in practice, once the system got under way, most global transactions were conducted in sterling or other major currencies. Britain was the dominant global economy at the time and sterling was the major world 'reserve currency' – much as the United States dollar is today. Foreign exchange surpluses would be offset against other foreign exchange deficits and only imbalances that couldn't be settled through offsets were settled by the movement of gold between countries. The system worked against persistent imbalances by putting downward pressure on a country's income and prices if it was suffering persistent balance-of-payments deficits. This downward pressure was not good for the country's economic growth and job creation – and generally gave the affected country little economic policy leeway or autonomy – but it did make its exports more competitive and lowered its hunger for imports, both of which tended to correct its balance-of-payments position. The role of Britain was crucial to the workings of the system. Britain tended to run trade deficits but had net income from its overseas loans and investments that more than compensated for the trade deficits. Britain had a structure of global trade and global loans and investment that ensured its balance-of-payments imbalances never got too small or too large.[2] The presence of a large, dominant, moderating economy like Britain's, whose balance-of-payments imbalances never got too much out of whack, was a major factor behind the effective operation of this early exchange rate system (and the absence of such a large, moderating economy was a major factor behind the ineffectiveness of the later revived gold standard system and the subsequent Bretton Woods system). Britain kept itself in the middle of the global currency/balance-of-payments see saw of the first system and was able to absorb the fluctuations of the rest of the world; as a result its currency commanded a lot of confidence during this period. However, the start of the First World War, and the sharply divided camps into which it forced the world's major economies, saw the end of this successful gold standard system.

The gold standard system from the mid-1920s to the early 1930s

After the disruption of the First World War there was a short-lived attempt to revive the gold standard exchange rate system from the mid-1920s to the early 1930s. Its short life was mainly a result of the disappearance, by the mid-1920s, of the unique conditions that had allowed the first gold standard to work so well before the First World War. The most important changed conditions were: the weaker postwar trade performance of Britain, the transformation of Germany from a large pre-war creditor nation (that is, one that had money invested in other countries) to a large post-war debtor nation (that is, one that owed a lot of money to other countries), a French economy that sucked in large amounts of gold from the rest of the world through persistent balance-of-payments surpluses, and the emergence of the United States after the First World War as the dominant global economy.

For a short time the revived gold standard worked well with US trade surpluses with Europe, on the one hand, balanced out by a high level of foreign investment by the US in Europe and a large trade deficit between the US and its non-European trading partners on the other.[3] The system pivoted around the United States just as the pre-war system pivoted around Britain. But the US was not able to fill the shoes of Britain. It had less experience than Britain as a global investor, its money market was less connected to changes in its balance of payments, and its global trade was less important to it than it had been to the British.[4] All of this made the US less outward-looking than the British economy had been and less able to absorb the economic fluctuations of the rest of the world. This became all too apparent in 1929 when increased US interest rates and a boom in its stock market saw its lending and investment withdrawn from the rest of the world with the result that the delicate balance of global payments came crashing down. The crippling effect of the withdrawal of US funds was compounded by the collapse of the delicate financial relationship that existed between major European countries after the First World War. Before the First World War there had been little inter-governmental borrowing between the world's major economies, but after the war Europe's major economies had large debts with each other and with the United States in particular.[5] European economies sought to cover their loans repayments with war reparations from Germany but when those collapsed the whole European/US loan web came unstuck. In September 1931 the British withdrew sterling from the revived gold standard and the whole system basically came to an end. The termination of the scheme and the delicate web of balances it supported was confirmed at a World Economic Conference held in 1933 where newly elected US President Roosevelt said he would put the interests of the (then very depressed) US economy before those of the global economy.[6]

The Bretton Woods exchange rate system

As detailed in Chapter 2, in July 1944 some 730 delegates from 44 countries met in the New Hampshire town of Bretton Woods to map out a post-war global economic system. A paramount aim of the conference was to design a system that would avoid the extremes of the Great Depression. Central to this was to be the creation of a new fixed exchange rate system. The system that the conference (in reality mainly the United States) came up with was one that linked all the world's major currencies to the US dollar via (relatively) fixed exchange rates with the US dollar which in turn was convertible into gold. The new fixed exchange rate system was central to a US desire to create a post-war economic environment of uninhibited world trade – the biographer of John Maynard Keynes, Robert Skidelsky, says the Bretton Woods agreement was shaped 'by the US desire for an updated gold standard as a means of liberalising trade'.[7] In many ways the new system was similar to the earlier gold fixed exchange rate systems except that it was squarely centred on the United States and it allowed for more exchange rate variability than the earlier systems had – in many ways the system was a compromise between the rigid gold standard system that operated from the 1870s to the First World War and the laissez-faire system that mainly operated throughout the 1920s and 1930s.[8] The Bretton Woods exchange rate system was meant to be the mechanism that would nudge the balance of payments of different economies back to neutral; money available from the International Monetary Fund – which was also created at Bretton Woods – would give them the short-term foreign exchange needed to make the adjustment back to balance-of-payments neutrality.

From the end of the Second World War until the late 1950s and early 1960s – when the currencies of Western Europe and Japan became convertible into other currencies again – the system worked well although in reality it was little tested because of the lack of Western European and Japanese currency convertibility. But from the mid-1960s onwards the system came under attack on two fronts. The first was a massive expansion in the volume of cross-border financial transactions. From the early 1960s, more and more transnational banks became vehicles for large flows of global finance. In 1965 only 13 US-based banks had overseas branches but by the end of 1974 125 did – this allowed them to borrow from each other instead of seeking more formal loans. The assets of the overseas branches of US banks rose from about US$9 billion in 1965 to over US$125 billion in 1974.[9] The large increase in overseas branches and overseas assets of US banks meant the country rapidly became connected with the newly globalising world economy. The second front of attack was the economy of the United States itself. There were two problems there. One was that by the late 1960s the US dollar was significantly overvalued, partly because of inflation caused by its spending on the Vietnam War[10] and President Johnson's Great Society programme (a government initiative that included enhanced civil rights and increased welfare spending). The overvaluation led to an outflow of investment from the US and a deteriorating trade balance which in the 1970s began to slip consistently into deficit for the first time in the twentieth century.[11] The second problem was the attitude of the United States government towards these problems. Much as in the 1930s, it tended to be dismissive of the impact of its economic policies on the rest of the world; it tended to be fairly relaxed about its deteriorating balance-of-payments situation because it knew the rest of the world would keep propping it up through the status of the US dollar as the global reserve currency. This caused resentment in Europe and Japan, resentment which was compounded by their view that much of the US government's excessive deficit spending went on belligerent unilateral wars[12] (in an eerie pre-echo of today's situation). Until 1965 the Bretton Woods system still looked like it had a long-term future, but growing inflation in the US fuelled by its refusal to cover increased government spending by increased taxes (another pre-echo of today) and the ever-deteriorating US balance-of-payments situation sent the Bretton Woods system into paralysis in 1968. But the US continued to be relaxed about its ongoing deteriorating balance of payments, thinking the rest of the world would keep coming to its rescue. The then US Under Secretary of the Treasury, Beryl Sprinkel, even infamously told the world in 1971 'it may be our dollar, but it is their problem'.[13] In the spring and summer of 1971, however, there was a run on the US dollar and the US government was finally forced to act. On 15 August 1971 US President Nixon ended the Bretton Woods exchange rate system when he announced that the US dollar would no longer be convertible into gold and that the US would impose a new 10 per cent tariff on imports. Panicked, Nixon had not bothered to consult with the other major members of the global monetary system. The Bretton

Woods system was dead and buried and a new *ad hoc*, laissez-faire system of global exchange rates took its place.

The experience of the three fixed exchange rate systems used between the 1880s and the 1970s demonstrated that they didn't necessarily guarantee benign balance-of-payments balances. Both the 1930s and the Bretton Woods exchange rate systems failed to deliver on that front. They were only a partial insurance against large balance-of-payments imbalances because they depended on the dominant global economy of the time to moderate global imbalances. Britain was able to fill that role in the first fixed exchange rate system but was too weak after the First World War to do so any longer, and the US also was unable to fill it in the second and third attempts at using the system. Fixed exchange rate systems are a clumsy and unreliable method of ensuring the world doesn't slip into unsustainable balance-of-payments imbalances. They only work when the right ingredients exist – the world therefore needs a more surefire method of restraining global balance-of-payments imbalances.

Today's laissez-faire exchange rate system

Although the Bretton Woods system disappeared, the forces that saw to its demise did not. By 1973 it had been replaced by a system of floating exchange rates where basic demand-and-supply forces determined the value of national currencies. Although this system made for less certainty about currency values it was meant to self-correct any persistent balance-of-payments imbalances. The theory was that countries with large balance-of-payments deficits would experience a declining currency value that would make their exports cheaper, and more competitive, and at the same time the imports into their economies would become more expensive, and therefore less competitive with locally made alternatives. The reality, however, has been that the world's large balance-of-payments imbalances have not gone away, and the US balance-of-payments problem has stubbornly persisted and even got worse. The floating exchange rate system has only tinkered with the system; it has not addressed its fundamental underlying flaws.

During the 1970s the world's major economic powers began having regular meetings to coordinate the new laissez-faire floating exchange rate system. Exchange rate coordination was meant to replace exchange rate regulation. The major economic powers held a major meeting in the United States in 1971, straight after Nixon's decision, and in 1975 they began having their regular annual G7/G8 economic summits. The new system was put under a lot of strain in 1974 by the first of the two major oil price rises induced by OPEC. The OPEC price rises resulted in a large amount of Middle Eastern oil-related money coming on to the world's capital markets; a huge amount of money washed across the world's borders through a new lightly regulated Eurodollar currency market that increased the speculative pressure on the newly globalised world economy. The new volumes of oil-related capital washing around the world also allowed low-income countries to start borrowing large amounts of foreign funds for the first time (borrowing that came unstuck in the Third World debt crisis that began in the early 1980s). The US dollar generally drifted lower during the 1970s, but despite that the US trade balance stayed in deficit and the currency commanded less and less confidence with the result that it became less popular as a global reserve currency (although a majority of global foreign reserves continued to be held in US dollars). Despite well-intentioned efforts by the Carter administration in the second half of the 1970s, a panic sell-off of the US dollar in 1978 following an exchange rate accord agreed to in Bonn in the same year underscored how reluctant most economies (particularly the US) were about making adjustments that would restore faith in the global financial system.[14] The panic sell-off also showed how unreliable exchange rate coordination really was as a replacement to the Bretton Woods exchange rate system.

In 1979 the US introduced a new, monetarist policy of curbing inflation that employed high interest rates. The new policy suddenly pushed up the value of the US dollar and had several other unintended knock-on effects. One was that it pushed many low-income foreign debtor countries to the brink as they suffered simultaneous higher interest payments and lower raw material export prices. Another effect was that the higher value of the dollar played havoc with the already lacklustre US trade balance. It demonstrated in all too stark terms how intertwined trade flows and capital flows had become in the ever-globalising world – each kept interfering with the other and neither could be treated separately to the other any more. The US trade deficit blew out from US$35 billion in 1979 to more than US$100 billion by 1984.[15] By 1985 the world's exchange rates were seriously misaligned and huge balance-of-payments imbalances had opened up. The situation was made worse, once again, by: chronic US government overspending, high US economic growth sucking in large volumes of imports, the shift of the US economy from being a net global creditor/investor to being a net global debtor, and the unilateralist attitude towards economic issues adopted by the Reagan administration. In 1985 another major summit was held to coordinate global exchange rates – this one in New York – that would lower the value of the dollar. The New York accord, like the 1978 Bonn exchange rate accord, had mixed results and caused a lot of disagreement about exchange rates among the world's major economic powers. The accord was successful in dramatically lowering the value of the dollar (it fell by nearly 30 per cent in the second half of the 1980s) but Japan felt it had fallen too far while the US wanted it to fall further. A follow-up conference to resolve the differences was held in France in 1987, but fear that the meeting hadn't managed to resolve very much contributed to the global stockmarket collapse later that year and generally gave global exchange rate coordination a bad name. The large fall in the US dollar did vastly improve the US trade balance, however, and its overall balance-of-payments imbalance was back to modest levels by the early 1990s so it looked for a short time as if the US balance-of-payments problem had gone away and that therefore the future of world trade was fairly secure.

A major US gripe from those days – one that persists to this very day – is that the US shoulders much of the responsibility for world economic growth by pursuing high-growth policies whereas, from a US perspective, the Europeans and Japanese do not promote high growth enough and live off the US. The Europeans and Japanese, however, see the US economy as ill-disciplined, unable to live within its means and ultimately reckless with the health of the global economy. Both points of view are legitimate ways of looking at the US balance-of-payments dilemma.

After the brief hiatus at the start of the 1990s the US trade balance and its balance-of-payments situation deteriorated again throughout the 1990s. By the end of the decade the US balance-of-payments problem had well and truly returned (after a strengthening of the dollar in the second half of the 1990s) but it is now much worse than it has ever been before. Current account deficits are basically the sum of trade deficits and deficits on the interest and dividends that enter and leave a country. In the mid-1980s the US current account deficit was equal to about 3 per cent of its gross domestic product but by 2004 it was equal to double that – about 6 per cent of its GDP (over 90 per cent of which is accounted for by its trade deficit) – the highest it has ever been. In 1995 the annual US trade deficit was US$172 billion but by 2004 it had blown out to more than three times that at US$569 billion.[16] One of the ironies of the widening US current account and trade deficits is that both grew considerably worse during the presidency of the free trade champion Bill Clinton, who was instrumental in bringing the Uruguay Round to a close and in establishing the North American Free Trade Agreement. Another irony is that the US trade deficit got much worse during the life of the WTO. By 2004 – a decade after the establishment of the WTO – the US trade deficit was five times larger than it had been in 1994. The *Economist* magazine says the US economy today 'resembles a rich man who has discovered credit-card bingeing late in life'.[17] It is very difficult, in fact, not to liken the US profligacy with oil to its profligacy with global money. It's hard to not to conclude that the US is irresponsible in its use of both. Catherine Mann, of the US-based Institute for International Economics, even predicts that by 2010 the US current account will blow out to more than 12 per cent of its gross domestic product – a level of major economy balance-of-payments imbalance the world has never experienced before.[18] A US current account deficit of this size will put enormous strain on the world economy. In past decades the US

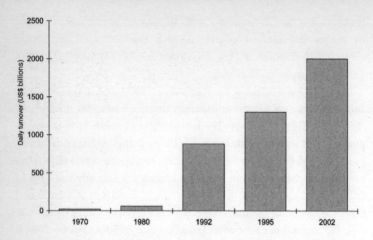

Figure 8.1 Increase in world currency turnover, 1970 to 2002

Note: Currency turnover is all foreign currency bought and sold around the world on any one day for any purpose including for international trade, investment and borrowing.
Source: The *Economist*, 23 September 1995, p. 73, for 1970, 1980 and 1995 figures.

economy would not have been able to sustain current account deficits of this size but particularly since the early 1990s the world's currency markets have become highly integrated, with increasing exchange of national currencies, and it is now easier for the US to call on the rest of the world to finance these deficits than it has ever been before.

During the 1980s the US often blamed its large trade deficits on West Germany and Japan (even though they frequently financed the United States' current account deficits), then after German reunification and the end of the Cold War the US tended to blame just Japan. Now they blame China (even though China only accounts for about 10 per cent of all US imports and about a fifth of the US trade deficit). As in the 1980s, the worsening US balance-of-trade in the 1990s was aggravated by an overvalued dollar. Today the global loan balance is just as precarious and fragile as was the balance of intergovernmental loans after the First World War; and things could spectacularly fall apart as they did after the stockmarket crash of 1929. Since late 2000 Japan, China, South Korea and Taiwan have doubled their holdings of

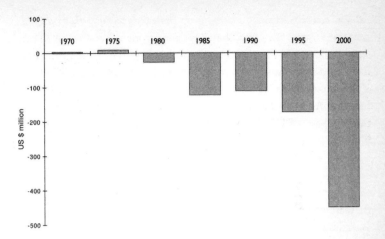

Figure 8.2 The US balance of trade, 1963 to 2003

Source: Data downloaded from www.datastream.com/welcome.htm in 2004.

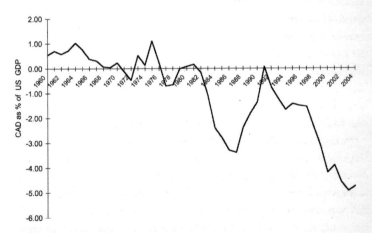

Figure 8.3 The US current account deficit (CAD), 1960 to 2004

Source: OECD, *Economic Outlook No. 74*, Paris, 2003

foreign reserves through chalking up persistent balance-of-payments surpluses;[19] since the 1990s they have gone from holding about 30 per cent of the world's foreign reserves to holding more than half. They have used their large foreign reserve stocks to purchase US dollars. This means that today a lot of trade money is pouring out of the US into East Asia and then being recycled back into the US economy via the purchase of US dollars by the central banks of East Asia. They purchase large volumes of US dollars because keeping the US dollar at a relatively high level means their currencies can stay at relatively low, competitive levels (several East Asian currencies are even pegged to the US dollar). East Asian businesses are very enthusiastic traders and they are therefore generally keen to keep their currency values low and competitive. In 2003 alone, central banks throughout Asia financed more than half the US current account deficit.

The US, for its part, feels that East Asian currency values are being kept at levels that are far too low and that the Chinese yuan, in particular, needs to appreciate. And the US government continues to feel that it is propping up the rest of the world by providing much of its economic growth. Since 1995 almost 60 per cent of the world's cumulative economic growth has taken place in the United States.[20] To some extent the US government feels the rest of the world has a duty to keep financing its ever-widening balance-of-payments deficits. But we now have a very fraught financial co-dependency between East Asian surplus economies and the US deficit economy. The co-dependency could come unstuck at any moment and could cause a massive economic slowdown in the US, and therefore around the world, when it does.

Jim O'Neill, chief economist at the global US investment bank Goldman Sachs, claims the delicate balance could end when East Asia decides the American market isn't so important to it any more and therefore from their perspective isn't worth propping up any longer. He says East Asian central banks will then drop the dollar, which will then come crashing down with 'potentially catastrophic' consequences.[21] Other commentators argue that over time Asian savings rates will decline because of Asia's ageing population and the more free-spending habits of the younger generation, and that this decline will also reduce the East Asian banks' ability to keep propping up the US current account deficits. The central banks may also stop holding US dollars if they fear the currency will lose a lot of value. If, and when, any of these happen the rest of the world will suffer along with the US. For some time the US has been becoming more protectionist about trade. During the 2004 presidential elections the Democrat challenger, John Kerry, often spoke about 'Benedict Arnold corporations' that leave the US to set up in lower-wage countries; President George W, Bush, meanwhile, has extended various forms of protection to US industries including steel and agriculture. Even if the United States doesn't turn decidedly more protectionist, a major fall in the dollar will at the very least induce a major loss of confidence in the US economy which will dramatically lower both US and global economic growth.

The United States is not the only high-income country to have had a large balance-of-payments deficit. Other high-income countries such as Australia, New Zealand, Portugal, Greece and Ireland currently run large current-account deficits, and in the nineteenth century then quite well-off countries such as Canada and Argentina ran large balance-of-payments deficits. But two things set the current situation of the United States apart. One is that the US is the world's largest economy (equal to 21 or 31 per cent of the world's total gross domestic product depending on what currency conversion method you use), and the other is that its heavy global borrowing is happening during a new age of unprecedented availability of global money in which the rules and boundaries are uncertain and untested. Today money is more globally mobile than it has ever been before but no one knows what the limits of the availability of global money for a high-income country are. Money markets haven't bailed out in a big way on any high-income economy over the past twenty years like they did the East Asian economies during the meltdown of 1997 or the Argentinian economy during its debt crisis of 2002 or the Mexican economy during its debt crises of 1982 and 1994. But such a high-income-economy panic could yet happen, and it is most likely to happen with the United States. If and when it does happen it will bring both US and global economic growth – and US and global trade – down with it. The ever-widening US current account deficits are not only making the US more protectionist but also threatening long-term confidence in the world's largest trade market – this does not bode well for global trade.

Keynes's alternative balance-of-payments proposal

There have been many proposals for systems that could act as brakes on large and persistent balance-of-payments imbalances. Fixed exchange rate systems are not a reliable insurance against large balance-of-payments imbalances, and the world needs something that is. The best-known system to moderate balance-of-payments imbalances was developed by John Maynard Keynes, the famous British economist best known for his work on post-First World War reparations in the 1920s, for his 1936 landmark book, *The General Theory of Employment, Interest and Money*, and for his part in the 1944 Bretton Woods conference. In 1941 Keynes developed a scheme that would place significant limits on the extent to which countries could run up large balance-of-payments deficits or surpluses. At the time he developed his scheme there was concern that Britain would finish the Second World War with large balance-of-payments deficits and that the United States would come out of the war with large balance-of-payments surpluses that it would horde and not use in a way that could help other countries, like Britain, climb out of their deficits. Keynes thought it was important to have a global balance-of-payments adjustment system that would put equal pressure on both deficit and surplus countries. He thought one of the major reasons for the failure of the 1930s gold standard scheme was that adjustment was '*compulsory* for the debtor and *voluntary* for the creditor'.[22] He also argued – in eerie anticipation of the Third World debt crisis that began in the 1980s – that simply providing loans to countries with balance-of-payments problems (as the International Monetary Fund does) doesn't necessarily solve balance-of-payments problems unless those loan funds generate new sources of foreign exchange.[23] Keynes's balance-of-payments scheme was inspired by a pre-war German scheme developed by the German finance minister Hjalmar Schacht, who developed a system of bilateral 'barter trade' in which the exports from one country to another would necessarily be balanced by the return exports back from that country.[24]

Skidelsky claims that what Keynes was best at was 'constructing a realizable utopia'.[25] The balance-of-payments scheme Keynes developed was very much an example of this. He wanted to challenge the United States and argued that his scheme assumed 'a higher degree of understanding' and 'bold innovation'.[26] His proposal was encapsulated in what he called an 'International Currency Union'. The International Currency Union would seek adjustment by both surplus and deficit economies. All international transactions that resulted in either balance-of-payments surpluses or deficits would have to be settled through 'clearing accounts' held in what he called the 'International Clearing Bank'.[27] All nations would have a quota with the bank equal to half their average trade over the previous five years. Countries that ran balance-of-payments deficits equal to more than half their quota would be 'supervised' and required to depreciate their currency as well as to sell the International Clearing Bank any free gold they had. They would also be prohibited from allowing any flight of money to overseas havens. Interest would be charged on large deficits and a country that persistently ran up large deficits could be expelled from the International Currency Union.[28] Conversely, Keynes also proposed that any economy that persistently ran up large surpluses would be required to appreciate its currency, unblock its foreign exchange reserves and overseas investments, and be required to pay interest on surpluses that were equal to more than a quarter of its quota. Surpluses that exceeded 100 per cent of a country's quota at the end of a year would be confiscated and transferred to the bank.[29] Above all, the aim of Keynes's scheme was to maintain balance-of-payments equilibrium between countries.

In recent years some members of the global justice movement, including British author George Monbiot (see Chapter 9) have begun calling for a reconsideration of Keynes's scheme. The floating exchange rate theory that currencies will automatically adjust to a level that will ensure balance-of-payments equilibriums has not worked. High-income countries such as the United States, Australia and Portugal have had balance-of-payments deficits for decades now while other countries, including Germany, Japan and China, have had equally persistent balance-of-payments surpluses. The 'invisible hand' of Adam Smith simply isn't working in today's global economy, and we need a more interventionist system in place before our laissez-faire system catches up with us. The time to revisit Keynes's visionary proposal is well and truly upon us.

The trade plight of least developed countries

It is not just large, rich countries such as the United States that have a problem with persistent balance-of-payments deficits. At the other end of the spectrum least developed countries (LDCs) – the poorest of the low-income countries – do as well. There are currently 191 members of the United Nations of whom about 50 – roughly a quarter – are considered LDCs. Poverty estimates undertaken by both the World Bank and UNCTAD indicate that almost half the combined population of the LDCs live on less than US$1 per day.[30] The number of people caught in LDC poverty is currently about a third of a billion and is forecast to rise to about half a billion by 2015.[31] Like the United States nearly all the LDCs have high and persistent trade deficits. In 1999–2001 the combined trade deficit of the LDCs was equal to 23 per cent of their imports.[32] This is massive by anyone's standards. During the same period, in 25 of 44 LDCs for which data is available the trade deficit was equal to more than 10 per cent of their gross domestic products and in 8 of them the trade deficit was equal to more than 20 per cent of GDP.[33] These huge trade deficits are generally financed by debt, foreign aid and remittances from local workers working in foreign countries.

Restriction of trade is not the reason for the large LDC trade deficits. During 1999–2001 the combined value of LDC imports and exports equalled 51 per cent of their GDPs which is higher than the equivalent percentage for high-income countries (which averaged 43 per cent over the same period).[34] There has been extensive liberalisation of trade in LDCs since the late 1980s, generally as part of IMF and World Bank loan conditionality, and very little further liberalisation can be undertaken in their economies.[35] The bleak LDC trade situation is compounded by the fact that most LDCs are losing trade share and what trade they do manage to hang on to isn't reducing their poverty levels. Amongst those LDCs that mainly export agricultural products, by 2001 their share of world trade was only 56 per cent of its level in 1980; amongst those that mainly export minerals it was only 16 per cent of its 1980 level.[36] Loss of trade market share is particularly acute for Africa. In 1980 Africa exported 6.3 per cent of all global merchandise exports but by 2000 this share had collapsed to 2.5 per cent.[37]

UNCTAD says that amongst LDCs 'it is clear that the potential role of trade in poverty reduction is not working as expected'.[38] What UNCTAD called 'the virtuous trade effect' of poverty reduction was present in only 22 of the 51 LDC cases they examined.[39] During the 1990s export growth was even associated with declining per capita GDPs in about a third of all LDCs.[40] UNCTAD says the ability of trade to reduce poverty in LDCs is breaking down 'because export expansion is not associated with an inclusive form of economic growth that is poverty-reducing'.[41] UNCTAD argues that export growth often takes place in LDCs in enclaves that have weak links with the rest of the economy, particularly with the agricultural sector where most of the population of LDCs work.[42] UNCTAD says 'it is unlikely an export-led growth strategy will of itself lead to a virtuous trade–poverty relationship in the LDCs', and it concurs with an LDC representative to the United Nations and WTO who once described most LDCs as 'galloping in the darkness'.[43]

The perils of raw material export dependency

The big trade problem for LDCs is that most are dependent on raw materials for the bulk of their export income, and the prices of raw materials for a very long time have been on a long-term slide. Raw materials are a very weak export base for a country to have. Of the 30 countries in the world with the lowest human development index (an index that combines economic and social indicators) 26 are highly dependent on agricultural produce or minerals for a large part of their export income.[44] In 2001 three agricultural crops alone made up 63 per cent of the exports of Kenya; three export crops – also made up 68 per cent of Rwanda's exports, 42 per cent of Tanzania's, 70 per cent of Malawi's, 75 per cent of Ethiopia's, 89 per cent of Burundi's and 51 per cent of Guinea-Bissau's.[45] In 1996 some 23 nations derived 80 per cent or more of their total export income from one raw material; another 21 derived 60 to 80 per cent from one raw material and a further 21 derived 40 to 59 per cent.[46] UNCTAD says that out of 141 low-income countries in the world, 95 rely on raw materials (including oil) for at least half their export income.[47]

Raw materials are on a long-term losing streak. Although they have experienced small price rises over the past few years, in the long term they are losing value. According to the World Bank, over the period from 1990 to 2003 the prices of non-energy raw materials coming from low-income countries in general (not just LDCs), fell by 8.5 per cent.[48] Throughout the twentieth century there was an even more pronounced long-term downward trend in the prices raw material exports fetched – with only occasional interruptions. Today non-fuel raw materials only command, on average, prices about half what they commanded in the mid-1970s and only one third of their levels of 1900.[49] The *Economist* magazine has kept an index of industrial commodities (raw materials, excluding oil and precious metals) since 1845 – today it is a massive 75 per cent below its starting point back then.[50]

The main problem behind the long-term slide in raw material prices is that the world demand for raw materials is getting seriously out of line with world supply. On the supply side, poor-country shortages of foreign earnings, needed to pay for imports and debt servicing, have meant poor countries have a big incentive to keep pouring raw materials on to the world market, almost regardless of price, in the desperate hope that sheer quantity will make up for falling prices (with often disastrous consequences for the environment whose resources are plundered for ever-diminishing returns). Coffee is one of the worst examples of this – between 1980 and 2000 global exports of coffee increased by 60 per cent but the total earnings from coffee over that period declined by 18 per cent.[51] Ever more sophisticated development technology has allowed poor countries to open up new mines, develop new plantations and extract more produce from existing farms etcetera, all of which has increased global raw material supply. But on the demand side, the world is consuming raw materials in more and more efficient ways or is increasingly consuming goods and services that don't use a lot of raw materials. The amount of wheat needed to make a given quantity of bread is falling, the amount of iron ore needed to make a given quantity of steel is falling and the world produces ever-increasing volumes of paper without increasing its wood use. Plastics and synthetics are replacing metals and natural fibres, while increasingly affluent consumers are buying services rather than raw-material-intensive goods as their post-war parents did. None of this makes for good news on the raw material export price front.

UNCTAD says that, if anything, trade liberalisation in LDCs has made their raw material dependency worse. It argues that 'in general, the process of trade liberalisation in the LDCs has reinforced specialisation in commodity [raw material] exports rather than promoted a shift to manufactured exports'.[52] It also argues that 'the major sin of omission in the current international approach to poverty reduction is the failure to tackle the link between commodity dependence and extreme poverty'.[53] UNCTAD says resolving the problem of declining raw material export prices is pivotal to eradicating the world's worst poverty and that 'any measures in relation to commodities are likely to have a high poverty-reduction intensity in the LDCs'.[54]

Raw material export price stability schemes

The problem of the slide in raw material export prices has been around for a long time, and there have been two major attempts to establish schemes that would stabilise raw material prices – these attempts took place in the 1930s and the 1970s. The 1930s saw steep declines in raw material prices, so during that decade agreements were struck between leading raw material export countries and major raw material import countries that covered the production and marketing of particular raw materials. These agreements covered raw material such as tin (1931), sugar (1931), tea (1933), wheat (1933), rubber (1934) and copper (1936).[55] The schemes partly grew out of agreements struck in the 1920s between private raw material cartels as a result of attempts by some governments to deal with raw material surpluses. The schemes varied in their effectiveness but had a significant influence on the prices of tea, tin and rubber while having a moderate influence on the prices of sugar and copper.[56] The schemes were generally well organised and were a good example of what intergovernmental cooperation could achieve during a period that was famous for its lack of such cooperation. The schemes were finally killed off by the outbreak of the Second World War.

During the 1970s a second round of attempts aimed at stabilising raw material prices was stimulated both by the success of OPEC in raising oil prices during that decade and by the decline in raw material prices during the mid-1970s (although the idea first took root in the 1950s – stabilisation schemes for coffee, sugar, tin and wheat were established in the 1950s and 1960s). During the 1944 Bretton Woods negotiations, raw material price stabilisation schemes were considered but were ultimately dropped.[57] The 1970s schemes were mainly cooperative agreements between exporting countries and did not involve agreements struck with importing countries. Producer organisations were established for a number of raw materials. The agreements generally attempted to influence raw material prices through some, or all, of three different mechanisms: increases in raw material export taxes; restriction of raw material supply and management of raw material buffer stocks.[58] In 1980 it was proposed that the agreements be augmented by the establishment of a Common Fund for Commodities – a central raw materials financing mechanism that was promoted by UNCTAD – but it never got off the ground because of insufficient support within the United Nations. Some of the schemes were quite successful but many only had limited effectiveness and most fell apart by the end of the 1980s. The first major agreement to fall apart was the World Tin Agreement in 1985; the rest soon followed. Among the several reasons for their failure were that some countries wanted to break ranks to get larger market shares, raw material transnational corporations resisted the schemes, higher raw material prices resulted in lower demand and competition from substitute materials. A major factor that finally killed off the schemes was the start of the Third World debt crisis in 1982. The debt crisis hugely increased the power and influence of the World Bank and the IMF over low-income countries. They generally pursue a free-market agenda that is fundamentally opposed to schemes like the raw material price stabilisation schemes. Amongst other things, interventions by the IMF and World Bank have seen an end to the government-run raw material marketing boards in low-income countries that could have helped facilitate raw material price stabilization schemes. About 40 per cent of the world's economies have been under the management of the World Bank or the IMF since the start of the Third World debt crisis.

Despite the IMF and World Bank opposition to 'anti-market' raw material price stabilisation schemes, many non-government groups, including Oxfam, have started calling for their reintroduction (see Chapter 9). People are realising that there is never likely to be an end to the slide in raw material prices and the call for a third wave of price stabilisation schemes is getting louder and louder. A major problem in resuscitating such schemes is the fact that transnational corporations (TNCs) have tightened their grip on the trade in raw materials since the 1970s. Today just five TNCs control more than 80 per cent of the global banana market[59], just six control about 85 per cent of the world grain trade, eight control up to 60 per cent of world coffee sales and seven account for 90 per cent of all the tea drunk in Western countries.[60] But TNC power should not stop such schemes being established.

For both high- and low-income countries the current laissez-fare approach to global balance of payments imbalances is creating a huge problem that is getting worse. The time has come for sensible regulation of global balance of payments through both a scheme like Keynes's International Currency Union and through raw material price stabilisation schemes. Such regulation shouldn't stifle global trade initiative but it should recognise that persistent imbalances have a price – a price that, ultimately, all the world's citizens have to pay.

Notes

1   A.G. Kenwood and A.L. Lougheed, *The Growth of the International Economy 1820–1990: An Introductory Text*, Routledge, London, 1983, p. 107.

2   Ibid., p. 116.

3   Ibid., pp. 184–185.

4   Ibid., p. 186.

5   Roger E. Backhouse, *The Penguin History of Economics*, Penguin Books, London, 2002, p. 216.

6   James Foreman-Peck, *A History of the World Economy: International Economic Relations since 1850*, Barnes and Noble Books, Totowa (New Jersey), 1983, p. 247.

7   Robert Skidelsky, *John Maynard Keynes 1883–1946: Economist, Philosopher, Statesman*, Pan Books, London, 2003, p. 767

8   Robert Gilpin, *The Challenge of Global Capitalism: The World Economy in the 21st Century*, Princeton University Press, Princeton, 2000, p. 59.

9   Joan E. Spero and Jeffrey A. Hart, *The Politics of International Economic Relations: Fifth Edition*, Routledge, London, 1997, p. 16.

10 Ibid., p. 18.

11 Ibid., p. 21.

12 Ibid., p. 19.

13 Robert Gilpin, *The Challenge of Global Capitalism*, p. 230.

14 Spero and Hart, *The Politics of International Economic Relations*, p. 35.

15 Ibid., p. 38.

16 *Economist* 1 April 1995, p. 135, and *Economist*, 3 July 2004, p. 93.

17 'Flying on one engine: A survey of the world economy', *Economist*, 20 September 2003, p. 8.

18 Fred Bergsten, 'The risks ahead for the world economy', *Economist*, 11 September 2004, pp. 63–64.

19 'Competitive sport in Boca Raton', *Economist*, 5 February 2004, p. 62.

20 'Flying on one engine: A survey of the world economy', *Economist*, p. 3.

21 'A Central Question', *Economist*, 13 December 2003, p. 72.

22 Robert Skidelsky, *John Maynard Keynes: Volume Three, Fighting for Britain 1937–1946*, Macmillan, London, 2000, p. 204.

23 Ibid.

24 Skidelsky, *John Maynard Keynes 1883–1946: Economist, Philosopher, Statesman*, pp. 672–673.

25 Skidelsky, *John Maynard Keynes: Volume Three, Fighting for Britain*, p. 208.

26 Ibid., p. 205.

27 Ibid., p. 206.

28 Ibid.

29 Ibid.

30 United Nations Conference on Trade and Development, *The Least Developed Countries Report 2004: Overview by the Secretary-General of UNCTAD*, United Nations, New York and Geneva, 2004, p. 2, downloaded from www.unctad.org in 2004.

31 Ibid.

32 United Nations Conference on Trade and Development, *UNCTAD Handbook of Statistics 2002*, United Nations, New York and Geneva, 2002, p. 33.

33 United Nations Conference on Trade and Development, *The Least Developed Countries Report 2004*, p. 6.

34 Ibid., p. 5.

35 Ibid., p. 16.

36 Ibid., p. 9.

37 United Nations Conference on Trade and Development, *Economic Development in Africa: Trade Performance and Commodity Dependence*, United Nations, New York and Geneva, 2003, p. 5, downloaded from www.uncatd.org in 2004.

38 United Nations Conference on Trade and Development, *The Least Developed Countries Report 2004*, p. 10.

39 Ibid.

40 Ibid., p. 11.

41 Ibid., p. 12.

42 Ibid., p. 12.

43 Ibid., p. 23.

44 Thomas Lines, *Commodities Trade, Poverty Alleviation and Sustainable Development: The Re-emerging Debate*, published by author, Oxford, 2004, p. 5 (available by sending an email to: tlines@globalnet.co.uk).

45 Ibid., pp. 29–31.

46 Worldwatch Institute, *Vital Signs 2001–2002: The trends that are shaping our future*, Earthscan, London, 2001, p. 122.

47 United Nations Conference on Trade and Development, *Issues in Brief*

Number 3, Commodities: Bold Solution Needed, p. 1, downloaded from www.unctad.org in 2004.

48   Lines, *Commodities Trade, Poverty Alleviation and Sustainable Development*, p.6.

49   Worldwatch Institute, *Vital Signs 2001–2002*, p. 122.

50   Pam Woodall, 'The Dragon and the Eagle: A Survey of the World Economy', *Economist*, 2 October 2004, p. 12.

51   Lines, *Commodities Trade, Poverty Alleviation and Sustainable Development*, p. 13.

52   United Nations Conference on Trade and Development, *The Least Developed Countries Report 2004*, p. 19.

53   Ibid., p. 27.

54   Ibid.

55   Kenwood and Lougheed, *The Growth of the International Economy 1820–1990*, p. 206.

56   Ibid.

57   Skidelsky, *John Maynard Keynes 1883–1946: Economist, Philosopher, Statesman*, p. 757.

58   Spero and Hart, *The Politics of International Economic Relations*, pp. 306–312.

59   Lines, *Commodities Trade, Poverty Alleviation and Sustainable Development*, p. 16.

60   John Madeley, *Hungry for Trade: How the Poor Pay for Free Trade*, Zed Books, London, 2000, p. 91.

9

The policies of the global justice movement

Rarely a month goes by these days without the media carrying a story about an anti-globalisation protest. They are ubiquitous. The World Trade Organisation, like the leaders of the G-8 countries and the European Union, can't meet without being greeted by massive protests. Many people think the groups behind these protests are just anarchists and rabble-rousers but in fact a large network of sophisticated, articulate organisations backs the protests. These groups are becoming a major challenge to global trade in particular and to globalisation in general and must be examined when considering the future of global trade. Some refer to this network of organisations as 'the anti-globalisation movement' but this tag emphasises what they are against rather than what they are for and doesn't do justice to the policy stance of the movement. Although many alternative labels for the movement are suggested from time to time, this book will refer to it as 'the global justice movement' because at the end of the day that is what the groups are most about – justice for people and justice for the earth.

Origins of the global justice movement

The lineage of the global justice movement reaches back at least until the 1960s and 1970s. Those two decades saw the first major questioning since the 1930s of the direction of human development. In contrast to the social unrest of the 1930s the unrest of the 1960s and 1970s took place during a time of abundance – a time of high employment and unprecedented economic prosperity. For the first time people dared to question the impact development and technology were having on the environment and on our future as a species. In 1962 Rachel Carson wrote the ground-breaking book *Silent Spring* about chemical pollution, in 1968 Paul Ehrlich wrote *The Population Bomb* about overpopulation, and in 1972 the Club of Rome wrote *The Limits to Growth* about the increasing scarcity of the world's natural resources. All posed questions that people had not hitherto dared to ask, and all helped catalyse the protest movement of the 1960s that focused on issues like the Vietnam and Algerian wars. The protest movement of the 1960s paved the way for the global justice movement of the 1990s which focused on a broader range of issues including global trade. From the 1960s through to the 1990s a reaction to modernism was mounting. Post-modernism found a voice not only in art and design but in politics as well. Modern no longer meant good.

Post-modern thinking reaches beyond the issues taken up in the 1990s, it also reaches into the very structure of the global justice movement. From the start of the twentieth century right through until the 1960s left-wing groups had a near monopoly on the organisation of protest politics. Although the left sometimes paid (dubious) homage to figures such as Stalin and Mao, it had good organisational skills and was generally economically articulate and good at presenting a robust, articulate case for economic redistribution and compassion for the poor. But the new protest movement of the 1960s and 1970s was more secular and didn't necessarily align itself with the left. It focused on issues, at times, that the left wasn't necessarily strong on, like the environment and feminism, and it was far less centralised and much more atomised than the left had been. This new political and organisational *modus operandi* has continued through to today. The global justice movement is made up of thousands of different organisations some of which don't even necessarily see themselves as part of a movement. They focus on a myriad issues including the rights of indigenous people, saving forests, rivers and animals, global warming, the rights of

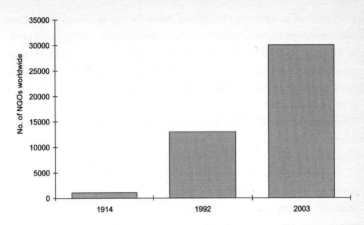

Figure 9.1 Growth of non-government organisations around the world

Source: Mike Moore, *A World Without Walls*, Cambridge, Cambridge University Press, 2003, p. 188.

women, global poverty, Third World debt relief, foreign aid, overpopulation, genetic engineering, war and non-violence, and sustainable energy to name just a few. The movement is very dispersed and decentralised both in its focus and in its structure in stark contrast to the traditional more centralised makeup of the left which tended to concentrate on a narrower range of issues.

Although the global justice movement is dispersed and seemingly chaotic at times, five broad trends have emerged within it over the past ten years. The first is that the movement is becoming increasingly dominated by non-government organisations (NGOs). These are formal organisations that often provide particular services and express political views. Aid organisations are the most conspicuous NGOs. They are generally backed up by sizable bureaucracies, have significant budgets and invariably command a high degree of community trust. In recent years they have exploded in number. In 1914 there were only about 1,000 such organisations, by the start of the 1990s there were about 13,000 and now there are about 30,000.

A second trend is that more and more groups in the global justice movement are taking root in low-income countries. Traditionally most of the organisations in the movement have been based in high-income countries, but increasingly there are protest/ advocacy groups based in low-income countries. Via Campesina, a group that represents subsistence farmers in poorer countries, as well as the vibrant Focus on the Global South organisation (based in Thailand) and the Third World Network (based in Malaysia) are examples of dynamic global justice movement groups based in low-income countries.

A third trend is that groups within the movement are becoming better at cooperating with each other. This is an important development. It means the decentralised nature of the movement can be retained but the advantages of size can also be had through better inter-group coordination. Groups are forming coalitions around key issues and key events – this gives them a louder voice without the disadvantages of centralisation.

A fourth trend is that the movement is becoming more economically articulate. Traditionally the global justice movement has not been as well versed in economics as the left and has often relied on emotion and rhetoric to carry its case. More and more, however, the movement is able to put clear economic arguments and as a result is winning increased respect.

A fifth trend has been the size and frequency of the global justice movement's protests. Protests have become the movement trademark. It was the massive protest against the WTO's meeting in Seattle in November 1999 that really put the movement's protests on the map. All hell broke loose at Seattle with 50,000 people hitting the streets to voice their opposition to the trade talks. For the first time the now familiar images of clouds of tear gas and police dressed like front-line, high-tech soldiers flooded on to people's television screens. Many thought the 'battle for Seattle' might be a one hit wonder. But the protests continued in Washington (against an IMF–World Bank meeting in April 2000), in Chiang Mai (against a meeting of the Asian Development Bank in May 2000), in Melbourne (against a meeting of the World Economic Forum in September 2000), in Prague (against an IMF–World Bank meeting in

September 2000), in Quebec City (against the Summit of the Americas in April 2001) and in Gothenburg (against a European Union summit in June 2001) amongst many other sites. The largest protest was in Genoa, Italy, in July 2001 when a massive 200,000 to 300,000 people hit the streets to protest against a G8 meeting. Two months after, the September 11th terrorist attacks in New York and Washington took place. Although confidently predicted by some as the death of the global justice movement, they ended up having only a temporary effect. Big global justice protests began again in 2002 including large ones in Washington (against IMF–World Bank meetings), Sydney (against a WTO mini-ministerial meeting) and Johannesburg (against the World Summit on Sustainable Development). The size of the protest (250,000) against the G8 meeting in Gleneagles, Scotland, in July 2005, was recent evidence of the continuing vigour of the global justice movement.

The Seattle protest wasn't the first big protest the global justice movement had staged. In 1990 trade talks held by GATT, in Brussels, were met by thousands of protestors.[1] In 1997 about 50,000 people demonstrated outside a meeting of the G8 in Birmingham[2] and again in the same year about 10,000 turned out against WTO trade talks in Geneva that included birthday celebrations for the 50th anniversary of the start of the post–Second World War free trade system.[3]

The protests have ended up being both a blessing and a blight for the global justice movement. The hugely increased profile they delivered to the movement was undoubtedly a blessing but they created an impression for some that the movement was only about opposition. Many have become convinced that the movement is all about negativity. When it comes to global trade in particular, commentators like the *Economist* magazine thunder that 'today's militant critics of globalisation … present no worked-out alternative to the present economic order. Instead, they invoke a utopia free of environmental stress, social justice and branded sportswear, harking back to a pre-industrial golden age that did not actually exist'.[4] The global justice movement *is* working up coherent alternatives, however – alternatives that go well beyond mere protest. Although there is still considerable internal disagreement, alternatives *are* taking shape within the movement.

Policy formulation by the global justice movement

The development of viable, well-articulated policy alternatives by the global justice movement has gathered great pace since the Seattle protests and has taken place on several fronts. One front has involved huge improvements in the production and dissemination of information and critiques about global trade and globalisation. Many organisations in the movement now act as vibrant clearing houses of volumes of information about global trade. Many operate powerful webpages where information and analyses about global trade are readily available. Another front has involved the successful staging of a number of large policy forums. The forums that seem to work best are ones that don't bind participants to come up with one single group view on the future direction of global economics. Respect for diversity invariably makes for more productive dialogue. The most high-profiled of these forums have been the Social Forums which have been held at both regional and international levels since 2001. World Social Forums have been held in Porto Alegre, Brazil, in 2001, 2002, 2003 and 2005, and in Mumbai, India, in 2004. After attracting about 20,000 people in 2001 they now attract over 100,000 each year. The success of the World Social Forums spawned a number of regional social forums including a Middle East Social Forum in Beirut, an African Social Forum in Belem, an Australian Social Forum in Sydney, an Indian Social Forum in Hyderabad and a European Social Forum in Genoa.

A further front of policy development has developed within the NGOs of the global justice movement. These groups are arguably at the cutting edge of policy development within the movement and over the past few years in particular they have produced some very cogent and authoritative reports on the possible future of global trade. Increasingly NGOs are attracting sharp, articulate analysts who are doing a lot to improve the economic literacy of the global justice movement. The remainder of this chapter will concentrate on the trade policies proposed by NGOs in the movement. It must be said, however, that sometimes there is unease within the movement about the increasing influence NGOs have over policy development: many feel they often dominate too much. There is no denying, however, their command of effective arguments and their ability to find the resources to articulate them to a large audience.

Common trade policies of the global justice movement

No new trade issues

The global justice movement is a very broad church, a fact that becomes immediately apparent when one reviews its trade policies. There is at least as much that divides the movement, policywise, as there is that unites it. However, some central tenants of trade policy virtually all members of the movement agree on. One of these is that no new issues, including the Singapore issues, should be introduced into trade talks (see Chapter 2). The movement is united in the belief that too many issues have already been introduced into global trade talks. In the second half of the 1990s a broad network of groups in the global justice movement formed themselves into the Our World Is Not For Sale Network (originally to fight the Multilateral Agreement on Investment being proposed by the OECD). In 2001 and 2002 they circulated a petition around the world that attracted hundreds of thousands of signatures. One of the points in the 'WTO: Shrink or Sink' petition flatly said 'there should be no new trade negotiation rounds and no new issues should be embraced by the WTO'.[5] Aileen Kwa, from Focus on the Global South, similarly argues that 'developing countries should insist on dropping the Singapore issues from the Doha Development Agenda and from the WTO since there was no explicit consensus to launch any of the negotiations at the Fifth Ministerial, as instructed in the Doha Declaration'.[6] Martin Khor of the Third World Network similarly says about the Singapore issues that 'the best option is to decide to take these issues out of the WTO negotiating agenda for once and for all'.[7]

The global justice movement's hostility to new trade issues extends to a deep unease about past expansions of the global trade agenda including the TRIPS and GATS agreements. The movement generally feels that both these agreements should be scrapped or at the very least significantly limited in their effect. Friends of the Earth simply says that it 'opposes the continuation of the WTO's General Agreement on Trade in Services (GATS)'.[8] The World Development Movement advocates something similar, arguing that 'no further GATS negotiations should take place while there are still grave concerns over the impact of the agreement on the poor'.[9] The 'WTO: Shrink or Sink' petition also said the GATS agreement should be scrapped and that issues such as health, education, energy distribution and other basic human services should not be subject to international free trade rules.[10]

The movement's position on the TRIPS agreement is somewhat more qualified than its blanket opposition to the GATS agreement but is still largely oppositional. Christian Aid echoes the position of many groups in arguing that 'intellectual property issues should be negoti-ated through the UN, not the WTO'.[11] World Vision says the TRIPS agreement needs to be brought into line with the Convention on Biodiversity and that innovative solutions are needed to ensure low-income countries are not left with major financial burdens from high-income country patents.[12] Greenpeace simply says 'there should be no patents on life forms'.[13] Oxfam has a quite detailed policy on intellectual property rights. It says the duration of patents operating in low-income countries should be reduced, that low-income country public health interests should have priority over patent rights (including being able to access drugs from the cheapest possible source), that plants essential for food should not be patentable, that low-income countries should be able to develop their own unique plant patent systems, and that the TRIPS agreement should be brought into line with the UN Convention on Biological Diversity and the International Treaty on Plant Genetic Resources for Food and Agriculture.[14]

Special and different treatment for low-income countries

Another consensual plank of global justice movement trade policy concerns the issue of special trade agreement rights for low-income countries. The movement generally believes low-income countries should be more leniently treated by global trade rules than high-income countries are. They believe that low-income countries cannot necessarily compete in trade markets as ably as high-income countries can and should therefore receive concessionary treatment. They feel low-income countries should receive what is known as 'special and different treatment'. Christian Aid asserts that 'developing countries must be given special and different treatment, which allows them to use trade policy in an interventionist and flexible manner'. [15] World Vision similarly argues that 'developing countries require special and different treatment in the provisions of WTO rules and their implementation'.[16] Oxfam argues for the 'strengthening of the WTO's provisions for the "special and different treatment" of developing countries'.[17]

Agricultural protectionism

The belief that low-income countries should get special and different trade treatment is particularly applied by the global justice movement to the agricultural industries of low-income countries. Nearly all organisations in the movement feel that low-income countries should be able to protect their agricultural markets.

On protection of agriculture in low-income countries Action Aid – a global alliance of organisations working to promote structural change to eradicate poverty and injustice – believes low-income countries should be given the flexibility to exempt farm products from global tariff reductions.[18] Oxfam (despite its general support for open trade) similarly advocates that 'developing countries have the right to protect their domestic agricultural sectors'.[19] Christian Aid argues that low-income countries should be 'free to choose effective import tariffs to ensure they are not flooded with cheap and disruptive food imports'.[20] Similarly Anuradha Mittal, policy director of the US-based anti-hunger organisation Food First, says 'each country has a right to protect basic food production as it sees fit'.[21]

Some groups in the global justice movement are also prepared to make a special case for farm subsidisation in high-income countries.

The Worldwide Fund for Nature says an enlightened WTO agriculture agreement would 'end harmful subsidies while permitting support for agriculture that furthers environmental or development needs'.[22] A joint paper by ActionAid, Cafod, Forum Unwelt und Entwicklung and German Watch says that 'in order to preserve and improve important societal benefits from agriculture … it is important to give targeted support to sustainable agriculture'.[23] Colin Hines, a high-profile British-based economist who was once head of Greenpeace's International Economics Unit, also supports agricultural subsidisation:

> The truth is that most countries subsidise their farmers, but they do it in different ways and for different reasons. And why not? Does the state have a responsibility to ensure that its citizens are fed? Surely the experience of wars, trade wars and economic recessions all justify a nation in ensuring that a good quality diet is reliably available for its citizens?[24]

The International Forum on Globalization (IFG), a US-based research and educational institution that brings together researchers, activists and economists from over twenty countries, adds its voice in favour of agricultural subsidisation. John Cavanagh, vice-president of the IFG, has said:

> We think Japan should be able to decide to protect its rice, we think that Mexico should be able to protect its corn. For cultural reasons – for other reasons – we believe in a set of rules that allow that kind of diversity – that kind of democracy to flourish![25]

A variation on the agricultural protectionist proposals advanced by some groups in the global justice movement is a proposal to establish a 'development box' – much like the current blue, green and amber boxes – in the WTO's Agreement on Agriculture which a low-income country could use to protect its poor farmers and which would provide a range of measures (including increased tariffs), many of which requiring exemption from WTO rules. The measures would be specifically targeted at poor farmers and would not cover large agribusinesses operating in low-income countries.[26] The proposal is a targeted form of the general global justice movement support for farm protectionism.

Controls on capital

The global economy basically has two arms: trade and capital (which includes foreign direct investment, loans and share market (portfolio) investment). Although the capital part of the global economy is qualitatively different from and separate to the trade arm, as we have seen it is inextricably linked to trade because investment, in particular, often drives the structure of trade and affects key variables such as exchange rates. Because of this interconnectedness, high-income countries have been very keen to link investment agreements to global trade agreements. Although the global justice movement is fairly divided on whether more or less trade would make the world economy more sustainable, it is united in its belief that the movement of global capital should be more regulated than it is at present. The French-based Association for the Taxation of Financial Transactions in the Interests of the Citizen (ATTAC) argues 'it is therefore necessary to introduce capital control measures on an international scale'.[27] The International Confederation of Free Trade Unions says there should be a 'recognition of the rights of governments to control foreign capital flows in the interest of macroeconomic and social stability'.[28] The Congress of South African Trade Unions similarly argues for the introduction of 'rules on movement of capital that will not only challenge the speculative character of many portfolio flows, but will shift the balance of power that capital has gained through free movement of capital back to democratic institutions'.[29]

Many aid organisations take a somewhat narrower policy stance on global capital flows, a stance that mainly focuses on the regulation of foreign investment, rather than capital in general; most of these aid organisations believe that low-income countries, in particular, should have the power to regulate foreign investment. Oxfam says 'integration through trade is not the same as integration through capital markets' and argues that 'governments should retain the right to regulate foreign investors'.[30] World Vision says foreign investment should not be uncritically accepted by low-income countries but should, instead, be subject to comprehensive economic and social cost–benefit analysis.[31] Christian Aid echoes Oxfam and World Vision by advocating that low-income countries have full regulatory power over foreign investment.[32]

Differences on trade policy within the global justice movement

Despite their common ground, major trade policy differences exist within the global justice movement which, to a large extent, echo differences in the broader community. As more alliances are built within the movement, the differences tend to narrow but still a significant number differentiate different groups from each other. Many of the differences involve the structure and administration of global trade.

Access to high-income country trade markets

The most vexed trade policy divide within the global justice movement involves the issue of whether trade should be made more sustainable by increasing or by decreasing its flows between high- and low-income countries. Some organisations argue (quite passionately) that greater access by low-income countries to high-income country markets would definitely make low-income countries wealthier and would therefore make the system fairer; other organisations argue (equally passionately) that such increased trade would make an already bad situation even worse and that true sustainability will only come through greater national self-reliance and less trade. Organisations that believe greater trade holds the answer to eliminating world poverty and inequality are sometimes known as the 'fair trade school' while those that believe in greater self-reliance and less trade are sometimes known as the 'localisation school'.

Oxfam is the standard-bearer for those organisations that believe greater trade, particularly through greater low-income country access to high-income countries, is the answer to trade sustainability – the fair trade school. In 2002 Oxfam launched its high-profiled Make Trade Fair campaign with a report, *Rigged Rules and Double Standards: Trade,*

Globalisation, and the Fight against Poverty, in which it unambiguously argued that 'the increasing integration of developing countries into the global trading system offers the promise of more rapid progress towards poverty reduction and improved standards of living'.[33] The report specifically predicted that if Africa, East Asia, South Asia and Latin America were each to increase their share of world exports by 1 per cent 128 million people could be lifted out of poverty[34] (equal to about 10 per cent of those who currently live on less than US$1 per day). The well-known global economics commentator and correspondent for the British *Guardian* newspaper, George Monbiot, argues that in his ideal trading system 'rich countries ... would be required to pull down their barriers to trade. They would be permitted neither to subsidise their industries nor to impose tariffs or other restraints upon imports from poorer countries'.[35] The Congress of South African Trade Unions similarly sees greater trade access as crucial to low-income country development and advocates the 'lifting of trade barriers against African products by industrialised societies'.[36] World Vision states that 'for the most part, trade offers very significant net static and dynamic gains over the long terms to all countries'.[37]

Many in the global justice movement, however, have major doubts about this policy. Many think, at the very least, that the benefits for low-income countries from greater access to high-income country markets have been exaggerated. Via Campesina is quite explicit about the issue and argues that 'increasing liberalisation and market access do not resolve problems of poverty and social exclusion of millions of people in the world. On the contrary this will worsen the situation'.[38] Mark Weisbrot and Dean Baker from the Center for Economic and Policy Research in the United States argue 'some of the most widely used economic models show that many developing countries will actually lose from trade liberalisation in important sectors, such as agriculture and textiles'.[39] Christian Aid says that 'evidence does not show that the faith in trade liberalisation has been well placed ... evidence from multi-country studies shows that, far from being a solution to problems of growth and poverty, liberalisation can sometimes be part of the problem'.[40]

The source of much of the suspicion about the benefits of greater low-income country access to high-income country markets is a fear that high-income countries will demand greater access to low-income country markets in return and that this will inevitably devastate a lot of low-income country industries, particularly damaging their agricultural and manufacturing industries. Weisbrot and Baker argue that the removal of low-income country trade barriers is 'likely to lead to large disruptions in agriculture. In most developing countries a large portion of the population is still tied to the agricultural sector. If barriers to agricultural imports are removed too quickly, it can lead to large-scale displacement of the rural population.'[41] A 2003 report co-commissioned by the United Nations Development Fund, the Heinrich Böll Foundation, the Rockefeller Foundation and the Wallace Global Fund, *Making Global Trade Work for People*, reached similar conclusions. It said as many as 70 per cent of the jobs in poorer low-income countries and 40 per cent of jobs in richer low-income countries are in agriculture and that these jobs are threatened by the fact that 'with rapidly growing trade, developing countries have become much more dependent on food imports'.[42] The report claimed that between 1974 and 1997 the share of world agricultural exports of low-income countries had only grown from 30 to 34 per cent while their share of imports had grown from 28 per cent to 37 per cent; this had resulted in a net US$13 billion deficit in agricultural trade for low-income countries in general in 1997.[43] This nervousness about the impact that more access to high-income country markets would have is echoed by Action Aid, which argues (from a slightly different angle):

> Many developing country governments see increased access to developed country markets as extremely important, but Action Aid is more cautious because of concerns that this could fuel an explosion of export-orientated agriculture in developing countries at the expense of small-scale producers and the environment. This trend has been seen in Brazil with a rapid expansion in soybean production and in Indonesia and Malaysia in relation to oil palm production for export. Also, typically, produce from low-income farms is sold on local and national markets and so for small-scale farmers increases in export markets is to a large extent irrelevant.[44]

It should also be kept in mind that many low-income countries are net importers of agricultural produce and that many may therefore benefit from subsidised high-income country agricultural exports – 33 of the 49 poorest countries in the world are net agricultural importers.[45]

Protection of trade markets

Groups like Oxfam are at one end of the trade policy spectrum of the global justice movement. At the other are organisations that believe true trade sustainability will only come through restricting trade to its bare essentials, and that regions and countries should become more self-reliant through a process called 'localisation'. Advocates of this trade-restricting policy draw a distinction between internationalisation and globalisation. They argue the world should retain the benefits of inter-nationalisation, such as its global communication linkages and general global awareness, but that trade (and capital) linkages between the world's countries should be reduced.

The standard-bearer for the localisation school of policy thought is Colin Hines, author of two books on localisation entitled *Localization: A Global Manifesto* and *The New Protectionism: Protecting the Future Against Free Trade*. He has also co-authored a localisation manifesto – entitled *Time to Replace Globalisation: A Green Localist Manifesto for the World Trade Organisation Ministerial* – with Caroline Lucas, British member of the European Parliament for the Green Party. In *The New Protectionism* Hines says, 'we look to less trade … every effort should be made to meet requirements from local sources first, then nationally, then regionally, and only after that internationally'.[46] In *Localization* Hines advocates the use of tariffs to bring about localisation and says that 'they send a clear message to all exporters that they need to reori-entate their production towards more local markets'.[47] Hines is by no means alone in his advocacy of localisation. The International Forum on Globalization says 'economic systems should favour local produc-tion and markets rather than invariably being designed to serve long distance trade'.[48] Friends of the Earth argues that a distinction needs to be made between free trade and the freedom to trade; it also argues that one of the key principles around which twenty-first-century economics should be based is 'economic and political subsidiarity – devolving power and authority to the most local level appropriate'.[49]

Like the call for greater trade access, localisation has its fair share of doubters within the global justice movement. Oxfam bluntly proclaims that 'a retreat into isolationism would deprive the poor of the opportunities offered by trade'.[50] It also argues that '"national sovereignty", without a systematic strategy for poverty reduction, is little more than a one-way street leading to self-sufficient misery'.[51] World Vision feels much the same, arguing 'workers should not artificially and selfishly protect domestic jobs at the expense, not only of impoverished workers elsewhere in the world, but at the expense of their own citizens'.[52]

A very astute observation about the merits, or otherwise, of localisation/protectionism versus open trade comes from Claire Melamed from Christian Aid. She believes that 'evidence indicates that it is managed trade, rather than liberalisation, that has (traditionally) contributed most to development' but warns that undirected restrictive trade systems can be just as detrimental as undirected free trade systems. She says:

> What all success stories in trade policy and development have in common is that governments managed markets to ensure that the incentive structure faced by the private sector reflected development goals. A closed system with no incentives has not been shown to be particularly helpful in advancing economic growth and poverty reduction. Likewise, an open system where incentives are left entirely to market forces has not had conspicuous success in fostering growth or poverty reduction.[53]

Raw material price support schemes

While most in the global justice movement believe low-income countries should be able to protect their domestic agriculture industries, few have given much thought to the broader question of what measures could be taken to stop the long-term slide in the raw material export prices of low-income countries. One individual who has, however, is Peter Robbins.

Peter Robbins is a former advisor to the United Nations and the African National Congress as well as a one-time commodities trader and an expert on raw materials trade. Robbins believes the only way that prices for raw materials will ever pick up again is through restricting their supply. In his book, *Stolen Fruit: The Tropical Commodities Disaster*, he argues:

> It has now become self-evident that none of the various strategies currently being used to address the disaster caused by the collapse of tropical commodity [raw material] prices will make a significant impact on the problem of oversupply. The obvious solution is to cut the volumes of supplies until they are, once more, balanced by volumes of demand at price levels that are high enough to deliver a fair reward to producers but not so high that they deter consumers from buying the products. In other words, it is necessary to manage supplies of these commodities.[54]

Robbins has also said that 'complicated as the logistical, administrative and political difficulties may be, I believe this to be the only solution'.[55]

Like Robbins, Oxfam believes that there needs to be more proactive management of the world's traded raw materials. It argues that 'in the longer term, there needs to be a renewed effort by producing and consuming nations alike to bring supply into line with demand, on a more systematic basis, across a range of commodities'.[56] Oxfam believes the Secretary-General of the United Nations should establish a special high-level task force to analyse the causes of the crisis in raw material prices and deliver a report to the UN and the G8 within a year.[57] In the longer term Oxfam believes an international institution should be established that would deliver reform in the four key areas of: market intervention and long-term supply management, diversification and value-adding in exporting countries, the use of insurance for farmers to manage the risk of price collapse; and funding to deliver these three measures. Oxfam believes that one funding option for a raw material in crisis would be to tax its imports when its price slumped and to tax its exports when its price increased.[58] Oxfam also believes the task of stabilising prices should be separated from that of increasing prices: it believes that it was the confusion of these two goals that led to the failure of price support schemes in the 1970s.[59]

Labour and environmental clauses

Another major global trade issue that frequently divides organisations in the global justice movement is the use of labour and environmental clauses in trade agreements. These are clauses built into global trade agreements that threaten retaliatory trade action against a country if it fails to uphold minimum labour or environmental standards. Even though the movement generally believes no new issues should be introduced into trade agreements, nonetheless a number of organisations, particularly in the fair trade school, believe it is permissible for labour and environmental clauses to be included. There are also a number of organisations both within and outside the global justice movement, that strongly oppose such clauses.

Like many trade union groups, the International Confederation of Free Trade Unions is an advocate of the inclusion of labour clauses in trade agreements. It argues 'the WTO must fully integrate a social, labour, developmental, gender and environmental dimension into the WTO system'.[60] Greenpeace similarly advocates the use of trade agreements to achieve environmental ends. It believes the precautionary principle should be built into decision making by the World Trade Organisation and that the WTO's disputes settlement mechanism should be used to achieve implementation of the Kyoto protocol on greenhouse gas emissions. It even says 'if the United States continues to refuse to ratify the Kyoto protocol WTO member states who support Kyoto should … consider bringing that country before a WTO dispute settlement panel'.[61]

Attempts were made by high-income countries to include labour clauses in WTO agreements at the WTO Seattle ministerial in 1999 and during the closing stages of the Uruguay Round in 1994. But many low-income country governments and organisations oppose them. The Non-Aligned Movement of low-income countries is one low-income country organisation that often voices its opposition to such trade clauses. A high-profile activist within the global justice movement who has long campaigned against labour and environmental trade clauses is Martin Khor, director of the Malaysian-based Third World Network. He believes labour and environmental clauses run the risk of penalising low-income countries and are 'fraught with the dangers of protectionism'.[62] He also argues that trade-related labour and environmental clauses should not be negotiated through the WTO and that while many high-income country unions support the inclusion of labour clauses in trade agreements many low-income country unions oppose them. He says many low-income country governments see their low labour costs as legitimate comparative advantages rather than evidence of the exploitation of workers.[63]

Ahwini Sukthankar and Scott Nova from the US-based Workers Rights Consortium have no time for Khor's line of argument. They argue:

> Many developing-world governments, unions and workers have attacked the call for linking trade to labour standards as ill-disguised protectionism. It is worth disaggregating the opposition to enforceable labour standards, given some governments' motivations have not been particularly altruistic. Claims about how labour standards are a neocolonial encroachment on sovereignty, or culturally inappropriate, or protectionist, all too often mask a resistance to international scrutiny of outdated laws, unimplemented policies, or corrupt institutions.[64]

The Focus on the Global South group has held a number of 'roundtable' meetings of different organisations in the global justice movement which, in part, have attempted to iron out differences over labour clauses. The meetings have generally managed to find common ground over the desirability of upholding workers' rights – including upholding the aims of the International Labour Organisation – but they have not managed to sort out the best way of enforcing such rights.[65]

Trade-balancing mechanisms

One issue that unfortunately gets scant attention from most organisations in the global justice movement is the potential use of interventionist mechanisms to ensure that a country's global trade and its overall balance of payments do not become too unbalanced (as detailed in

Chapter 8). Most organisations in the movement have policies that hold great promise for improving the trade balances of low-income countries but few have policies that would necessarily ensure balanced trade and low balance-of-payments imbalances. The idea of having interventionist trade-balancing mechanisms is fairly radical in an age that has become used to laissez-faire economics and persistent, long-term global trade imbalances, but it is because such imbalances have become so entrenched that the issue needs to be addressed. Two commentators who have given the issue considerable thought are Herman Daly and the British writer George Monbiot.

Herman Daly was once senior economist at the World Bank and Professor of Economics at the University of Louisiana State University in the United States. He believes balanced trade flows around the world are crucial – he thinks if trade can be balanced then international borrowing need not exist (putting an end to Third World debt). He argues: 'balanced trade and capital immobility are two sides of the same coin. The way a country borrows in real terms is to import more than it exports. If that is forbidden, then so is international lending and borrowing'.[66] Daly advocates a system of auctioned import licences to achieve balanced trade. He says 'perhaps the simplest way to balance trade is to limit imports to rough equality with expected exports by issuing import quota licenses, and auctioning them to competing import firms. Resale of the quota license could be permitted during the time period for which it is valid. The subsequent time period would begin with another auction'.[67]

Like Daly, George Monbiot believes balancing trade is fundamental to a sustainable world economy. He says the world should look at resuscitating the idea of an International Clearing Union as presented by John Maynard Keynes to the 1944 Bretton Woods conference (see Chapter 8). Monbiot believes Keynes's proposal would fundamentally change how nations with trading surpluses operate by making their exports less attractive because of rising currency values, by stopping the flow of capital from trade deficit countries into those with surpluses, and by encouraging surplus countries to introduce policies that would increase their imports.[68]

Reform or abolition of the World Trade Organisation

A very vexed issue within the global justice movement is the question of how reformable the WTO is. All organisations in the movement believe that the rules of global trading, and the organisation that manages them, need to be changed but the movement is divided about whether this can be best achieved by reforming or by abolishing the WTO. Nearly all organisations agree, however, on the desirability of international trade rules.

On the side of those who think the WTO can be reformed, Action Aid says it 'agrees that a fair rules-based international trading system would indeed be a positive force for good'.[69] It says it would like: the proposals for WTO reform put forward by low-income countries to be adopted, high-income countries to stop their bullying tactics at trade talks, all WTO members to automatically de-restrict their WTO documents, WTO public consultation to be improved and WTO members to disclose all trade negotiation access given to outside bodies (especially businesses).[70] Greenpeace says 'transparency, openness and consultation at the WTO urgently need to be improved'.[71] The World Development Movement maintains the WTO needs to be 'radically reformed'.[72] Dot Keet, from the Africa Trade Network, believes the nature and roles of the WTO need to be reformed and that it should be made subordinate to the United Nations.[73] The APM World Network says there needs to be an international trade appeals court established that is independent of the WTO.[74] Oxfam says the WTO needs to be democratised and that part of that democratisation should be the creation of a fund (of about US$250 million) that would enhance the trade negotiating capacity of poor countries. It also advocates WTO reviews of the impact of trade rules on employment standards.[75] Christian Aid sums up the feeling of many organisations in the movement by arguing that the WTO needs not so much to be reformed as to have its focus narrowed so that its rules no longer impinge on national sovereignty. It also says that 'all major decisions must be taken with the active participation of all WTO members, ending the practice of rich countries agreeing deals behind closed doors'.[76]

Those that advocate the more radical option of abolishing the WTO include Colin Hines, the International Forum on Globalization (IFG) and Walden Bello of the Focus on the Global South organisation. Often advocacy of abolition of the WTO goes hand in hand with support for localisation/self-reliance.

Colin Hines believes the WTO should be replaced by what he calls a 'World Localisation Organisation' that would administer radically rewritten trade rules enshrined in a new trade agreement he calls the 'General Agreement for Sustainable Trade'.[77] The IFG is less categorical than Hines and gives three options for the replacement of the WTO:

- the creation of an International Trade Organisation, of the sort envisaged at the Havana trade conference in 1947, that embraced global full employment and anti-monopoly goals;

- a return to the type of global trade management that existed before the WTO, where there were non-binding rules and there was no permanent international trade management body;

- an end to all global trade management and its replacement by a network of regional trade bodies.[78]

The IFG also argues that 'global trade bureaucracies and international finance agencies should not have authority over state or national decision making when it comes to the commons, national heritage resources, the preservation of national choice in domestic services, or fundamental human rights'.[79]

Walden Bello has consistently argued against reform of the WTO and believes abolition is the only answer. He also gives three replacement options for the WTO, all of which are more radical than those of the IFGs:

- a complete decommissioning of the WTO;

- a 'neutering' of it through its conversion into a purely research-based organisation;

- a radical reduction of its powers, turning it into one of 'just another set of actors co-existing with and being checked by other international organisations, agreements and regional groupings'.[80]

Bello often campaigns on the theme that the WTO, as well as the IMF and the World Bank, is driving world economic policy and therefore world social and environmental policy as well. He consistently argues these three organisations shouldn't have this power but instead should be one of a number of global public policy institutions that should keep each other in check. He says if other international agreements and agencies – such as the UNCTAD, multilateral environment agreements, the International Labour Organisation and regional trade authorities such as the Mercosur and ASEAN groupings – had more authority they could balance out the power of the IMF, the WTO and the World Bank (or their replacements) and that would make for 'a more fluid, less structured, more pluralistic world with multiple checks and balances' that would also make for more sustainable low-income country development.[81] Bello cautions against policies of reforming the WTO by arguing that replacing one set of centralised global rules and institutions with another, albeit a more enlightened set, 'is likely to reproduce the same Jurassic trap that ensnared organisations as different as IBM, the IMF and the Soviet state'.[82] Noreena Hertz, author of *The Silent Takeover: Global Capitalism and the Death of Democracy*, like Bello advocates the creation of global organisations that can counter the force of the WTO. She argues, 'we need to set up a World Social Organisation (WSO): an organisation which will counter the dominance of the World Trade Organisation and will establish rules and ensure the long-term protection of human rights, labour standards and the environment'.

Ideological battles within the global justice movement

When it comes to global trade policy and globalisation policy in general, more unites the global justice movement than divides it. But sharp differences do exist, particularly over trade policy, and from time

Figure 9.2 Distinguishing features of the agenda of the localisation school

Self-reliance

National and regional economies should be the focus of economic management, not the international economy. Production and investment should be carried out as close to the point of economic activity as possible through a general regime of self-reliance.

Trade

Trade should be as locally based as possible through protectionism using mechanisms like tariffs and quotas.

Investment and capital markets

Investment should be as locally based as possible and capital markets should be regulated in favour of local investment through local content and ownership laws etcetera.

Abolition of the World Trade Organization (WTO)

The WTO should be abolished and replaced with a more democratic, less powerful, more narrowly defined and transparent body concerned with local production rather than free trade. Alternatively, the WTO could be replaced by regional trade bodies.

General world economic management

There should generally be more pluralism in world economic management with international non-financial organisations providing checks and balances against international financial institutions.

Greater regulation of transnational corporations (TNCs)

TNCs should be more regulated through: restrictions on international profit repatriation, compulsory reporting in non-financial areas, site-here-to-sell-here requirements, restrictions on patenting and factory closures, tax policies that favour local businesses, anti-monopoly laws, greater liability for any social and environmental damage they cause and greater shareholder power.

Figure 9.3 The agenda of the fair trade school

Rich-country protectionism
Rich-country protectionism, particularly against poor-country imports, should cease. Rich countries should also stop subsidising agricultural exports.

Special and different treatment
Poor countries should be given 'special and different treatment' with regard to trade.

Poor-country protection of their agricultural industries
Poor countries should be able to protect their domestic agricultural industries against imports.

Social and environmental trade clauses
Labour and environmental clauses should be attached to international trade agreements that could be used to pressure exporting countries to raise their employment and environmental standards.

Raw material export price support schemes
There should be mechanisms or agreements to stop the ongoing slide in global raw material export prices.

No new issues
No new issues should be introduced into present or future global trade negotiations. Trade liberalisation should not be pushed any further.

Containment of the Trade Related Aspects of Intellectual Property (TRIPS) agreement
The TRIPS agreement should not allow rich countries either to patent poor-country practices or plant species or to stop poor countries from having access to essential generic pharmaceuticals.

Reform of the World Trade Organisation (WTO)
The WTO needs to be made more democratic and accountable, with poor countries more able to engage with it. There should be no more backroom trade agreement decision making by a select few countries.

Regulation of foreign investment and capital markets
There should be greater regulation of the world's foreign investment, if not of the global capital market in general.

Transnational corporation (TNC) regulation
TNCs should be more regulated and accountable and exposed to stronger international competition laws.

---

to time they break out into fairly nasty brawls. Over the past few years there have been particularly vexed arguments about the trade policies of Oxfam and Colin Hines.

The tension between those in the global justice movement who basically believe that low-income countries can trade their way out of poverty – given the right incentives and access to high-income country markets – and those who feel that more localised production, and less global production, is the answer came to a head with the 2002 launch of Oxfam's Make Trade Fair campaign and its accompanying *Rigged Rules and Double Standards* report. As mentioned above, the report made no secret of its support for a greater amount of (properly managed) world trade. It also dismissed those who did not share their enthusiasm for the policy (whom they called 'globaphobes'); and rather brazenly claimed that 'globaphobia is refuted by the evidence of history' and that 'a retreat into isolationism would deprive the poor of the opportunities offered by trade'.[83] The report went on to claim that globaphobia played well in high-income countries because of insecurity bred by economic globalisation.[84]

The *Rigged Rules* report sparked a major ideological brawl within the global justice movement. Although the debate was heated at times, Walden Bello thought it did a great service to the movement by 'pushing the question of our strategy on the trade front to centre stage'.[85] Colin Hines said Oxfam's report read like a 'bland script unquestioningly accepting the trade theory of comparative advantage'.[86] The well-known antiglobalisation campaigner Dr Vandana Shiva (who is a board member of the International Forum on Globalization) said Oxfam's policies were the same as the 'export first' policies of the World Bank except that Oxfam dressed them up in the WTO language of 'market access'.[87] Food First, a US-based organisation that campaigns for food security, said it was disappointed that Oxfam had 'chosen to undermine the demands of social movements and think tanks in the south such as Via Campesina, MST, Third World Network, Focus on the Global South, and Africa Trade Network which have demanded that governments must uphold the rights of all people to food sovereignty and the right to food rather than industry-led export-orientated production'.[88] Walden Bello said Oxfam had the wrong focus and was acting like an agent for the Cairns group of trade liberalisers.[89]

Oxfam wasted no time in hitting back. Kevin Watkins said 'the extreme element of the antiglobalisation movement is wrong … trade can deliver much more (to poor countries) than aid or debt relief'.[90] Watkins denied that Oxfam promoted World Bank-style trade liberal-isation and said Oxfam did not 'argue for export-led agriculture'.[91] He also said trade market outcomes reflect the policy choices and power relations that lie behind them.[92] He defended his report as one that 'attacks the current course of economic globalisation as a motor of greater inequality and poverty'.[93] Above all, Watkins said, he makes 'no apologies for attaching importance to improved market access'.[94]

The 2003 book by George Monbiot *The Age of Consent: A Manifesto for a New World Order* also sparked a heated ideological debate, this time about localisation and the merits of restricting trade. In his book Monbiot was openly critical both of localisation and of Colin Hines. Of localisation he wrote that 'many of the localisers have demanded measures which are the mirror image of those promoted by the market fundamentalists' and while 'there is an argument for per-mitting the poor nations to protect their economies against certain imports in order to incubate their own industries … there is no argument founded on justice for permitting the rich countries to do so'.[95] In a column for the *Guardian* newspaper in Britain Monbiot even wrote that '[localisation] is as coercive, destructive and unjust as any of the schemes George Bush is cooking up'.[96] Monbiot claimed 'Colin Hines is in good company, however, because, though it pains me to say so, the approach of many of the most prominent members of the global justice movement in the rich world has been characterised by a staggering inconsistency'.[97]

Colin Hines wasted little time in hitting back. He said that Monbiot 'seriously misrepresents what localisation is' and that 'George Monbiot's solution actually has in it the seeds of its own destruction'.[98] About Monbiot's proposed trade-led solutions – which were similar to Oxfam's – Hines said 'George Monbiot says virtually nothing about the devastating effects on third world exporters of south-south competition for the more open markets of the north'.[99] And about Monbiot's argument that rich countries shouldn't be able to protect their markets Hines said 'to callously write off, as George Monbiot does, the ability of working people throughout northern countries to have a right to protect and rebuild their economies ... frankly beggars belief'.[100] Hines linked the disagreement with Monbiot to the controversy the year before over Oxfam's *Rigged Rules* report by saying 'George Monbiot's one-sided protectionism shares Oxfam's central call of 'complete market access to rich country markets for low income countries".[101] The Oxfam and Hines/Monbiot controversies both underlined how much work the global justice movement has yet to do on its trade policies.

A separate area of conflict within the global justice movement concerns policy differences between high-income country groups and low-income country groups. Low-income country groups within the movement tend to be more radical about trade and globalisation policy than high-income country groups. The greater daring of low-income countries is a product of several factors, one of which is that they have generally been hit harder by trade and globalisation than high-income countries have. They invariably have first-hand experience of what it is like to have already meagre health or education services cut back because their countries have been under IMF management. Some low-income country groups even liken globalisation to colonialism. Vandana Shiva argues that 'globalisation is completing the project of colonisation that led to the conquest and ownership of land and territory'.[102] Another factor behind the policy divide between high-income and low-income country groups is the fact that global justice movement activists from high-income countries tend to be supporters of the poor whereas in low-income countries they are more likely to be poor themselves (a distinction that reinforces differences about actual experience of the downsides of trade and globalisation).[103] An example of this policy tension was played out at the inaugural international meeting of Green parties held in Canberra, Australia, in 2001 (the Global Greens Conference). At the conference a charter was debated that was intended to be an international policy statement of Green parties. The sections dealing with economic globalisation ended up being some of the most hotly debated parts of the charter – in particular a section dealing with reform of the WTO. Conference delegates from low-income countries generally wanted to abolish the WTO while delegates from high-income countries generally wanted to reform it. For some time it looked as though no compromise could be reached, but the United States Greens successfully proposed a policy that said that Green parties 'support abolition of the WTO unless it is reformed to make sustainability its central goal, supported by transparent and democratic processes and the participation of representatives from affected communities'.[104]

Overview of the trade policies of the global justice movement

In terms of policies despite the internal disagreements there is definitely more that unites the global justice movement than divides it. Its trade policies are rapidly assuming more and more maturity and have become a major influence on global trade policy. The movement is also successfully managing to move beyond mere protest. On four major issues there is broad agreement within the movement:

1 New issues, including the Uruguay Round new issues of intellec-

tual property rights and services, and the Singapore issues of investment, competition, government procurement and trade facilitation, should not be part of global trade negotiations. They should either be negotiated separately or, preferably, not at all.

2 Low-income countries deserve special trade rules treatment; in particular they should be given more lenient implementation requirements than high-income countries and should be able to protect their agricultural industries.

3 There should be controls on the movement of global capital, especially on foreign investment but also, possibly, on other forms of global capital as well.

4 There should be greater regulation of transnational corporations, particularly in relation to their penetration of local markets, their labour practices, their environmental policies and their transfer pricing structures.

In a further two areas there is (probably) a high degree of agreement within the movement but, as yet, only limited policy development. These are:

1 The need for supply management of globally traded raw materials, probably through global supply restriction and possibly aided by global financial contributions.

2 The need for a global interventionist mechanism that would ensure long-term balance of national trade and mitigation of long-term balance-of-payments imbalances (possibly like the International Clearing Union idea proposed by John Maynard Keynes at the 1944 Bretton Woods Conference).

The movement is still quite divided, however, about: whether labour and environment clauses should be attached to trade agreements; whether the WTO should be reformed or abolished; and whether more trade and more low-income country access to high-income country markets is the answer to long-term trade sustainability or if more localised production, and less trade, is the answer.

On the issue of labour and environment clauses it is inconsistent for the global justice movement to insist that there should be no new issues attached to trade agreements and then for parts of it to turn around and say that environment and labour issues should still be attached. This is opportunistic. If other issues, such as intellectual property rights, should be negotiated separately to trade agreements then so too should labour and environment clauses/conditions.

The issue of whether to reform or abolish the WTO is not as vexed as it might appear. Nearly all organisations in the global justice movement agree that rules should be applied to global trade; for them it is just a question of finding the best way of administering them. At times the movement gets too preoccupied with means rather than ends in this issue. Whether to abolish the WTO or not is a debate about means, not ends.

The issue of whether the world should have more or less trade will be the most challenging one for the movement to resolve in future years. The movement doesn't necessarily need to have all organisations saying exactly the same thing on this issue but at the moment there is too much disagreement on it. As with the debate about whether to reform or abolish the WTO, organisations in the movement need to focus more on ends and less on means in this debate, and all sides need to be prepared to make more exceptions to their hard-line philosophies. All sides concede that low-income country agriculture should be protected. Occasionally some groups or commentators in the localisation school concede there are practical limits to what can be produced locally, but these limits need to be spelled out much more. The fair trade school needs to be much more cognisant of the environmentally damaging effects of trade and needs to realise that this necessarily must place limits on the amount of trade the world can sustain. The fair trade school also needs to be more prepared to concede that more trade between low and high-income countries would almost certainly force low-income countries to open their markets more to high-income countries and that this could devastate many parts of their population, especially their farming populations.

These issues can be resolved by the global justice movement. There is no doubt that the most creative and cutting-edge thinking on the future of trade is taking place within the movement and that the world will look to it for the ideas it needs about the long-term sustainable management of world trade.

Notes

1 Richard Peet (ed.), *Unholy Trinity: The IMF, World Bank and WTO*, Zed Books, London, 2003, p. 192.

2 Jonathan Neale, *You Are G8, We Are 6 billion: The Truth behind the Genoa Protests*, Vision Paperbacks, London, 2002, p. 9.

3 Peet, *Unholy Trinity*, p. 192.

4 'Marx after Communism', *Economist*, 21 December 2002, p. 19.

5 Our World Is Not For Sale Network, 'WTO: Shrink or Sink' petition, downloaded from www.speakeasy.org in 2002, point 1.

6 Aileen Kwa, *The Post-Cancun Backlash, and Seven Strategies to Keep the WTO off the Tracks*, p. 3, downloaded from www.focusweb.org in 2003.

7 Martin Khor, *TWN Briefings for Cancun 1*, p. 3. downloaded from www.twnside.org.sg in 2003.

8 Friends of the Earth International, *Stop the GATS!: WTO's general agreement on trade and services will undermine social and environmental sustainability*, p. 1, downloaded from www.foei.org/cancun in 2003.

9 World Development Movement, *If It's Broke, Fix It*, p. 8, downloaded from www.wdm.org.uk in 2002.

10 Our World is Not for Sale Network, 'WTO: Shrink or Sink' petition, point 1.

11 Mark Curtis, *Trade for Life: Making Trade Work for Poor People*, Christian Aid, London, 2001, p. 10. downloaded from www.christian-aid.org in 2003.

12 Brett Parris, *Trade for Development*, World Vision, East Burwood (Australia), 1999, p. vi, downloaded from www.wvi.org in 2002.

13 Greenpeace International, *Safe Trade in the 21st Century, 2001*, p. 10, downloaded from www.greenpeace.org in 2002.

14 Kevin Watkins et al., *Rigged Rules and Double Standards: Trade, Globalisation and the Fight against Poverty*, Oxfam International, Washington DC, 2002, pp. 236–237.

15 Claire Melamed, *What Works? Trade, Policy and Development*, Christian

Aid, London, 2002, p. 1, downloaded from www.christian-aid.org in 2003.

16 Parris, *Trade for Development*, p. v.

17 Watkins et al, *Rigged Rules and Double Standards*, p. 15.

18 Action Aid/Axione Aiuto, *The WTO Agreement on Agriculture*, p. 3, downloaded from www.actionaid.org in 2003.

19 Watkins et al, *Rigged Rules and Double Standards*, p. 120.

20 Curtis, *Trade for Life*, p. 9.

21 Sarah Anderson (ed.), *Views from the South: The Effects of Globalisation and the WTO on Third World Countries*, Food First/Institute for Food and Development Policy, Oakland CA, 2000, p. 173.

22 Worldwide Fund for Nature, *Agriculture: 5th WTO Ministerial Conference, Cancun, WWF Briefing Series*, p. 1, downloaded from www.panda.org in 2003.

23 Tim Rice et al., *Post-Cancun Reflections on Agriculture: Joint NGO Sub mission to the European Commission*, p. 3. downloaded from www.actionaid.org in 2003.

24 Colin Hines and Tim Lang, *The New Protectionism: Protecting the Future against Free Trade*, Earthscan, London, 1993, p. 96.

25 September 9th Panel in Cancún 'Alternatives to Economic Globalisation and the WTO', published by Deb Foskey via WTO watch email list (debf@webone.com.au), 15th September 2003 (No. 201), p. 1, (For archive copy, see www.nwjc.org.au/avcwl/lists/ archives.html).

26 Michael Woodin and Caroline Lucas, *Green Alternatives to Globalisation: A Manifesto*, Pluto Press, London, 2004, p. 168.

27 William F. Fisher and Thomas Ponniah (eds.), *Another World is Possible: Popular Alternatives to Globalisation at the World Social Forum*, Zed Books, London, 2003, p. 44.

28 The International Confederation of Free Trade Unions, *Global Unions' Statement: The Role of the IMF and World Bank*, 2001, p.10, downloaded from www.icftu.org in 2002.

29 Fisher and Ponniah, *Another World is Possible,* p. 69.

30 Watkins, *Rigged Rules and Double Standards*, pp. 24, 238.

31 Brett Parris, *Foreign Direct Investment and Corporate Codes of Conduct in National Development Strategies*, World Vision, East Burwood (Australia), 2001, p. 5, downloaded from www.wvi.org in 2002.

32 Curtis, *Trade for Life*, p. 9.

33 Watkins, *Rigged Rules and Double Standards*, p. 239.

34 Ibid., pp. 3.

35 George Monbiot, *The Age of Consent: A Manifesto for a New World Order*, Flamingo, London, 2003, p. 218.

36 Fisher and Ponniah, *Another World Is Possible*, p. 76.

37 Parris, *Trade for Development*, p. iv.

38 Via Campesina, *Press Release Via Campesina After 'Cancún'*, p. 3, downloaded from www.viacampesina.org in 2003.

39 Mark Weisbrot and Dean Baker, *The Relative Impact of Trade Liberalization on Developing Countries*, Center for Economic and Policy Research, Washington, 2002, p. 1, downloaded from www.cepr.net in 2003.

40 Melamed, *What Works? Trade, Policy and Development*, p. 6.

41 Weisbrot and Baker, *The Relative Impact of Trade Liberalization*, p. 2.

42 Kamal Malhotra et al., *Making Global Trade Work for People*, Earthscan, London, 2003, pp. 109, 126.

43 Ibid., p. 126.

44 Action Aid/Axione Aiuto, *The WTO Agreement on Agriculture*, p. 11.

45 'Punch-up over handouts', *Economist*, 26 March 2005, p. 70.

46 Colin Hines and Tim Lang, *The New Protectionism*, p. 128.

47 Colin Hines, *Localization: A Global Manifesto*, Earthscan, London, 2000, p. 65.

48 The International Forum on Globalization, *Report Summary – Alternatives to Economic Globalisation: A Better World is Possible*, p. 12, downloaded from www.ifg.org in 2002.

49 Friends of the Earth International, *Towards Sustainable Economies: Challenging Neoliberal Economic Globalisation*, pp. 8, 10, downloaded from www.foei.org/cancun in 2003.

50 Watkins, *Rigged Rules and Double Standards*, p. 16.

51 Ibid., p. 24.

52 Parris, *Trade for Development*, p. 56.

53 Melamed, *What Works? Trade, Policy and Development*, pp. 1, 7.

54 Peter Robbins, *Stolen Fruit: The Tropical Commodities Disaster*, Zed Books, London, 2003, p. 61.

55 Ibid., p. 62.

56 Watkins, *Rigged Rules and Double Standards*, p. 171.

57 Ibid., p. 170.

58 Ibid., p. 171.

59 Ibid.

60 The International Confederation of Free Trade Unions, *Joint Statement on Globalisation and the WTO*, 2001, downloaded from www.icftu.org in 2002.

61 Greenpeace International, *Safe Trade in the 21st Century, 2001*, p. 9, downloaded from www.greenpeace.org in 2002.

62 Anderson, *Views from the South*, p. 44.

63 Ibid., p. 47.

64 Ahwini Sukthankar and Scott Nova in Lori Wallach and Patrick Woodall, *Whose Trade Organisation?: A Comprehensive Guide to the WTO*, The New Press, New York, 2004, p. 225.

65 Ibid., p. 231.

66 Herman E. Daly and John B. Cobb, Jr, *For the Common Good: Redirecting the Economy Toward Community, the Environment and a Sustainable Future*, Beacon Press, Boston, 1989, p. 230.

67 Ibid.

68 Monbiot, *The Age of Consent*, p. 163.

69 ActionAid/AzioneAiuto, *Food Rights: WTO Democracy and Reform*, p. 2. downloaded from www.actionaid.org in 2003.

70 Ibid., p. 8.

71 Greenpeace International, *Safe Trade in the 21st Century, 2001*, p. 10.

72 World Development Movement, *If It's Broke, Fix It*, p. 1.

73 Fisher and Ponniah, *Another World Is Possible*, p. 52.

74 Ibid., p. 169.

75 Watkins, *Rigged Rules*, pp. 4, 16, 204.

76 Curtis, *Trade for Life*, pp. 8, 10.

77 Hines, *Localization*, p. 260.

78 International Forum on Globalization, *Report Summary – Alternatives to Economic Globalisation*, p. 20.

79 The International Forum on Globalization, *Alternatives to Economic Globalisation: A Better World Is Possible*, San Francisco, Berrett-Koehler, 2002, p. 54.

80 Walden Bello, *Deglobalisation: Ideas for a New World Economy*, London, Zed Books, 2002, pp. 116–117.

81 Walden Bello, *Why Reform of the WTO is the Wrong Agenda*, p. 8, downloaded from www.focusweb.org in 2002.

82 Bello, *Deglobalisation*, p. 115.

83 Watkins, *Rigged Rules*, pp. 16, 23.

84 Ibid., p. 24.

85 Walden Bello, 'The Oxfam Debate: from Controversy to Common Strategy', published by Deb Foskey via WTO Watch email list (debf@webone.com.au), 7 June 2002 (No. 63), p. 1. (For archive copy see www.nwjc.org.au/avcwl/lists/archives.html).

86 Colin Hines, 'Oxfam's Jekyll and Hyde Approach to Trade Will Worsen the Plight of the Poor', published by Deb Foskey via WTO Watch email list (debf@webone.com.au), 30 April 2002 (No. 55), p. 2. (For archive copy see www.nwjc.org.au/avcwl/lists/archives.html).

87 Vandana Shiva, 'Export at any Cost: Oxfam's Free Trade Recipe for the Third World', published by Deb Foskey via WTO Watch email list

(debf@webone.com.au), 18 May 2002 (No. 59), p. 2. (For archive copy see www.nwjc.org.au/avcwl/lists/archives.html).

88 Nick Parker, 'New Oxfam Campaign Contradicts Developing Country Demands for WTO Reform', published by Deb Foskey via WTO Watch email list (debf@webone.com.au), 17 April 2002 (No. 51), p. 1. (For archive copy see www.nwjc.org.au/avcwl/lists/ archives.html).

89 Walden Bello, 'What's Wrong With the Oxfam Trade Campaign', published by Deb Foskey via WTO Watch email list (debf@webone.com.au), 1 May 2002 (#55), pp. 1—2. (For archive copy see www.nwjc.org.au/avcwl/lists/archives.html).

90 Patrick Bond, 'Moderates Wilt But Radical South Africans Struggle On', published by Deb Foskey via WTO Watch email list (debf@webone.com.au), 21 April 2002 (No. 53), p. 1. (For archive copy see www.nwjc.org.au/avcwl/lists/archives.html).

91 Kevin Watkins, 'Response to Patrick Bond article', published by Deb Foskey via WTO Watch email list (debf@webone.com.au), 25 April 2002 (No. 53), p. 1. (For archive copy see www.nwjc.org.au/avcwl/lists/archives.html).

92 Ibid., p. 1.

93 Ibid., p. 2.

94 Kevin Watkins, 'Oxfam's Response to Walden Bello's Article on Make Trade Fair', published by Deb Foskey via WTO Watch email list (debf@webone.com.au), 9 May 2002 (No. 57), p. 2. (For archive copy see www.nwjc.org.au/avcwl/lists/archives.html).

95 George Monbiot, *The Age of Consent: A Manifesto for a New World Order*, pp. 52–54.

96 George Monbiot, 'I was wrong about trade', *Guardian*, 24 June 2003.

97 Monbiot, *The Age of Consent*, p. 53.

98 Colin Hines, *Understanding and Explaining Localisation*, p. 1, downloaded from www.sovereignty.org.uk in 2003.

99 Ibid., p. 6.

100 Ibid.

101 Ibid.

102 Anderson, *Views from the South,* pp. 92, 93.

103 John Madeley, *A People's World: Alternatives to Economic Globalisation*, Zed Books, London, 2003, p. 13.

104 Margaret Blakers (ed), *The Global Greens: inspiration, ideas and insights from the Rio+10 international workshop and Global Greens 2001*, The Australian Greens and Green Institute, Canberra, 2001, p. 196.

270

10
Global trade:
lessons for the future

Global trade is massive these days. Making generalisations about it is dangerous but the following conclusions can be fairly made about where it has come from and where it probably needs to go to. The history of global trade will, to a large extent, drive its future – we will either keep making the same mistakes or we will learn from them and create a new future of sustainable global trade.

The evolution of global trade

These conclusions are most evident from the history of global trade:

- empires and energy have been major determinants of the shape of global trade;

- at best the expansion of global trade, and the spread of globalisation in general, at least over the past two decades, has had no net global economic benefit in terms of reducing global inequality;

- two of the greatest threats to the ongoing expansion of global trade are the increasing scarcity of oil and the growth of global balance-of-payments imbalances;

- low-income countries are separating into 'third' and 'fourth' worlds with very different trade and development needs and agendas;

- there is growing deep-seated unease amongst many people in both high- and low-income countries about the costs of global trade;

- in terms of resource use and trade clout, some low-income countries are catching up with high-income countries;

- the environment is paying a huge subsidy to global trade.

Empires and energy have been the major determinants of the shape of global trade

Ever since the voyages of Vasco da Gama and Christopher Columbus, empires and energy have been major architects of global trade. It is clear that the British, French, Dutch, Spanish and Portuguese colonial networks were hugely influential in establishing new raw material supply chains. The age of colonial empires is over, and therefore their trade power no longer exists, but the free trade agreements that the US and Europe have signed with various low-income countries, and the tendency for both these regions – as well as Japan – to locate their client-state labour-intensive/low-value-adding manufacturing plants in low-income countries, mean that commercial empires are to a large extent just as much in existence today as they ever were. While violence is no longer used in global trade, as it once was by the Spanish and Portuguese, a huge amount of force still is, particularly during WTO negotiations. Like empires, energy technology has also been hugely influential in shaping global trade: the development of steam transport – in the form of ships and trains – in the early nineteenth century massively expanded the world's trading opportunities, as did the opening of the Suez and Panama canals and the development of the diesel engine. Energy supplies and energy technology are the arteries of today's global trade network.

At best the recent expansion of global trade, and the recent spread of globalisation in general, have had no net global economic benefit in terms of reducing global inequality

The supporters of free trade, as well as some in the global justice movement who see much poverty-relieving potential in trade, are always keen to emphasise that trade can increase prosperity. The measure of global inequality developed by former World Bank economist Branko Milanovic, which encapsulates inequality changes both within and between countries, shows that over the past two decades there has been no net decrease in global inequality. The World Bank's own poverty statistics reveal only modest reduction in global poverty over the same period. In global inequality and poverty terms no conspicuous, recent net benefit has flowed from the expansion of global trade. In regional terms the now decade-long operation of the North American Free Trade Agreement has not managed to lift Mexican wages although it must be acknowledged that global trade has helped a number of Eastern Asian countries rise out of poverty. But East Asia is the exception: it is the only collection of low-income countries that has consistently won from global trade. Africa and the Middle-East have been consistent losers with the rest of the low-income world having mixed results. The worsening terms of trade for low-income countries, the tendency for labour-intensive export manufacturing to bring little value-adding to low-income countries and the ongoing long-term slide in raw materials export prices all suggest that the poor-to-mediocre recent trade performance of most low-income countries won't change any time soon.

The two greatest threats to continuing expansion of global trade are the increasing scarcity of oil and the growth of global balance-of-payments imbalances

Since the Second World War in particular, global trade has expanded at breakneck pace with nothing seemingly able to stop it, but oil and global balance-of-payments imbalances may end up becoming major blocks to the further expansion of global trade. After flat global oil demand throughout the 1980s, global oil demand looks set to double between the early 1990s and 2020 while the discovery rate of new oilfields is less than half the world's ongoing usage. With increased transport accounting for most of the steep rise in global oil demand, trade is playing a significant part in radically changing the supply and demand outlook for oil for the worse. Cheap oil can no longer be taken for granted, and thus the ongoing expansion of global trade isn't a certain thing either. Energy made global trade and energy can break it. At the moment it looks like oil scarcity has the potential to curtail global trade significantly, and if that happens the world may have to radically rethink the place of trade: it may have to rely on global trade much less and on local production much more. Even if oil doesn't reduce global trade, the ever-increasing balance-of-payments imbalances being experienced by the US and most least-developed countries have as much potential to reduce it. If the US keeps increasing its trade and current account deficits then, eventually, the rest of the world is likely to panic and may not be prepared to bail it out anymore. This may force the US to correct its trade imbalances through increased protectionism and through turning its back on its post-war role of being a champion of free trade. Similarly if least-developed countries keep experiencing ever-increasing balance-of-payments difficulties, the IMF and World Bank may be forced to rethink the free trade prescriptions they keep forcing those countries to adopt. Oil scarcity may combine with growing balance-of-payments imbalances to induce a major rethink of global trade. We could be living through the last period of pervasive global trade.

Low-income countries are separating into 'third' and 'fourth' worlds with very different trade and development needs

Throughout the 1960s and 1970s in particular, low-income countries had a reasonably common trade and development agenda and managed to stick together in pursuing their trade aspirations. The emergence of the G22 group of low-income countries at the 2003 Cancún meeting of the WTO was seen by many as a return to that cohesion, but the reality is that either through changes in income and/or through changes in size, low-income countries are much less homogenous than they once were and are separating into vastly different 'third' and 'fourth' worlds as a result. When it comes to trade, the larger and/or more prosperous Third World low-income countries are keen to play a limited form of the free trade game that high-income countries have played for some time. They aren't interested in most of the Singapore issues but they are interested in deepening global free trade in agriculture, in many services and in a lot of manufactured products. The poorer 'fourth-world' countries, however, are more interested in protecting their fledgling manufacturing industries and fear that the consequences of more liberalised agricultural trade could devastate the majority of their population who eke out existences as peasant farmers. The concerns of the poorer countries are very different to the trade agenda of wealthier low-income countries but poorer ones risk getting caught up in that trade agenda and pulled down by it.

There is growing deep-seated unease amongst many people in both high- and low-income countries about the costs of global trade

In both high and low-income countries a significant proportion of the population – if not a majority – has become very concerned about the costs of global trade. The concern is no longer hidden; increasingly it is being taken to the street and the ballot boxes. Global trade is becoming a political liability and politicians advocate even more of it at their peril.

In terms of resource use and trade clout, some low-income countries are catching up with high-income countries

High-income countries have traditionally been able virtually to dictate global trade rules by dismissing low-income countries as reasonably insignificant traders and consumers of the world's resources. But those days are fast receding. China has recently overtaken Japan as the world's second-largest user of oil, and India and Brazil were two of the five principal countries that negotiated the 2004 framework agreement for the Doha Round of trade talks. This new clout gives some low-income countries a lot more power than they have had in the past, but they risk being coopted by the trade system they have railed against for so long. Low-income countries need to develop their own rules instead of living by the old rules of high-income countries.

The environment is paying a huge subsidy to global trade

The single-world marketplace that global trade has created has had a devastating impact on the worldwide environment. The enormous amount of energy that is required to keep traded goods moving around the world has been a major contributor to the fourfold increase in global carbon emissions since 1950 and the global warming crisis it has brought on. Transport has also been responsible for an explosion in expensive and environmentally destructive infrastructure such as roads, railways, airports and shipping ports. The single-world market-place has also meant that if a country runs out of timber or fish or coal it can simply source it from somewhere else in the world instead of developing its own substitutes. This has forced most countries to adopt industrial farming and mining techniques. Global trade rules have also made it harder for measures that are good for the environment to be implemented and they have given global investors enormous power which is often wielded at the expense of the environment.

The future of global trade

The conclusions that are most apparent about the future of global trade are:

- The current global trading system will probably face a major crisis before there is meaningful change;

- there should not be a one-size-fits-all solution to global trade – sustainable trade should be multi-optional;

- poverty relief and sustainable development need to be much more specifically targeted in trade policy;

- there may be a lot of trade tension between different groups of low-income countries in the future;

- protectionism and self-reliance should be given more legitimacy for both low- and high-income countries;

- raw material management schemes and Keynesian-type balance-of-payments schemes have to be part of future trade;

- the WTO needs major reform if not abolition;

- transnational corporations need more regulation;
- the global justice movement needs more consistent trade policies;
- more focus needs to be applied to the quality of trade, not its quantity, and the benefits of trade need to be more holistically assessed.

The current global trading system will probably face a major crisis before there is meaningful change

Although it would be nice to think that morality alone will change the course of global trade, it probably won't. Global trade may need to face a major crisis before the world is forced to accept the need for change. Protests etcetera by the global justice movement will help but they may not, of themselves, change global trade. The big crisis that could radically change global trade is a crisis in the balance-of-payments of the United States, which could well happen if its trade and current account deficits keep expanding and if the rest of the world decides they won't keep financing those deficits any more. This may force the US to engage in a significant rethink of its free trade policies but it may also force it to become more protectionist (which is starting to happen already) which may bring on a major implosion of the global trade system. In the longer term, more expensive oil may also curtail our current system of global trade.

There shouldn't be a one-size-fits-all solution to global trade – sustainable trade should be multi-optional

Too many books and manifestos published by the global justice movement, and similar organisations, read as though they want to replace the one-size-fits-all free trade policies of today with alternative one-size-fits-all trade policies. This approach has the potential to be just as anti-democratic and unsustainable as the current free trade system is. For trade to be sustainable it is important to give countries and people choice. Some cultures are much more innately disposed towards trading than others, and it is important that those cultures be allowed to trade (within the bounds imposed by sustainability). We need to heed the 1870 view of Thomas Leslie who argued, as had an earlier German school of economic thought, that economic laws are not universal but vary from place to place.[1] Sustainable trade policy should be post-modern and multi-optional. It shouldn't be afraid to take from past experience when trade policies have proved effective. It also shouldn't be afraid to take the best parts from the left and right of politics. The left is correct in arguing that governments need to keep a steady hand on economic management, and the right has a fair case when arguing that entrepreneurial spirit needs a certain amount of freedom in which to flourish.

Poverty relief and sustainable development need to be much more specifically targeted in trade policy

Trade is not an end unto itself, it is a means to an end. For too long it has been assumed that trade necessarily reduces poverty but there is too much evidence that it does not necessarily do so. There have been only modest reductions in global poverty despite the explosion in trade volumes that has taken place in recent decades; low-income countries, like Mexico, that have now had extensive experience of free trade have had no major reductions in poverty and have, in fact, seen significant increases in inequality. The biggest single problem with global trade is that its supporters are obsessed with boosting trade as a policy goal unto itself. In some instances this may help relieve poverty but in other instances it won't, particularly if it simply wipes out a local industry that previously produced the same goods and services that newly imported goods provide. Trade is not the aim, relieving poverty and creating sustainable development are, and trade policy needs to reflect this more keenly. Global trade is a means, not an end.

There may be a lot of trade tension between different groups of low-income countries in the future

There is little doubt that some of today's low-income countries are set to have more and more influence in global trade politics in coming decades consistent with their growing share of global GDP and global trade. But it is possible that low-income countries may divide into two camps. One camp – including countries such as China, India, Brazil and South Africa – may pursue a limited form of free trade while another camp – including most African countries – may want a more protectionist attitude towards global trade. There may end up being as much trade friction between the two camps as there currently is between high- and low-income countries.

Protectionism and self-reliance should be given more legitimacy for both low- and high-income countries

Although it is heinous to say so these days, protectionism and self-reliance should be seen as legitimate, possible trade strategies to be used when fighting poverty and achieving sustainable development. They should be allowable in the global trade network. They worked well for today's high-income countries when they were in earlier stages of development, and elements of them worked well for several Eastern Asian countries during the 1980s. Even if there is no way current world trade politics could ever look sympathetically upon protectionism and self-reliance, it may be forced to if the world ends up facing a major balance-of-payments crisis and if cheap oil runs out. It is important to heed the words of Claire Melamed of Christian Aid, however, who said in relation to the need for trade systems to reflect development goals:

> what all success stories in trade policy and development have in common is that governments managed markets to ensure that the incentive structure faced by the private sector reflected development goals. A closed system with no incentives has not been shown to be particularly helpful in advancing economic growth and poverty reduction.[2]

A protectionist trade policy that is not targeted towards specific development aims could be as bad as free trade. Protectionism has not necessarily been done very well in the past – it has often tended to be implemented in conjunction with large government bureaucracies and large industrial projects that weren't particularly suited to the development needs of the country they were situated in. But manufacturing systems have become a lot more flexible in recent decades and some can be adapted to small scales that may be sympathetic to the development needs of many low-income countries. Moreover, economic structures drive technological development to a large extent these days: protectionist structures are likely to stimulate development of more small-scaled manufacturing systems and could create a whole new 'small-is-beautiful' technology sector.

Raw material management schemes and Keynesian-type balance-of-payments schemes have to be part of future trade

The two problems that the global trade system has been spectacularly unable to solve have been the ongoing slide in raw material export prices and the chronic and persistent balance-of-payments imbalances faced by many low- and high-income countries. These problems have continued for decades and will probably not go away without active intervention. Free trade is not solving the problem of the ongoing slide in raw material prices, and interventionist, government-led supply management needs to be seriously considered if the slide in raw material prices is to be arrested. Export raw materials need active global supply management. Similarly, the world is crying out for a balance-of-payments management system, like that proposed by John Maynard Keynes at the 1944 Bretton Woods conference, in which penalties are applied to countries that run persistent balance-of-payments surpluses as well as to those that run persistent deficits. At the moment only deficit countries are penalised (by those that finance their deficits).

Both these measures could be perceived as anti-free-market. Herman E Daly, a former senior economist at the World Bank, and professor of philosophy and theology John B. Cobb, have insightful observations about the free market. They argue that 'for allocating resources among commodity uses, the [free] market is the most efficient institution we have come up with thanks to its ability to use information'; however they also argue 'those who want to rely on the market for allocation will only weaken their case if they expect the market to also solve the independent problems of distribution and scale'.[3]

The WTO needs major reform if not abolition

The WTO has become a monstrous organisation obsessed with forcing the world to embrace free trade. It is run by high-income countries and a small group of low-income countries that are blinkered about the benefits of free trade. Medium and small low-income countries, in particular, have little effective say in the WTO: agreements are invariably stitched up between high-income countries and strategic, large low-income countries. WTO rulings always find in favour of free trade and always find against measures that might help development or the environment. The WTO is possibly unreformable and its abolition needs to be considered. Whether it is reformed or not, it is vital that it become an equal partner in a 'family' of United Nations organisations where each one can act as a check and balance on the others. At the moment the WTO rules supreme and is unchecked by any UN organisation.

Transnational corporations need more regulation

Transnational corporations (TNCs) have as much influence over the shape of global trade as the WTO, if not more. They are responsible for at least two-thirds of global trade, with about a third taking place between different arms of the same TNC. There needs to be much more global regulation of TNCs, especially with regard to their labour practices, their environmental impact, their transfer pricing and profit-shifting practices, their preparedness to develop links with local businesses, their merger and takeover policies, and their attitude towards the shifting of investments from one low-income country to another. Global TNC regulation needs to be effective across borders and will need a high degree of cooperation between countries before it can take place. The United Nations has a code of conduct for TNCs (which grew out of the infamous Nestlé baby formula case) but it is a toothless tiger and needs replacement with regulations that have real bite. TNCs should not be stifled or unnecessarily regulated but they must accept more global and social responsibility than they do at present. They should also lose a lot of the influence they currently have over global trade policy.

The global justice movement needs more consistent trade policies

The global justice movement is at the cutting edge of alternative trade policy, but at the moment it is deeply divided about the future of trade. Some within the movement – like Oxfam and George Monbiot – see more trade, with more rules, as the answer to global poverty, while others – like Colin Hines – see global trade as one of the major causes of global poverty and advocate less trade, not more. These policies are hugely divergent and do the credibility of the movement no favours. The different organisations in the global justice movement don't necessarily have to have exactly the same policy on trade. On other issues, like foreign investment and global capital, there are differing degrees of radicalism within the movement, but at least the policies move in the same general direction. With trade they don't, and much greater dialogue between the opposing camps within the movement is needed.

More focus needs to be applied to the quality of trade, not its quantity, and the benefits of trade need to be more holistically assessed

There is nothing inherently evil about global trade but much, much more emphasis needs to be placed on its quality. At the moment the world is obsessed with the sheer quantity of global trade but we need much greater focus on those areas where trade is of strategic importance rather than assuming that all trade is necessarily good. The world needs a holistic assessment of trade that takes into account its impact on people and the environment. Before the Doha Round began, low-income countries asked for an assessment of the impact of the Uruguay Round – that assessment never happened but still desperately needs to happen. One of the greatest failings of global trade in recent decades has been that it has gone from being something that was resorted to when a region or country couldn't produce something for itself to being something that is allowed regardless of whether it is needed or ~t. When the decision is taken to allow in imported products, it no ~r matters that an area may already be able to produce something. ~eeds to return to being a mechanism of last resort.

Conclusion

If one thing is reasonably clear from the history of world trade it is that after five centuries world trade may be reaching its limits to growth. There are simply too many wolves at its door now. Global warming is a wolf at its door, the imminent end of cheap oil is a wolf at its door, persistent major balance-of-payments imbalances are wolves at its door, high global poverty levels and high global inequality are wolves at its door and (successful) low-income country resistance to the spread of trade agreements into new areas – like the Singapore issues – is yet another wolf at the door of global trade. This doesn't mean that global trade will cease to exist – it won't – but its role in overall economic development may be seriously re-evaluated in years to come. It is probably unlikely to keep filling the role it has had since the Second World War. The past may well catch up with it.

Enhanced contact between people is not always good. The enhanced human contact that global trade has brought has not always been a positive force largely because its benefits have been unevenly spread and because it hasn't been assessed in very holistic terms. We still have an enormous amount to learn about how to manage global economic integration sustainably. There have only been two short periods when the management of the world economy has looked even vaguely sustainable – in the three or four decades before the First World War and in the two decades after the Second World War. Even in those two periods, major issues of inequality, poverty, resource use and pollution existed but were ignored. Today we live in a period of laissez-faire global economic management that is a very long way from being sustainable. The global trading system may be heading for a big crash. This may not be all bad, however – the Bretton Woods system grew out of the economic crash of the 1930s, and a more enlightened global trading system may grow out of the current system's demise.

During the nineteenth century a new modernist consciousness around the world was produced by the growth of cities which, like global trade, enhanced human contact. Living in cities changed attitudes from those that prevailed when most people lived in the country. People now saw politics differently, their democratic rights differently, the arts differently, the environment differently and even poverty differently. A similar change in consciousness is happening as the world becomes more interconnected and as internationalisation and globalisation spread their tentacles. Telecommunications, freight, travel, global capital and global trade are all drawing us closer together and it is reasonably inevitable that this will change our thinking yet again. The future of global trade will necessarily get caught up in such changed thinking. Global society now stands at a crossroads where we either start making daring decisions about our future as a race or we sink into a mire created by our past mistakes. We must hope that the new global consciousness will be daring and courageous, especially when it comes to economics.

The world needs a new humility and a preparedness to learn from past mistakes. John Maynard Keynes once said that humankind 'will always do the right thing but only after exhausting all other possible alternatives'. At the moment the global trading system is very much in the throes of 'exhausting all other possible alternatives'; once we have done so the survival of our economies and the survival of our species will probably depend on us taking daring decisions that correct past mistakes. We don't have to be prisoners of our past, but in order to avoid being so we have to bring a new mindset to global trade. As Albert Einstein once said, 'we cannot solve a problem with the same consciousness that created it'.

Notes

1   Roger E. Backhouse, *The Penguin History of Economics*, Penguin Books, London, 2002, p. 178.

2   Claire Melamed, *What Works? Trade, Policy and Development*, Christian Aid, London, 2002, pp. 1,7 downloaded from www. christian-aid.org in 2003.

3   Herman E. Daly and John B. Cobb, *For the Common Good: Redirecting the Economy towards Community, the Environment and a Sustainable Future*, Green Print, London, 1990, pp. 46, 60.

Suggested reading

Akyüz, Yilmaz (ed.), *Developing Countries and World Trade: Performance and Prospects*, London: Zed Books, 2003.

Anderson, Sarah (ed.), *Views from the South: The Effects of Globalization and the WTO on Third World Countries*, Oakland (California): Food First/Institute for Food and Policy Development, 2000.

Bello, Walden, *Deglobalization: Ideas for a New World Economy*, London: Zed Books, 2002.

Bello, Walden, Nicola Bullard and Kamal Malhotta (eds.), *Global Finance: New Thinking on Regulating Speculative Capital Markets*, London: Zed Books, 2000.

Blakers, Margaret (ed.), *The Global Greens: Inspiration, Ideas and Insights from the Rio+10 International Workshop and Global Greens 2001*, Canberra: Australian Greens, 2001.

Daly, Herman and John B. Cobb, *For the Common Good: Redirecting the Economy towards Community, the Environment and a Sustainable Future*, London: Green Print, 1990.

Dunkley, Graham, *Free Trade: Myth, Reality and Alternatives*, London: Zed Books, 2004.

Fisher, William F. and Thomas Ponniah (eds.), *Another World is Possible: Popular Alternatives to Globalization at the World Social Forum*, London: Zed Books, 2003.

Gilpin, Robert, *The Challenge of Global Capitalism: The World Economy in the 21st Century*, Princeton: Princeton University Press, 2000.

Goldsmith, Edward and Jerry Mander (eds.), *The Case Against the Global Economy and for a Turn Towards Localization*, London: Earthscan, 2001.

Heinberg, Richard, *The Party's Over: Oil, War and the Fate of Industrial Societies*, Gabriola Island (Canada): New Society Publishers, 2003.

Held, David and Koenig-Archibugi, Mathias (eds.), *Taming Globalization: Frontiers of Governance*, Cambridge: Polity Press, 2003.

Hertz, Noreena, *The Silent Takeover: Global Capitalism and the Death of Democracy*, London: Arrow Books, 2002.

Hines, Colin, *Localization: A Global Manifesto*, London: Earthscan, 2000.

Hoogvelt, Ankie, *Globalization and the Post Colonial World: The New Political Economy of Development*, Houndmills (UK): Palgrave, 2001.

Houtart, Francois and Francois Polet, *The Other Davos: The Globalization of Resistance to the World Economic System*, London: Zed Books, 2001.

Hugill, Peter J., *World Trade since 1431: Geography, Technology and Capitalism*, Baltimore: The John Hopkins University Press, 1993.

International Forum on Globalization, *Alternatives to Economic Globalization: A Better World Is Possible*, San Francisco: Berrett-Koehler Publishers, 2002.

Jawara, Fatoumata and Kwa, Aileen, *Behind the Scenes at the WTO: The Real World of International Trade Negotiations*, London: Zed Books, 2003.

Kenwood, A.G. and A.L. Lougheed, *Growth of the International Economy 1820–1990: An Introductory Text*, London: Routledge, 1992.

Khor, Martin, *Rethinking Globalization: Critical Ideas and Policy Choices*, London: Zed Books, 2001.

Kingsnorth, Paul, *One No, Many Yeses: A Journey to the Heart of the Global Resistance Movement*, London: The Free Press, 2003.

Klein, Naomi, *No Logo*, London: Flamingo, 2000.

Klein, Naomi, *Fences and Windows: Dispatches from the Front Line of the Globalization Debate*, London: Flamingo, 2002.

Lal Das, Bhagirath, *The WTO and the Multilateral Trading System: Past, Present and Future*, London: Zed Books, 2003.

Lang, Tim and Hines, Colin, *The New Protectionism: Protecting the Future Against Free Trade*, London: Earthscan, 1993.

Lucas, Caroline and Colin Hines, *Time to Replace Globalization: A Green Localist Manifesto for the World Trade Organisation Ministerial*, London: The Greens/European Free Alliance, 2001.

Madeley, John, *Hungry for Trade: How the Poor Pay for Free Trade*, London: Zed Books, 2000.

Madeley, John, *Food for All: The Need for a New Agriculture*, London: Zed Books, 2002.

Madeley, John (ed.), *A People's World: Alternatives to Economic Globalization*, London: Zed Books, 2003.

Malhotra, Kamal et al., *Making Global Trade Work for People*, London: Earthscan, 2003.

Milanovic, Branko, *Worlds Apart: Measuring Global and International Inequality*, Princeton: Princeton University Press, 2005.

Monbiot, George, *The Age of Consent: A Manifesto for a New World Order*,

London: Flamingo, 2003.

Moore, Mike, *A World Without Walls: Freedom, Development, Free Trade and Global Governance*, Cambridge: Cambridge University Press, 2003.

Neale, Jonathan, *You Are G8, We Are 6 billion: The Truth behind the Genoa Protests*, London: Vision Paperbacks, 2002.

Peet, Richard et al., *Unholy Trinity: The IMF, World Bank and WTO*, London: Zed Books, 2003.

Rifkin, Jeremy, *The Hydrogen Economy: The Creation of the Worldwide Energy Web and the Redistribution of Power on Earth*, Cambridge: Polity, 2002.

Robertson, Robbie, *The Three Waves of Globalization: A History of a Developing Consciousness*, London: Zed Books, 2003.

Robbins, Peter, *Stolen Fruit: The Tropical Commodities Disaster*, London: Zed Books, 2003.

Shiva, Vandana, *Protect or Plunder? Understanding Intellectual Property Rights*, London: Zed Books, 2002.

Singh, Kavaljit, *Taming Global Financial Flows: A Citizens' Guide*, London: Zed Books, 2000.

Skidelsky, Robert, *John Maynard Keynes 1883–1946: Economist, Philosopher, Statesman*, London: Pan Books, 2004.

Spero, Joan E. and Jeffrey A. Hart, *The Politics of International Economic Relations* (fifth edition), London: Routledge, 1997.

Stiglitz, Joseph E., *Globalization and Its Discontents*, London: Allen (Penguin Group), 2002.

Tracey, James D. (ed.), *The Rise of Merchant Empires: Long-Distance Trade in the Early Modern World 1350–1750*, Cambridge: Cambridge University Press, 1990.

Tracey, James D. (ed.), *The Political Economy of Merchant Empires: State Power and World Trade 1350–1750*, Cambridge: Cambridge University Press, 1991.

Wallach, Lori and Woodall, Patrick, *Whose Trade Organization? A Comprehensive Guide to the WTO*, New York: The New Press, 2004.

Watkins, Kevin *et al.*, *Rigged Rules and Double Standards: Trade, Globalisation and the Fight against Poverty*, Washington: Oxfam International, 2002.

Woodin, Michael and Lucas, Caroline, *Green Alternatives to Globalisation: A Manifesto*, London: Pluto Press, 2004.

World Watch Institute, *Vital Signs 2003–04: The Trends That Are Shaping Our Future*, London: Earthscan, 2003.

Yergin, Daniel, *The Prize: The Epic Quest for Oil, Money and Power*, New York: Free Press, 1992.

Index

Global Issues
in a Changing World

This new series of short, accessible think-pieces deals with leading global issues of relevance to humanity today. Intended for the enquiring reader and social activists in the North and the South, as well as students, the books explain what is at stake and question conventional ideas and policies. Drawn from many different parts of the world, the series' authors pay particular attention to the needs and interests of ordinary people, whether living in the rich industrial or the developing countries. They all share a common objective – to help stimulate new thinking and social action in the opening years of the new century.

Global Issues in a Changing World is a joint initiative by Zed Books in collaboration with a number of partner publishers and nongovernmental organizations around the world. By working together, we intend to maximize the relevance and availability of the books published in the series.

Participating NGOs

About this series

'Communities in the South are facing great difficulties in coping with global trends. I hope this brave new series will throw much needed light on the issues ahead and help us choose the right options.'
MARTIN KHOR, *Director,*
Third World Network, Penang

'There is no more important campaign than our struggle to bring the global economy under democratic control. But the issues are fearsomely complex. This Global Issues series is a valuable resource for the committed campaigner and the educated citizen.'
BARRY COATES, *Director,*
World Development Movement (WDM)

'Zed Books has long provided an inspiring list about the issues that touch and change people's lives. The Global Issues series is another dimension of Zed's fine record, allowing access to a range of subjects and authors that, to my knowledge, very few publishers have tried. I strongly recommend these new, powerful titles and this exciting series.'
JOHN PILGER, *author*

'We are all part of a generation that actually has the means to eliminate extreme poverty world-wide. Our task is to harness the forces of globalization for the benefit of working people, their families and their communities – that is our collective duty. The Global Issues series makes a powerful contribution to the global campaign for justice, sustainable and equitable development, and peaceful progress.'
GLENYS KINNOCK, *MEP*

The Global Issues series

ALREADY AVAILABLE

IN PREPARATION

Liz Kelly, *Violence against Women*

Alan Marshall, *A New Nuclear Age? The Case for Nuclear Power Revisited*

Paola Monzini, *Sex Traffic: Prostitution, Crime, and Exploitation*

Roger Moody, *Digging the Dirt: The Modern World of Global Mining*

Jonathon W. Moses: *International Migration: Globalization's Last Frontier*

Edgar Pieterse, *City Futures: Confronting the Crisis of Urban Development*

Peter M. Rosset, *Food is Not Just Another Commodity: Why the WTO Should Get Out of Agriculture*

Toby Shelley, *Nanotechnology: New Promises, New Dangers*

Vivien Stern, *The Making of Crime: Prisons and People in a Market Society*

For full details of this list and Zed's other subject and general catalogues, please write to: The Marketing Department, Zed Books, 7 Cynthia Street, London N1 9JF, UK or email Sales@zedbooks.demon.co.uk

Visit our website at: www.zedbooks.co.uk

Participating organizations

Both ENDS A service and advocacy organization which collaborates with environment and indigenous organizations, both in the South and in the North, with the aim of helping to create and sustain a vigilant and effective environmental movement.

Nieuwe Keizersgracht 45, 1018 vc Amsterdam, The Netherlands
Phone: +31 20 623 0823 • Fax: +31 20 620 8049
Email: info@bothends.org • Website: www.bothends.org

Catholic Institute for International Relations (CIIR) CIIR aims to contribute to the eradication of poverty through a programme that combines advocacy at national and international level with community-based development.

Unit 3, Canonbury Yard, 190a New North Road, London N1 7BJ, UK
Phone: +44 (0)20 7354 0883 • Fax +44 (0)20 7359 0017
Email: ciir@ciir.org • Website: www.ciir.org

Corner House The Corner House is a UK-based research and solidarity group working on social and environmental justice issues in North and South.

PO Box 3137, Station Road, Sturminster Newton, Dorset DT10 1YJ, UK
Tel.: +44 (0)1258 473795 • Fax: +44 (0)1258 473748
Email: cornerhouse@gn.apc.org • Website: www.cornerhouse.icaap.org

Council on International and Public Affairs (CIPA) CIPA is a human rights research, education and advocacy group, with a particular focus on economic and social rights in the USA and elsewhere around the world. Emphasis in recent years has been given to resistance to corporate domination.

777 United Nations Plaza, Suite 3C, NewYork, NY 10017, USA
Tel.: +1 212 972 9877 • Fax +1 212 972 9878
Email: cipany@igc.org • Website: www.cipa-apex.org

Dag Hammarskjöld Foundation The Dag Hammarskjöld Foundation, established 1962, organises seminars and workshops on social, economic and cultural issues facing developing countries with a particular focus on alternative and innovative solutions. Results are published in its journal *Development Dialogue*.

Övre Slottsgatan 2, 753 10 Uppsala, Sweden.
Tel.: +46 18 102772 • Fax: +46 18 122072
Email: secretariat@dhf.uu.se • Website: www.dhf.uu.se

Development GAP The Development Group for Alternative Policies is a Non-Profit Development Resource Organization working with popular organizations in the South and their Northern partners in support of a development that is truly sustainable and that advances social justice.

927 15th Street NW, 4th Floor, Washington, DC, 20005, USA
Tel.: +1 202 898 1566 • Fax: +1 202 898 1612
Email: dgap@igc.org • Website: www.developmentgap.org

Focus on the Global South Focus is dedicated to regional and global policy analysis and advocacy work. It works to strengthen the capacity of organizations of the poor and marginalized people of the South and to better analyse and understand the impacts of the globalization process on their daily lives.

C/o CUSPLI, Chulalongkorn University, Bangkok 10330, Thailand
Tel.: +66 2 218 7363 • Fax: +66 2 255 9976
Email: Admin@focusweb.org • Website: www.focusweb.org

IBON IBON Foundation is a research, education and information institution that provides publications and services on socio-economic issues as support to advocacy in the Philippines and abroad. Through its research and databank, formal and non-formal education programmes, media work and international networking, IBON aims to build the capacity of both Philippine and international organizations.

Room 303 SCC Bldg, 4427 Int. Old Sta. Mesa, Manila 1008, Philippines
Phone: +632 7132729 • Fax +632 716108
Email: editors@ibon.org • Website: www.ibon.org

Inter Pares Inter Pares, a Canadian social justice organization, has been active since 1975 in building relationships with Third World development groups and providing support for community-based development programmes. Inter Pares is also involved in education and advocacy in Canada, promoting understanding about the causes, effects and solutions to poverty.

221 Laurier Avenue East, Ottawa, Ontario, KIN 6PI Canada
Phone: +1 613 563 4801 • Fax +1 613 594 4704
Email: info@interpares.ca • Website: www.interpares.ca

Public Interest Research Centre PIRC is a research and campaigning group based in Delhi which seeks to serve the information needs of activists and organizations working on macro-economic issues concerning finance, trade and development.

142 Maitri Apartments, Plot No. 28, Patparganj, Delhi 110092, India
Phone: +91 11 222I0SI/2432054 • Fax: +91 11 2224233
Email: kaval@nde.vsnl.net.in

Third World Network   TWN is an international network of groups and individuals involved in efforts to bring about a greater articulation of the needs and rights of peoples in the Third World; a fair distribution of the world's resources; and forms of development which are ecologically sustainable and flilfil human needs. Its international secretariat is based in Penang, Malaysia.

121-S Jalan Utama, 10450 Penang, Malaysia
Tel.: +60 4 226 6159 • Fax: +60 4 226 4505
Email: twnet@po.jaring.my • Website: www.twnside.org.sg

Third World Network–Africa   TWN–Africa is engaged in research and advocacy on economic, environmental and gender issues. In relation to its current particular interest in globalization and Africa, its work focuses on trade and investment, the extractive sectors and gender and economic reform.

2 Ollenu Street, East Legon, PO Box AN19452, Accra-North, Ghana.
Tel.: +233 21 511189/503669/500419 • Fax: +233 21 511188
Email: twnafrica@ghana.com

World Development Movement (WDM) The World Development Movement campaigns to tackle the causes of poverty and injustice. It is a democratic membership movement that works with partners in the South to cancel unpayable debt and break the ties of IMF conditionality, for fairer trade and investment rules, and for strong international rules on multinationals.

25 Beehive Place, London SW9 7QR, UK
Tel.: +44 (0)20 7737 6215 • Fax: +44 (0)20 7274 8232
Email: wdm@wdm.org.uk • Website: www.wdm.org.uk

This book is also available in the following countries

CARIBBEAN
Arawak Publications
17 Kensington Crescent,
Apt 5,
Kingston 5
Jamaica
Tel: 876 960 7538
Fax: 876 960 9219

EGYPT
MERIC (The Middle East
Readers' Information Center)
2 Bahgat Ali Street,
Tower D/Apt. 24
Zamalek
Cairo
Tel: 20 2 735 3818/736 3824
Fax: 20 2 736 9355

FIJI
University Book Centre
University of South Pacific,
Suva
Tel: 679 313 900
Fax: 679 303 265

GHANA
Readwide Books Ltd
12 Ablade Road
Kanda Estates, Kanda
Accra
Tel: 233 244 630 805/
     208 180 310

GUYANA
Austin's Book Services
190 Church Street
Cummingsburg
Georgetown
Tel: 592 227 7395
Fax: 592 227 7396
Email: Austins@guyana.net.gy

IRAN
Book City
743 North Hafez Avenue
15977 Tehran
Tel: 98 21 889 7875
Fax: 98 21 889 7785
Email: Bookcity@neda.net

MAURITIUS
Editions Le Printemps
4 Club Road
Vacoas
Mauritius

MOZAMBIQUE
Sul Sensacoes
PO Box 2242
Maputo
Tel: 258 1 421974
Fax: 258 1 423414

NAMIBIA
Book Den
PO Box 3469
Shop 4, Frans Indongo
Gardens
Windhoek
Tel: 264 61 239976
Fax: 264 61 234248

NEPAL
Everest Media Services
GPO Box 5443, Dillibazar
Putalisadak Chowk
Kathmandu
Tel: 977 1 416026
Fax: 977 1 250176

NIGERIA
Mosuro Publishers
52 Magazine Road
Jericho, Ibadan
Nigeria
Tel: 234 2 241 3375
Fax: 234 2 241 3374

PAKISTAN
Vanguard Books
45 The Mall
Lahore
Tel: 92 42 735 5079
Fax: 92 42 735 5197

PAPUA NEW GUINEA
Unisearch PNG Pty Ltd
Box 320, University
National Capital District
Tel: 675 326 0130
Fax: 675 326 0127

RWANDA
Librairie Ikirezi
PO Box 443,
Kigali
Tel/Fax: 250 71314

SUDAN
The Nile Bookshop
New Extension Street 41
P O Box 8036
Khartoum
Tel: 249 11 463 749

TANZANIA
TEMA Publishing Co Ltd
PO Box 63115
Dar Es Salaam
Tel: 255 51 113608
Fax: 255 51 110472

UGANDA
Aristoc Booklex Ltd
PO Box 5130, Kampala
Road
Diamond Trust Building
Kampala
Tel/Fax: 256 41 254867

ZAMBIA
UNZA Press
PO Box 32379
Lusaka
Tel: 260 1 290409
Fax: 260 1 253952

ZIMBABWE
Weaver Press
PO Box A1922
Avondale
Harare
Tel: 263 4 308330
Fax: 263 4 339645